The Evolution of Regionalism in Asia

This edited volume looks at regional integration processes in Asia. Whilst integration in the region, defined as Southeast and East Asia, is not a new process, it has gained momentum in recent years. Two developments have acted as catalysts for integration. First, at the economic level, the Asian crisis of 1997 has been the watershed for most countries in the region. Ever since, there have been continuing search processes for sovereignty-enhancing types of economic policies, and the region is one location where policy makers look for new avenues to strengthen the position of their countries. The second major development is the continuing rise of China in the region. Today, China is not only the manufacturing powerhouse of the region, but it increasingly functions as a 'benign hegemon' in Asia.

Integration processes in Asia take place at several levels: in trade, finance and security affairs. This book analyses these dimensions of integration and sheds light on the prospects for successful integration. It investigates the puzzling, sometimes contracting trends of cooperation and integration in Asia.

The contributors to this volume look at a theme that is of growing importance to the discipline of political science as much as it is relevant for policy makers. By combining the analysis of the three dimensions of integration, *The Evolution of Regionalism in Asia* enables readers to gain a broad understanding of the theory and practice of the integration processes.

Heribert Dieter is a Senior Fellow at the German Institute for International and Security Affairs, Berlin, Germany. He is also an Associate Fellow at the Centre for the Study of Globalisation and Regionalisation (CSGR), University of Warwick, UK.

Routledge/Warwick Studies in Globalisation

Edited by Richard Higgott and published in association with the Centre for the Study of Globalisation and Regionalisation
University of Warwick.

What is globalisation and does it matter? How can we measure it? What are its policy implications? The Centre for the Study of Globalisation and Regionalisation at the University of Warwick is an international site for the study of key questions such as these in the theory and practice of globalisation and regionalisation. Its agenda is avowedly interdisciplinary. The work of the Centre will be showcased in this series.

This series comprises two strands:

Warwick Studies in Globalisation addresses the needs of students and teachers, and the titles will be published in hardback and paperback. Titles include:

Globalisation and the Asia-Pacific
Contested Territories
Edited by Kris Olds, Peter Dicken, Philip F. Kelly, Lily Kong and Henry Wai-chung Yeung

Regulating the Global Information Society
Edited by Christopher Marsden

Banking on Knowledge
The genesis of the global development network
Edited by Diane Stone

Historical Materialism and Globalisation
Edited by Hazel Smith and Mark Rupert

Civil Society and Global Finance
Edited by Jan Aart Scholte with Albrecht Schnabel

Towards a Global Polity
Edited by Morten Ougaard and Richard Higgott

New Regionalisms in the Global Political Economy
Theories and cases
Edited by Shaun Breslin, Christopher W. Hughes, Nicola Phillips and Ben Rosamond

Development Issues in Global Governance
Public private partnerships and market multilateralism
Benedicte Bull and Desmond McNeill

Globalizing Democracy
Political parties in emerging democracies
Edited by Peter Burnell

The Globalization of Political Violence
Globalization's shadow
Edited by Richard Devetak and Christopher W. Hughes

The Evolution of Regionalism in Asia

Economic and security issues

Edited by

Heribert Dieter

Routledge
Taylor & Francis Group

LONDON AND NEW YORK

E·S·R·C
ECONOMIC
& SOCIAL
RESEARCH
COUNCIL

CENTRE FOR THE
STUDY OF
GLOBALISATION AND
REGIONALISATION

First published 2007
by Routledge
2 Park Square, Milton Park,
Abingdon, Oxon OX14 4RN

Simultaneously published in the USA and Canada
by Routledge
270 Madison Ave, New York, NY 10016

Routledge is an imprint of the Taylor & Francis Group, an informa business.

First issued in paperback 2011

© 2007 Heribert Dieter

Typeset in Times New Roman by
Book Now Ltd

British Library Cataloguing in Publication Data
A catalogue record for this book is available from the British Library

Library of Congress Cataloging in Publication Data

The evolution of regionalism in Asia: economic and security issues/edited
by Heribert Dieter.
    p. cm—(Routledge/Warwick studies in globalisation; 16)
    Includes bibliographical references and index.
1. Asia—Politics and government—1945 2. Regionalism—Asia.
3. National security—Asia. I. Dieter, Heribert, 1961–
    JQ24.E96 2007
    337.1′5—dc22

                                                    2007024480

ISBN 10: 0–415–44684–8 (hbk)
ISBN 10: 0–415–66400–4 (pbk)
ISBN 10: 0–203–93743–0 (ebk)

ISBN 13: 978–0–415–44684–6 (hbk)
ISBN 13: 978–0–415–66400–4 (pbk)
ISBN 13: 978–0–203–93743–3 (ebk)

Contents

Preface

Since roughly the turn of the century, regionalism in Southeast and East Asia is changing dramatically. Previously, the influence of the United States on policies in the various fields was significantly higher, whilst China was not as important a player as it is today. With increasing speed, the traditional patterns are changing. The decline of the United States, at least relative to other players, continues, whilst the rise of China remains the most significant development in the region in this decade. Of course, the rise of China is not limited to one policy sphere, but stretches across them. In security as well as in economics, Southeast and East Asia are exposed to shifting configurations.

These changes pose a challenge for the analysis of political and economic developments in Asia. The contributors of this book, although coming from different disciplines, are engaged in the debate on regionalism in Asia. For us, the starting point has been the conference 'Regionalisation and the Taming of Globalisation? Economic, Political, Security, Social and Governance Issues', organised by the Centre for the Study of Globalisation and Regionalisation (CSGR), University of Warwick, from 26 to 28 October 2005. The conference in Warwick enabled the contributors to engage in substantive discussion on the evolution of regionalism in Asia. It also enabled us to further build our network of researchers that covers four continents. Chris Hughes, who co-ordinated the CSGR conference, contributed tremendously to this volume. He was both crucial in the development of the conference and he subsequently facilitated the development of this book. I am very grateful for his encouragement. I would also like to thank the CSGR staff in general and Denise Hewlett in particular for the smooth organisation of the conference.

The conference in 2005 as well as the work of CSGR has been generously funded by the Economic and Social Research Council (ESRC). This support is greatly appreciated.

I would also like to thank Heidi Bagtazo from Routledge for seeing the merit of this book. Many thanks also to Amelia McLaurin, who facilitated the production of this edited volume. Last but not least I wish to thank the founding director of CSGR, Richard Higgott, who has greatly supported this book project. In addition, he has been a critical and constructive player in the academic debate on regionalism in Asia.

Heribert Dieter
Berlin, July 2007

Illustrations

Figures

Tables

Boxes

Contributors

David Camroux is a Senior Research Associate at the Centre for International Research and Studies (CERI) and a Senior Lecturer seconded to the Institute of Political Studies (IEP), both at Sciences Po, Paris (France).

Heribert Dieter is a Senior Fellow at the German Institute for International and Security Affairs, Berlin (Germany) and an Associate Fellow at the University of Warwick (United Kingdom).

Derek McDougall is an Associate Professor in the School of Political Science, Criminology and Sociology at the University of Melbourne (Australia).

Thomas G. Moore is an Associate Professor in the Department of Political Science, University of Cincinnati (United States).

Golam Robbani is an Associate Professor at the Department of Finance and Banking, University of Rajshahi (Bangladesh) and a PhD Researcher at United Nations University–Comparative Regional Integration Studies (UNU–CRIS), Brugge (Belgium). For his PhD, he is affiliated with the University of Antwerp (Belgium).

Andrew Staples is an Associate Professor of Japanese Business and Economics at Kansai Foreign Language University, Osaka (Japan).

Takashi Terada is an Associate Professor, Institute of Asian Studies, Waseda University, Tokyo (Japan).

Douglas Webber is Professor of Political Science at the international business school INSEAD, based at its Europe campus in Fontainebleau (France).

Abbreviations

ABF	Asian Bond Fund
ABMI	Asian Bond Market Initiative
ACFTA	ASEAN–China Free Trade Agreement
ADB	Asian Development Bank
AFC	Advanced Fuel Cell [vehicle]
AFTA	ASEAN Free Trade Area
AIA	ASEAN Investment Area
AICO	ASEAN Industrial Cooperation Scheme
ANZUS	Australia, New Zealand and United States Security Treaty
APEC	Asia-Pacific Economic Cooperation
APT	ASEAN Plus Three
ARF	ASEAN Regional Forum
ASEAN	Association of Southeast Asian Nations
ASEM	Asia–Europe Meeting
AUSFTA	Australia–United States Free Trade Agreement
BBC	Brand to Brand Complementation
BIMSTEC	Bay of Bengal Initiative for Multisectorial Technical and Economic Cooperation
BIS	Bank for International Settlements
CBU	Completely built-up [vehicles]
CIE	Centre for International Economics
CKD	Completely knocked down [vehicles]
CLMV	Cambodia. Laos, Myanmar, Vietnam
EAEC	East Asian Economic Caucus
EAEG	East Asian Economic Grouping
EAS	East Asia Summit
ECOWAS	Economic Community of West African States
ECSC	European Coal and Steel Community
EEC	European Economic Community
EMEAP	Executives' Meeting of East Asia and Pacific Central Banks
EU	European Union
EVSL	[APEC's] Early Voluntary Sectoral Liberalisation [scheme]
FDI	Foreign Direct Investment

FoBF	Fund of Bond Funds
FTA	Free Trade Agreement
GATS	General Agreement on Trade in Services
GATT	General Agreement on Tariffs and Trade
GM	General Motors
GMS	Greater Mekong Subregion
GSP	Generalised System of Preferences
HMC	Honda Motor Company
HMCI	Honda Motor (China) Investment Co., Ltd
HS	Harmonized System
ICT	Information and Communications Technology
IFIs	International Financial Institutions
ILO	International Labour Organisation
IMF	International Monetary Fund
IIMV	International Innovative Motor Vehicle
INTERFET	International Force for East Timor
ISIS	Institute of Strategic and International Studies
JSEPA	Japan–Singapore Economic Partnership Agreement
MCSEAD	Ministerial Conference on Southeast Asian Development (disbanded in mid-1970)
MERCOSUR	*Mercado Común del Sur*
METI	[Japan's] Ministry of Economy, Trade and Industry
MITI`	[Japan's] Ministry of International Trade and Industry
MMC	Mitsubishi Motor Corporation
MNC	Multinational Company
MPV	Multi-purpose vechicle
NAFTA	North American Free Trade Agreement
NGO	Non-Governmental Organization
NIC	Newly Industrializing Countries
NIE	Newly Industrialized Economy
OCA	Optimum Currency Area
OECD	Organization for Economic Cooperation and Development
PAFTA	Pacific Free Trade Area
PAFTAD	Pacific Trade and Development
PAIF	Pan-Asian Bond Index Fund
PAS	*Parti Islam SeMalaysia*
PBEC	Pacific Basin Economic Council
PBS	Pharmaceutical Benefit Scheme
PECC	Pacific Economic Cooperation Council
PFP	Partnership for Progress
PRISE	Perceived Regional Implicit Security Enclave
PTA	Preferential Trading Agreement
RIS	Research and Information System [for Developing Countries]
RPN	Regional Production Network
RTA	Regional Trade Agreement

SAARC	South Asian Association for Regional Cooperation
SAEC	South Asian Economic Community
SADC	Southern African Development Community
SAFTA	South Asian Free Trade Area
SCO	Shanghai Cooperation Organization
SEATO	Southeast Asian Treaty Organization
SPNFZ	South Pacific Nuclear Free Zone
TAC	Treaty of Amity and Cooperation
TAFTA	Thailand–Australia Free Trade Agreement
TMC	Toyota Motor Corporation
TMMS	Toyota Motor Management Services
TNI	*Tentara Nasional Indonesia*
UMNO	United Malays National Organisation
UNTAET	United Nations Transitional Administration in East Timor
USSFTA	United States–Singapore Free Trade Agreement
WCO	World Customs Organization
WTO	World Trade Organization

Part I

Concepts of regionalism, inter-regional relations and the role of specific players

1 Introduction

Heribert Dieter

In the first decade of the twenty-first century, the shape of regionalism in Asia is changing rapidly. Whereas in previous decades regionalism was more limited, today both the scope of the cooperation and integration processes and the membership are being expanded. The contributions in this book aim at analysing these evolutionary processes.

Regionalism in Asia today covers a range of policy fields that, at first sight, appear to be unrelated. First, in trade we are seeing a large number of initiatives. Countries are engaging in a variety of trade schemes that differ from the previous decade. In the 1990s, larger integration projects, such as the Asia-Pacific Economic Cooperation (APEC) group or the ASEAN Free Trade Area (AFTA) were initiated and seemed to prosper, at least for a while. Today, however, these regional integration projects have given way to bilateral trade agreements. Since the turn of the century, virtually all countries in Asia have shifted the emphasis of their trade policy and have given preference to these bilateral arrangements.

Second, there is a strong trend toward financial and monetary cooperation in the region. Whilst there was very little, if any, cooperation in this field prior to 1997, the year the Asian financial crisis began, there has been a robust improvement of cooperation in this field in recent years. Third, there has been a significant change in the intra-regional division of labour. In particular, China has emerged as the region's most important location for manufacturing. However, China's rise has been accompanied by the deepening of intra-regional production networks. This, in turn, has enabled countries in the region to benefit from the economic upturn that China is enjoying. In some ways, in the monetary and financial fields in particular, the 1997 Asian crisis appears to be having similar effects to those that resulted from the 1973–74 shock in Europe: the catastrophic volatility of exchange rates and capital flows observed ten years ago concentrated minds and led to potentially useful revisions of regional policies.

Finally, the region is confronted with old and new challenges in the security domain. America continues to be the single most important player in security affairs, but the changes in American foreign policy since 9/11 have contributed to a severe revision of security policies of Asian countries.

Although these developments at first sight appear to be only loosely related, there are two common causes for these trends. In both economic and security affairs, the decisive factors are American foreign policy – including foreign economic policy – and the continuing rise of China. America's policies towards the institutions that govern the global economy – the World Trade Organization and the International Monetary Fund in particular – have contributed to raising the awareness of policy makers in Asian countries of their vulnerabilities. The shift of the United States in trade policy, where preferential trade agreements have been dominating George W. Bush's trade agenda in recent years, has been contributing to the interest of Asian policy makers to develop preferential agreements of their own. In finance, the policies of the International Monetary Fund – which was and is heavily influenced by the US Treasury – resulted in an unwarranted deepening of the crisis due to the reluctant provision of liquidity. Again, the primary source of change has been in Washington. The same, of course, is true for security affairs. The strong rhetoric that followed 9/11 has left its mark in the region. In particular, countries with large Muslim populations – such as Indonesia and Malaysia – have not followed America's war on terror.

The USA has not been part of the more recent efforts to create intra-regional networks in East Asia. A prominent example of the recent isolation of America has been the first East Asia Summit, which was held in Kuala Lumpur, Malaysia, on 14 December 2005. The meeting was attended by the ASEAN Plus Three (APT) countries as well as India, Australia and New Zealand. Russia attended as an observer, but, as T.J. Pempel observed, the 'strongest shaper of economic and strategic developments in the region, as well as a member of previously established Asia-Pacific groupings … had not been invited to attend' (Pempel 2006: 240).

At the same time, Washington's economic and security policies have facilitated the rise of China as a respected power in the region. In contrast to Washington's aggressive rhetoric, by comparison Beijing looked benign. In trade, China has opened its markets and today is the world's third largest importer. In finance, China has contributed to the termination of the Asian crisis by not devaluing its currency. Furthermore, China today is an active player in the various schemes in financial integration in the region. In security, China appears to be much less of a threat to stability in the region than in the 1990s.

Thus, China increasingly embraces and engages East Asia. In many East Asian countries the perception has grown, in particular during and since the financial crisis and 9/11, that they are pushed away by Washington. China has exploited this opportunity and filled the void. At the same time as America has put security issues in the centre of its foreign policy, China has demilitarized its rhetoric and policies. In contrast to previous decades, today it is China that promises a common future in harmony and prosperity. China's policy shift has resulted in a remarkable revision of perceptions in East Asia, as David Shambaugh has noted: 'Today China is an exporter of goodwill and consumer durables instead of revolution and weapons' (Shambough 2005: 65).

These developments raise important questions: Are we facing a major, structural trend leading to the appearance of new, region-wide economic and security arrangements, or is this just another rather meaningless, primarily rhetorical exercise? Does the political will to build effective and legitimate institutions and regimes exist in Asia?

In this volume, regionalism is defined as the ideational concept that underlies the emergence of regional identity and the policies that result from that concept. Regionalism drives regionalization, a term which also refers to the emergence of private-sector driven regional structures in the economic domain. Similar to the distinction between globalism and globalization, the latter can be measured, the former cannot. Although arguments continue about the adequate indicators for measuring regionalization and globalization, it is clear that we are evaluating the results of processes that have been inspired by regionalism and globalism.

Of course, a major problem is the geographical definition of the region. Which is the region we are examining in this volume? By looking at the various policy fields, it is becoming increasingly clear that there cannot be a single definition of 'Asia'. In security affairs, the region is comprised of a range of sub-regions. Northeast Asia, Southeast Asia and the South Pacific are areas with quite distinct and unrelated security matters. A number of non-Asian countries, e.g. Australia, have to be considered when analysing security affairs in the region. Above all, the United States continue to be the most important player in the security domain. In financial cooperation, there are a number of cooperation schemes that have over-lapping but not identical membership. Australia, for example, is playing an important role in regional cooperation of central bankers. By contrast, the United States is excluded from financial cooperation in Asia, at least when considering the more recent endeavours such as the Executive Meeting of East Asian and Pacific Central Banks (EMEAP). In trade, the mushrooming of bilateral agreements has resulted in a blurred picture. For the time being, there is no single large Asian integration project in trade.

Thus, the definition of an 'Asian region' depends on the policy field we are examining. Having said that, in this book the emphasis lies on those countries that represent the ASEAN+3 group, i.e. the member countries of the Association of Southeast Asian Nations, China, Japan and South Korea. This group of countries, all of them geographically located either in Southeast or Northeast Asia, constitutes the core of cooperation and integration processes in the whole of Asia. Whilst South Asia, India in particular, is gaining in importance, both in the economic and the security domain, South Asian countries have so far been only moderately successful in attracting attention for their regional cooperation projects. Nevertheless, India has been participating in the East Asia Summits in December 2005 and January 2007. In security affairs, South Asia – a sub-region characterized by enduring conflicts – is a useful geographic entity to consider.

Of course, the contributions in this edited volume aim to analyse more than the political statements that have been made on the issue of regional integration in Asia. In the various fields, we discuss interests and actors involved. The forces at work in favour of regional cooperation as well as those working for national solutions are identified. In the first decade of the twenty-first century, Asia experiences both dimensions simultaneously, and this book will shed light on these issues.

In Chapter 2, David Camroux demonstrates that the current focus on East Asian regionalism is somehow too narrow. By contrast, a conception of greater Asia including India becomes evident, if one analyses the historical evolution of the differing concepts and other factors than just economic integration and interests. He analyses two different aspects: the dynamics and evolution of Asian regionalism including the actors; and the different factors driving their behaviour. Situating the current regional integration process within the historical perspective and referring to the evolution of different concepts between the 1930s and today, Camroux specifies various important aspects: first, the process seems to be driven more by Realpolitik than by shared values; second, 'Asia' as a concept has been a Western invention, taken up by Asian elites, who, third, define themselves in opposition to colonialism (nowadays neo-colonialism). Therefore, different countries were – and still are – part of different concepts. The two important competing models are the Asian-Pacific model and the East Asian one; this can be seen today in the struggle between APEC and the idea of an East Asian Economic Group, today evolving as the ASEAN+3 group. Camroux stresses the importance of non-state actors and the emerging feeling of 'East Asian oneness'. He then takes a closer look at ASEAN+3 and its attempt to incorporate China, where a shift of importance from ASEAN to the '+3' seems to be dominant.

Chapter 3 by Thomas G. Moore seeks to answer the question how China has sought to use regional and global multilateralism in managing foreign policy challenges, or, to simplify it, whether the ultimate goal of Beijing's more active participation in multilateralism is integration or domination. Moore provides an outline of China's 'new multilateralism', i.e. its cooperation with various regional and global institutions and its pro-multilateralism rhetoric. He explores different approaches to explain this tendency towards multilateral cooperation, first by explaining it through a liberal internationalist perspective, then by challenging this analysis with the help of a realist approach and empirical findings, mainly based on interviews with Asian political leaders.

Moore addresses two important questions: Do the motives of China's active involvement in multilateral cooperation matter? Will its interests be transformed over time through the experience of active multilateralism (foreign policy learning)? Moore underscores the implications of the two different explanations of China's multilateralism. In accordance with liberal institutionalism, globalization is and will remain the driving force behind multilateral efforts, so that learning and value changing will take place. In contrast, a realist model suggests multilateralism as a means. Consequently, whether China will use and enhance this form of cooperation is not yet clear. On balance, Moore considers China's regional strategy to be part of its Grand Strategy and assesses that China cooperates to compete.

In Chapter 4 Takashi Terada emphasizes the central role Japan has played in the formation of various kinds of regionalism in Asia. Terada identifies three dimensions of regionalism in Asia that help to identify a distant Asian approach to regionalism. First, the involvement of governments occurs gradually. In early stages of regional integration in Asia, governments tend to play a very limited role. Second, the emphasis of regionalism has been changing from development facilitating to trade liberalization. Third, regionalism in Asia has been trying to integrate the emerging Asian economies as well as acknowledging the rising weight of Asian economies.

Of course, the rise of China has influenced the Japanese thinking on Asian regionalism. China creates difficulties for Japanese policy makers, because the establishment of a regional community in Asia for the time being cannot be based on values such as freedom, democracy or human rights. In ASEAN+3 a controversy arose between China and Japan over the question of membership of Australia, New Zealand and India. Terada argues that Japan's role as a bridge between Western and Asian countries is increasingly challenged. At the same time, Japan's leadership aspirations in the region are called into question by the rise of China.

In regional trade, the most significant developments in recent years have been the weakening of traditional processes of regional integration and the rise of bilateral free trade agreements. Even prior to September 11, Asian observers had increasingly evaluated APEC as a tool of American foreign policy. APEC's failure to provide any meaningful response to the biggest economic crisis in the Asia-Pacific region since 1945 made it, if not irrelevant, then less important, for many Asian members.

Frustrated with the lacklustre development of APEC, and in view of the emerging free trade agreement (FTA) networks of the European Union and the USA, Asian countries have begun to follow the bilateral trend. The implementation of discriminatory trade arrangements is arguably the most significant development in intergovernmental relations since the Asian crisis of 1997 (Ravenhill 2003: 300). However, these policies might be short-sighted for a number of reasons. First, preferential trade agreements might not make a significant contribution to the deepening of the international division of labour. Second, the emergence of bilateral trade agreements is accompanied by the need for the introduction of complex rules of origin, which is making international trade more, not less complex. Third, weaker partners in bilateral agreements may be gaining less than expected in these endeavours.

In Chapter 5 on bilateral trade, the recent policies of Australia, Singapore and Thailand are given specific consideration. Australia has been implementing an FTA with the United States, and this agreement is surprisingly asymmetric in favour of America. Singapore has been promoting bilateral trade agreements very actively, but this may have damaged the position of the country in the region. Thailand's cases show that the bilateral road is, when examined carefully, probably as complex as the multilateral regulation of trade.

The changing trade regimes in the region are of course a challenge for the private sector. In Chapter 6, Andrew Staples analyses the consequences of regionalism in Asia for corporate strategies. In particular, he analyses Japanese multinationals and their responses to the transformation of the East Asian political economy. Staples argues that the responses of multinational corporations to regionalism reflect the changing political economy within which firms operate.

This is evident when looking at the car industry. The regional production networks of Japanese manufacturers are structured in a manner that accommodates regional trade regulations. Trade policy has a decisive influence on corporate strategy.

Staples describes the international production networks of Toyota, Honda and Mitsubishi. He argues that the transformation of the political economy has not only resulted in the emergence of production networks that utilize national comparative advantage, but rather have led to the development of regional approaches in production and management. The central role of Thailand as a prime location for car manufacturing has been emerging as a consequence of the implementation of trade-facilitating measures. Staples examines in detail firm-level data which enables us to understand the issues central to the decisions of companies regarding investment, production and trading within a region.

In Chapter 7 on monetary regionalism, the progress in financial and monetary cooperation is analysed. Whilst the region did not cooperate in this field prior to the Asian crisis, since 1997 a number of initiatives have emerged. Although it is not clear whether Asian governments will continue to deepen their cooperation in this field, the example of the successful introduction of the euro as well as the unpleasant experience of 1997 are contributing to strengthen the support in the region for monetary regionalism. The various initiatives are analysed. Of particular importance are the Chiang Mai initiative, regional surveillance of financial markets and the recent schemes for the promotion of regional bond markets. Of course, as in the entire debate of regionalism in Asia, the specific role of China deserves special attention. The creation of a Greater Chinese Currency Union appears to be possible, although a distant prospect at this stage.

As mentioned before, the United States has been excluded from emerging institutions, such as the increasingly important EMEAP and from the Chiang Mai process that was started in the year 2000. EMEAP is not a purely Asian venture, because its membership includes – apart from the ASEAN+3 countries – Australia and New Zealand. The importance of EMEAP has not escaped the attention of Washington, but the USA is excluded from this scheme today. Of course, the United States and its currency continue to be of great importance in Asia. Nevertheless, the request of the American Federal Reserve to join was turned down by the Asian central bankers in EMEAP.

On a sceptical note, Douglas Webber argues in Chapter 8 that political integration in East Asia will not take place despite growing economic interdependence. Although economic factors in the region are conducive to political integration, certain other factors impede it: security doubts due to mistrust between the countries; the Sino-Japanese rivalry; political, economic and cultural heterogeneity; the actual or purported American opposition to integration; and fundamental strategic divergences. In particular, Webber argues that countries that view each other as security threats do not integrate politically.

Webber suggests that Asia cannot be seen as a 'bloc' comparable to the EU or NAFTA. The often cited example for political integration following economic integration – Europe – is reviewed and reinterpreted. Economic integration in

Europe might have been a necessary but not a sufficient condition; additionally there have been three other important factors: (1) the threat caused by the Soviet Union, (2) Germany tamed by its division, and (3) security guarantees by NATO. If such additional conditions are lacking, closer economic interdependence and growing political antagonism may co-exist for indeterminate periods of time.

In Chapter 9 Derek McDougall analyses the role of ASEAN and the Pacific Island Forum and shows which security threats exist(ed) in the respective region. The extent to which the regional organization influenced the situation is discussed. Regarding Southeast Asia, he identifies state-society and interstate tensions as the main threats. Given ASEAN member countries' strong commitment to national sovereignty, ASEAN did not play an active role in settling specific intrastate conflicts (for example East Timor). Besides, the ASEAN countries lack sufficient resources to deal with major crises, e.g. the Tsunami catastrophe of 2004. Instead, ASEAN contributes to the regional security by generating norms that diminish the probability of the future emergence of crises, e.g. the principle of peaceful interstate conflict resolution. Additionally, ASEAN had some influence in locating Southeast Asian security issues within a broader context by enhancing the importance of ASEAN countries in the 'Asia-Pacific' or 'East Asia'.

Finally, in Chapter 10 Golam Robbani explores the relationship between regional integration and regional peace and security. In this context, he examines the development of the European Coal and Steel Community and potential implications for South Asia. Robbani explains the validity of the commercial peace hypothesis on a regional level. Given the limited pacifying effect of bilateral economic integration – in a globalized world where countries can easily evade cooperation with difficult partners – and multilateral integration – where every country depends on the global systems rather than on particular countries – regional economic integration is seen to have the most intense pacifying impact.

Further, Robbani discusses the origins of European integration, in particular the several wars in Europe and their catastrophic consequences, the spread and threat of communism and the threat of US hegemony, and compares them with South Asian incentives for cooperation. Then, the applicability of the EU process to the Asian situation is considered. He highlights important differences concerning the regional situation but also the global structures. Nevertheless, Robbani evaluates the European model as principally applicable. Therefore, he proposes to develop a South Asian Economic Community.

The evolution of regionalism is, of course, a continuing process. If current trends continue, it is plausible to expect a much more central role for China in the region, as well as a less prominent role for the United States. The relationship between China and Japan is having a decisive role in that context. Until recently, any reconciliation between these two Asian powers appeared to be far-fetched and unrealistic. In 2007, however, both governments have displayed a longing for cooperation at an unprecedented level. If this reunion were to continue, regionalism in Asia may accelerate unexpectedly. In such a scenario, the currently separated process of regional cooperation in trade, finance and security could be amalgamated and regionalism in Asia could be leading to the emergence of a new pole in international affairs. At the same time, the analysis of the evolution of regionalism in Asia in this volume clearly demonstrates that there are many reasons for a more sceptical evaluation of the region's ability and willingness to deepen cooperation in economic and security affairs.

References

Pempel, T.J. (2006) 'The Race to Connect East Asia: An Unending Steeplechase', *Asian Economic Policy Review* 1(December): 239–254.

Ravenhill, John (2003) 'The New Bilateralism in the Asia Pacific', *Third World Quarterly* 24(April): 299–317.

Shambaugh, David (2005) 'China Engages Asia', *International Security* 29(Winter): 64–99.

2 'Asia, whose Asia?' Evolving conceptions of an Asian Community from the 1920s till today

David Camroux

Regionalization and regionalism in Asia

> What is the Pacific? It is necessary to define our terms by specifying *whose* Pacific – and when.
>
> (Dirlik 1998: 15)

Substituting 'Asia' for 'the Pacific' in the above quotation from Arif Dirlik's seminal edited volume on a previously fashionable geographical construction, provides some indication of the thrust of this chapter. The study of regional integration in Asia has developed apace since the 1990s linked to the rise of what has been described as the new regionalism (Gamble and Payne 1996; Söderbaum and Shaw 2004). Behind this literature is an underlying assumption that 'geography is destiny', to use Jessie Poon's (2001) prescient questioning formula. This broadening literature is increasingly sophisticated and interdisciplinary involving an examination of the inter-linkages between the economic, political and security dimensions (Beeson 2007; Katzenstein and Shiraishi 2006; Pempel 2005; Shambaugh 2005).

While it is not the purpose of this chapter to provide a critique of this contemporary literature, two fundamental points need to be underlined. First, the terms 'regionalism' and 'regionalization' are often used interchangeably, particularly by economists (Baldwin 2006), in describing the construction of regional entities in Asia. This involves a laudable attempt to bring the state back in, so to speak, by defining regionalism as a 'top down State led process' (Pempel 2005: 6; Kim 2004: 40). Certainly, while the state/non-state distinction needs to be acknowledged and incorporated in analytical grids, it should be removed as the defining element in differentiating 'regionalism' and 'regionalization'. Rather the state/non-state duality is valid for both phenomena.

In order to provide a more nuanced appreciation of Asian regional integration an analytical distinction is made between 'regionalism' and 'regionalization'. 'Regionalism' is defined as the development of identity construction across national boundaries. 'Regionalism' is conceptualized in relation to 'regionalization' – at the meso level (Gamble and Payne 1996) of international relations – what 'nationalism' is in relation to 'nation-building' at the micro level. 'Regionalism' is thus defined as being essentially ideational implying degrees of identity and the construction thereof.[1] This approach extends He's (2004) examination of the development of an Asian ideal. As with nationalism and Stato-national construc- tions, there are interactions between process and ideational/identity developments with, in practice, each feeding off the other. As Acharya (2004) has demon- strated, identity constructions and norm creation cannot be isolated from under- lying processes of regionalization in Asia, processes that involve convergences between market-driven actions and government policies. In this regard state actors are not the only custodians and vectors of ideas of regional identity. On the contrary, as the following analysis attempts to demonstrate, the idea of an Asian Community has also been the handiwork of public intellectuals and epistemic communities over the last century or so.

Relying on this new reformulation of 'regionalization' and 'regionalism' this chapter has two major objectives. First, it is an attempt to answer Hemmer and Katzenstein's (2002) appeal for an eclectic approach, both within and across dis- ciplines in the study of region. Second, it attempts to demonstrate that a longer- term historical perspective[2] calls into question an East Asian, and particularly sinocentric concept of both regionalization and, above all, of regionalism and would hint at the renewed relevance of concepts of a Greater Asia.

Pre-war Pan-Asianism[3]

As a number of authors have indicated, the notion of Asia dates from a Greek conception of a world that is described today as the Near or Middle East (Korhonen 1997; Milner and Johnson 1997). In the millennia of exchange between peoples in what are today geographically labelled as China, India and Southeast Asia with other peoples in the Middle East and then with Europe senses of difference developed, but not to the extent, it would appear, of engendering a sense of difference as one unique Asian people. That pre-colonial history remains relevant, at least rhetorically, in contemporary discourses on an Asian Community for they place a great deal of stress on trade, cultural and religious interchange as laying the grounds for distinct concepts of Asia today.[4]

Nevertheless, we really have to wait till the era of European imperialism to have a sense of an essentialized Europe being juxtaposed with an idealized Asia. In the latter half of the nineteenth century and early twentieth century intellectu- als in China, Japan and India began to present a vision of Europe (and the West) as an entity. In China, as Rebecca Karl (2002) has argued, nationalism at the turn of the twentieth century was impacted on by the language and consciousness of Western colonial exploitation and nationalist resistance movements in South Africa and the Philippines. The Filipino writer José Rizal's martyrdom inspired the first successful – and then betrayed – independence movement in Asia.[5]

The impact of the Russo-Japanese War of 1905 should also not be underesti- mated. The defeat of a European power by an Asian country demonstrated that the strength of Asian civilizations lay not only in the past, as the Orientalist per- ception would have it, but in a capacity to embrace modernity. The link between pan-Asian pride in glorious pasts and modern economic success continues to be an essential trope in Asian Community narratives a century later. Sun Yat Sen, in his famous speech in Kobe in November 1924, saw the victory of an Asiatic nation as demonstrating that '[Asian] blood was thicker than water' (Sun [1924] 1941: 143). For him, Asian peoples needed to unite around the principles of benevolence and virtue to free the oppressed. That vision was to be shattered when the Japanese answered his concluding rhetorical question – 'whether Japan will be the hawk of Western civilization of the rule of might' Sun [1924] 1941: 151) – with their invasion of China. Asian blood there was to be, but spilt not in an expression of solidarity but in fratricidal conflict.

While Mahatma Gandhi did not inscribe the struggle for Indian independence as part of a broader anti-colonial struggle for all of Asia, he did see it as a civilizational contest. On the eve of independence Gandhi advocated the concept of an Asian federation praising 'Asia's special message of spiritual enlightenment' (quoted in Jaffrelot 2003: 37). During the interwar period Rabindranath Tagore argued that all Asian countries shared the same characteristics of 'spiritual strength', 'simplicity' and a 'recognition of social obligation'. The writings of Tagore found a sympathetic audience in China and Japan (Hay 1970) laying the grounds for a vision of the Sino-Indic Asia prominent in Bandung and that re-emerged in the debates surrounding the Kuala Lumpur summit.

During the first congress of the League Against Imperialism held in Brussels in 1927 the first Sino-Indian expressions of Asian solidarity can be found in the meeting between Nehru and representatives from the Chinese Kuomintang (Samarani 2005). During the same interwar period Jawaharlal Nehru felt that, by stressing the notion of harmony with Nature, one shared by China, India had provided East Asia with a solid civilizational base that was in contrast to the materialism of the West. On the eve of independence in March 1947, he organized a Conference on Asian Relations bringing together 250 delegates from 25 countries, in effect proclaiming India as the leader of Asia's ineluctable common march towards independence.[6]

Turning to Japan, while the celebrated Westernizer of the Meiji restoration, Fukuzama Yukichi, felt that in order to develop Japan needed to 'escape from Asia and join Europe' (*Datsu A Nyû-Ô*), others, like the art historian Okakura Kakuzô, celebrated Japan's cultural bonds with the Asian continent in his assertion that 'Asia is One' (Ching 2001: 280). The point is that, either embraced or rejected, the idea of a modern Asia was already taking form. Yet as Tessa Morris-Suzuki (1998) points out the concept of 'Asia' was elastic, designed to fit the needs and purposes of the user. She further indicates that at the time of Bandung, the social critic Takeuchi Yyoshimi described 'Asia' as not something that possessed a cultural essence or innate spirit but as a 'means' or 'method' – '*hôhô toshite no Ajia*'. In other words, rephrased into the terminology previously proposed, we have allusions to both regionalism and regionalization.

The brutal experience, for many at least, of Japanese-inspired Pan-Asianism's geopolitical transfiguration into the Greater East Asia Co-Prosperity Sphere led the whole of the concept into disrepute. Yet at the time a significant number of non-Japanese willingly shared in this imperially led experiment in regional integration (Duara 2003; Young 1999). Be that as it may, for several decades economists have argued for the importance of the colonial infrastructure created by the Japanese in both Korea and Taiwan, as being an essential ingredient in the economic take-off of the first Asian tigers.

In the post-war period Japanese leaders were to disavow the rhetoric of Pan-Asianism. At Bandung the low level delegation headed by a technocratic Minister of State, Tatsunosuke Takashi, barely participated in the debates, let alone articulating a vision of Asian solidarity (Mackie 2005: 95). Nevertheless, for the leaderships of burgeoning Asian countries the same basic economic imperatives remain, which as will be argued later in the contemporary discourse of the Chinese leadership, can lead to similar ideological clothing. In Beijing today, as much as in Tokyo in the 1930s and 1940s, the rhetoric of anti-Western fraternity, as much as appeals to Asian co-prosperity, would appear to be relevant tools in soft power practice in promoting access to markets and raw materials.

The Asian African Conference in Bandung[7]

> Much will depend on whether Peking considers itself as more Asian than communist, or vice versa …
>
> > (*Times of India* 28 December 1954, quoted
> > in Mackie 2005: 62)

When one looks at the Bandung conference and, 50 years later, to the first two East Asian Community summits in Kuala Lumpur and in Cebu (in December 2005 and January 2007, respectively), it is a realist conception of international relations that comes to the fore. The concern of the Asian parties in Bandung in 1955, and particularly those of Nehru, was to socialize China as a responsible actor in the international community and thus, although this was not stated, to remove it as a threat to the perceived national interests of neighbouring Asian countries. Other Asian leaders at the time were preoccupied by two inter-related issues, namely, the PRC's support for Communist insurgencies in their countries and the allegiance of their minorities of Chinese origin. These two questions were to be resolved in the following years. Nevertheless, 50 years afterwards the same perennial questions of autonomy, tribute and suzerainty persist. At the summit held in Kuala Lumpur in December 2005, the same realpolitik concerns would seem to be at play. The same basic question remains: 'What are we to do with China?' Underlying this question is that posited at the beginning of this article, 'to whom does Asia belong?'

The first conference between African and Asian leaders was held in the euphoria of the post-independence period in Asia and as an instrumental lobby effort for decolonization in Africa. (Kahin 1956). Given developments in Asian regional integration over the ensuing 50 years, what is particularly striking at Bandung is the almost total absence of questions of economic relations. This can be explained, in part, by the then underdeveloped status of the participating countries as well as by the concern then with economic self-sufficiency as a necessary adjunct to political independence. Asianness in Bandung was conceptualized not only in relation to the West, but also in relation to the other continent participating, albeit in a token way, Africa.[8] In the words of one delegate: 'This Conference has represented an effort by these countries to regain their personality and international dignity and was an assertion of their personality vis-à-vis the West' (quoted in Kahin 1956: 38). The Asia of Bandung was essentially a political construct involving the newly independent nation-states spanning an arc from the Middle East to Indonesia.

The underlying importance of Bandung is that it was the culmination of a process of defining Asia within the struggle against colonialism. In the post-colonial period echoes of that struggle would linger in much of the discourse against neo-colonialism (Ingleson 1997). Certainly for Mahathir Mohamed, Prime Minister of Malaysia from 1981 till 2003, anti-neo-colonialism was the central element in his campaign for an East Asian Community (Mahathir 1999). Bandung's greatest legacy, however, was in defining the norms of non-interference, non-alignment and consensus decision-making that form the central elements of what came to be called the ASEAN way.[9] Those internationalist norms, however, sit uncomfortably with nationalistic capitalistic visions even in the most outward looking of Southeast Asian countries, namely Singapore (Amrith 2005).

Asia-Pacific versus East Asia: Competing regional concepts

In the decades following Bandung and, in particular, in the 1970s and 1980s two competing visions of Asia emerged: that of an Asia (limited to East Asia) for, and of, itself and that of an Asia as part of, one of the concentric circles of a larger entity, the Asia-Pacific. In institutional terms this can be seen as the contest between APEC, the Asia-Pacific Economic Cooperation forum, and EAEG, the East Asian Economic Group (Higgott and Stubbs 1995). The idea of a Pacific Community dates from the period after the First World War, in, for example, the work of the Institute of Pacific Relations (Woods 1993), but serious institutional proposals emerged only in the late 1960s and early 1970s amongst academics and business people in Japan and Australia (Ravenhill 2001).

From a realist perspective, this Canberra–Tokyo axis in the Pacific Community debate is not fortuitous: the two countries represent the two anchors of the US Alliance system in the Asia-Pacific, have mutually beneficial and balanced trade and investment relations and both suffer, for rather different reasons, from suspicions of their place as legitimate Asian actors. In the formulating of the Pacific Community idea both found a comfortable home, so to speak, at least in terms of a new geo-identity. More importantly, through its massive FDI and development assistance in Asia, the off-shoring of a great deal of Japanese production to the NICs and then to other Asian countries after the Plaza Agreement, Japan was able to develop the elements of its soft power in Asia (Katzenstein, 1997).

From the perspective of this chapter, what is particularly important in the evolution of Asia-Pacific regionalism is the role of, at least ostensibly, non-state actors (Woods 1993). The precursors to APEC, notably the Pacific Trade and Development (PAFTAD) Conference, the Pacific Basin Economic Council (PBEC) and the Pacific Economic Cooperation Council (PECC), generally had tripartite memberships involving business people, academics and public servants 'present in an unofficial capacity'. The creation of APEC in 1989 seemed a significant development, insofar as political leaders became involved and a degree of institutionalization initiated. Nevertheless, the ministerial meetings that begun the process and the annual summits that began in 1993 involve the leaders of the now 21 member economies (Ravenhill, 2001). The use of the term 'economies' rather than 'countries' is not insignificant: APEC is the only body in which the 'three Chinas' (the PRC, Taiwan and Hong Kong) are all present, a situation facilitated by the fiction of it as an economic forum.

Moreover, the original agenda of trade liberalization and economic development is one that achieves a broad minimal consensus. A realist perspective on geo-economic relations would seem to underlie the enthusiasm of the smaller countries, such as South Korea, Singapore and Australia, who have been the most supportive of the APEC project. Given the perception that the real tensions in trade relations are those between the United States and Japan and the United States and China, being in a forum in which all the three major players are present is seen as a way of making sure that their national interests are taken into account. According to Terada (1998) for Japanese governments in the 1970s and 80s, promotion of an Asia-Pacific concept of region was a second-best choice to that of an East Asian group, but one that was seen as a way of avoiding potential criticism that Japan was trying to revive the Greater Asian Co-prosperity Sphere of the Second World War.

The competing vision of an East Asian Economic Group (EAEG), first mooted by Malaysian Prime Minister Mahathir in 1990, also had a realist underpinning. For him, in order to achieve a balance of power in its favour in a bloc against bloc situation, East Asia needed to consolidate and strengthen its own regional market and, perhaps, institutions. Moreover, such a process of regionalization needs to be accompanied by the development of an East Asian consciousness, to use the expression of the late Noordin Sopiee (1995). Asian values and their purported superiority became inextricably bound up with the promotion of a process of regional integration. Mahathir's proposal was strongly opposed by the US Administration who ensured that it would not receive the backing of the Japanese government.[10] In institutional terms the EAEG proposal was watered down to become the East Asian Economic Caucus (EAEC), an informal meeting within the APEC framework. Nevertheless, at least at this juncture, Mahathir's proposal trumped APEC, returning in a new guise as ASEAN+3.

When one turns to the question of regionalism, the success has been more complete. The language of an East Asian consciousness was taken up by other Asian political leaders such as, in Singapore, Lee Kuan Yew and his successor Goh Chok Tong (2004), in the Philippines, Fidel Ramos and in Thailand, Thaksin Shinawatra. In Malaysia itself Mahathir's former deputy, Anwar Ibrahim, modified the Asian consciousness discourse in calling for an Asian renaissance in dialogue with the West (Anwar 1996a). Moreover, alongside the state vectors of East Asian regionalism a plethora of institutions such as the ASEAN-ISISs and of public intellectuals often linked to the former (e.g. Mahbubani 2002) propagated the ideal of an Asian identity.

Finally, the 1990s saw a breaking down of barriers in the area of popular culture. Forms of popular entertainment such as cinema, rock music, variety shows and television sit-coms have crossed frontiers and enjoy great popularity in neighbouring countries (Ching 2001). An unheralded and unquantifiable strengthening of an East Asian sense of oneness, i.e. an East Asian regionalism, through the vectors of popular culture is in train. Cultural transmutations, most recently with the enormous success of Korean popular music, cinema and sit-coms in both China and Japan and, to some extent, in Southeast Asia, are a much underrated element in the development of an Asian identity (Iwabuchi *et al.* 2004). Such pan-Asian cosmopolitanism – articulated in part through diasporic communities (Callahan 2006: Chapter 6) – combined with other material transformations has led to the development of a kind of pan-Asian middle-class lifestyle that Khoo (1999) and Shiraishi (2006) see as an essential element in the forcefulness of Asian regionalism. This being said, the Chinese role in facilitating Asian cultural regionalism remains a problematical work in progress.

Since 9/11 attempts by the Bush administration to 'politicize' APEC by using it as another forum to prosecute the war on terrorism, have led to a degree of disenchantment amongst its Asian members. Coupled with this is the tendency of the Bush administration to function at the micro level (i.e. bilaterally) or the macro level (multilaterally) when necessary, the meso level (i.e. regional processes, such as APEC) being less of an attractive option. In this regard, despite the rhetoric of open regionalism, APEC has been unable to hinder the proliferation of asymmetric bilateral PTAs in the region. While these are often presented as a 'latticework' on which an open trading region is to be constructed, the considerable evidence amassed by Christopher Dent (2006) would suggest that they have been antithetical to this objective. At the Hanoi APEC Summit of November 2006 proposals for an Asia-Pacific Free Trade sphere – after all the objective set at the first summit at Bogor in 1994 at the highest point of Asia-Pacific mobilizing rhetoric – were relegated to yet another study group and hopes for trade liberalization placed in a relaunching of the Doha Round. Caught between the Charybdis of multilateralism and the Scylla of bilateralism, it can be seriously asked whether APEC has lost its usefulness as a regional entity (Aggarwal and Kwei 2006).

Asia as 'ASEAN+3'

The Asian economic crisis of 1997–98 both coincided with, and impacted upon, long-term developments in the Asia-Pacific region. On a fundamental level it at least temporarily destroyed one of the tenants of the Asian values rhetoric, namely, that Asia's economic success is due to a number of specifically Asian cultural traits. Second, the crisis and its aftermath saw the departure, or the muting of the voices of a number of veteran political leaders such as Suharto, Lee Kwan Yew and, later,

Mahathir. Third, by not devaluing the yuan, the Chinese leadership demonstrated a degree of Asian solidarity. Fourth, the crisis revealed the weakness of the so-called ASEAN way, based on consensus and non-interference in the affairs of other member states. There was no pan-ASEAN response to the crisis and the political elites of Indonesia, Thailand and Malaysia all chose different paths to put their economies in order. Since the crisis the combined effects of uncontrolled burning and the ensuing pollution and environmental degradation, transnational terrorism and other soft security questions (such as piracy) have all contributed to calling into question ASEAN's weak form of intergovernmental regionalization.[11] ASEAN's internal coherence has also been sorely tested by its own enlargement to include Vietnam, in 1995, then of Burma/Myanmar and Laos in 1997 and finally of Cambodia in 1998. The inability of the peer pressure of other member countries to bring about even modest political change in Burma is but one manifestation of internal weakness. While describing ASEAN as a kind of 'regional delusion' (Martin Jones and Smith 2006) would be an exaggeration, still as these authors indicate, the shallowness of its institutionalization, and its lack of capabilities, limits its role as a regional actor.

In this context political and business elites in Southeast Asia have shown a concern to promote two complimentary agenda. On the one hand, to concentrate on developing ASEAN as a Free Trade Area pursuant to the AFTA agreement of 1992. On the other hand, as exemplified in declarations by the present Malaysian Prime Minister and the present Indonesian Vice-President, to try to maintain ASEAN as the core around which a putative East Asian Community can be built (Badawi 2004; Kalla 2006). Behind both objectives lies a concern to deal with the rise of China as a major economic and political actor. While some sectors of the ASEAN economies are clearly benefiting from China's economic growth, there is a strong perception that a north–south divide is opening up between Southeast and Northeast Asia, one that requires remedial action to ensure that Southeast Asia remains central to the regionalization process (Lim and Lee 2004).[12] Nevertheless, ASEAN leaders are seeking to tie China into more predictable economic relations through the signing of a Free Trade Agreement. In quite a realist strategy they are also seeking to balance Chinese influence and power through the signing of a similar agreement with Japan and through developed links with South Korea. In a sense what is sought is a reformulation of Mahathir's proposal for an East Asian Economic Group, but with ASEAN as its core (Hund 2003; Terada 2003).

Seen within a broader historical sweep, the essential question within Southeast Asia is the management of a relationship with China and, in the last century or so, Japan within the context of broader relations of trade, cultural contacts and political links extending to a larger world including India, Central Asia, the Middle East and Europe and, across the Pacific to the Americas. Put more prosaically, does being a crossroads constitute being central? The ASEAN+3 concept is particularly useful in this regard. The signing of an ASEAN–China Free Trade agreement demonstrates a capacity to negotiate in a unified way. Furthermore this agreement itself has become a bargaining chip in negotiations with the Japanese administration. Nevertheless, ASEAN's limited internal solidarity has been demonstrated by bilateral PTAs signed, or being negotiated, between Singapore and the United States and Australia, between Thailand and Australia and between the Philippines and Japan (Desker 2004). Moreover, since its post-Cold War enlargement to include authoritarian states, ASEAN's cohesiveness around a semi-democratic model of governance has been dissipated.

Within the regionalization processes at play, there are tendencies working, if not for the marginalization of Southeast Asian countries, at least to greater dependence on the '+3' of Northeast Asia. These changing balances are reflected in new conceptualizations within the domain of Asian regionalism. At its annual summit in November 2001, ASEAN+3 leaders accepted the proposal of then Korean President, Kim Dae Jung, for an East Asian Vision Group (2002) comprising eminent persons from the participating countries. A successor group involving officials from the same countries, the East Asian Study Group (2002), was also established to scrutinize the report of the former and, in practice, to tone down some of its proposals. The desirability, even inevitability, of an East Asian Community was strongly vaunted in both reports, although its membership was left unspecified.

Contesting Chinese centrality

> We need to integrate China into the regional economy in an orderly, win-win manner.
>
> > (Singapore Prime Minister, Lee Hsien Loong
> > 25 May 2005)[13]

Japanese involvement in determining the parameters of an Asian Community continues unabated with, for example, the proposals made by the Japan Forum on International Relations (2003) and the Council on (an) East Asian Community set up a year later. Chaired by former Prime Minister, Nakasone Yasuhiro, the latter involves participants from 12 major Japanese think-tanks, 14 of the largest Japanese corporations and 63 individual members from academia, the media and the public services. Its first report adopted in August 2005 stressed two elements confirmed by the praxis of the Koizumi government. The first, related to regionalization processes, concerns the 'principles of openness, transparency and inclusion' in defining the limits of an Asian Community.The second, on the level of regionalism, proposed that:

> a soft regional identity should be promoted in East Asia based on the recognition that the common characteristic of various cultures in East Asia is its hybrid composition of local, traditional and modern cultures with the increasing common influence of a common urban culture in East Asia.

The policy report then continues, in a direct rebuttal of a Mahathirian concept of Asia, by suggesting that 'the development of an identity focused primarily on differences with other regions would not be desirable' (Council on East Asian Community 2005: 7).

The problem for Japanese leaders – as for those in Australia (Richardson 2005) – is how to reconcile their participation in what the conventional jargon describes as two concentric circles of regional construction in the Asia-Pacific, namely the intra-East Asian and the extra-East Asian, across the Pacific.[14] This involves assuring themselves of the existing and cost-effective protection of the United States while advancing their economic and political interests with their neighbours. As Peter Katzenstein (2005) has demonstrated, Asian (and European) regionalization exists within a larger international regime where the United States as the only remaining hyper-power plays the major structuring role, in what he characterizes as an American Imperium. Other authors see this imperium functioning both through US hard and soft power mechanisms (Robison 2006) and also through transnational regulatory governance (Jayasuriya 2006).[15]

It would seem that for the Japanese leadership the most efficacious way to reconcile these seemingly contradictory demands is to ensure the enlargement of a putative Asian Community not only to include Australia and New Zealand but, more importantly, India. Indeed 'playing the India card' in relation to China fits rather conveniently into previous recommendations of the US policy community and the Bush administration as part of the 'congagement'[16] of China (Richardson 2002). Japan's investment in India has not been merely financial but also intellectual. A form of influence-building and agenda-setting in Southeast Asia[17] by such quasi-state bodies as the Japan Institute of International Affairs has been extended to India. For example, the Delhi-based think-tank most involved in propagating the concept of an Asian Community within India, the Research and Information System for Developing Countries (RIS), has had its activities generously supported by the Sasakawa Peace Foundation.

At the state level, there is a competition occurring between the political leaderships of China and Japan to enrol – or in the Japanese case to continue to enrol – the ASEAN countries as adjuncts to their own internal development. Despite at least a 30-year advantage in terms of economic and political engagement in Southeast Asia, it is the Japanese political and business elite that finds itself on the defensive at the beginning of the twenty-first century. One explanation for this is that millennial political and economic relations between China and Southeast Asia have reasserted themselves, at least rhetorically, to the detriment of Japan– Southeast Asia relations. The latter are not only less historically profound but continue to be poisoned, in China and South Korea at least, by continued reference for domestic political reasons, to Japanese behaviour during the Second World War. Certainly the need to somehow neuter Japan is part of contemporary regional practice. Japanese attempts at a more assertive security role in Southeast Asia – for example, in sending its Coast Guard to help patrol the Malacca Straits – have been ill received, while the Chinese proposal by Wen Jiaboa (2006) for security cooperation with ASEAN has been welcomed more favourably.

While Japanese proposals for a much broader Asian Community were most forcefully articulated by Koizumi (2002) himself, they also sprang essentially from METI, the same Ministry (as MITI) that previously argued for a purely East Asian regional construct. In Japan's 'new deal for Asia', to use the terms of METI's Vice-Minister Kitamura Toshiaki (2006), both a positive Japanese role in Southeast Asia and ASEAN centrality would appear to be dependent on containing China within a larger regional entity in which Indian membership is crucial. Kitamura's proposal for an Asian OECD financed by Japan, while on one level an effort in partnership and transparency, can also be seen as an effort to further socialize China and to maintain Japanese control of the regional agenda.

It is to this 'peaceful rise of China', to use the expression of the Chinese leadership, a rise engendering greater interdependence with other Asian countries (Ash 2005; Shambaugh 2005), that we shall now turn. The doctrine of China's peaceful rise (*heping jueqi*) developed from a new security concept elaborated in a number of Chinese think-tanks in the mid-1990s, many of whom were already involved in cooperative activities with similar security-oriented think-tanks in Asia and elsewhere. Emphasis is placed in the doctrine on the soft power means of promoting China's national interests – and its own internal development – in particular through multilateral and regional cooperation (Zhang and Tang 2005). Since its enunciation the term 'peaceful rise' has been modified in a way to embrace all of Asia (Suettinger 2005). Chinese willingness to engage in constructive dialogues with neighbouring partners has undoubtedly both quickened since the Asian financial crisis of 1997 and reflects, at the regional level, the normalization of Chinese behaviour as an international actor, symbolized at the multilateral level by Chinese entry into the WTO in 2001. As President Wen Jiaboa (2006) insisted with his hosts in Kuala Lumpur, 2004 had seen a 25 per cent rise in the ASEAN countries' exports to China. Chinese views of the East Asia Summit (Huang 2005; Pang 2005) echo completely the realist perspectives of their Asian partners with, however, a discordant objective, namely that a united Asia would both balance and socialize the United States![18]

One of the underrated vectors of Chinese engagement in regional construction has been the Boao Forum on Asia, vaunted as the Asian Davos. In the space of four years, the forum has established itself as a significant meeting place for political and business leaders from an Asia encompassing also the Indian sub-continent, Central Asia and Australasia. Other than the benefits brought to the tourist industry in Hainan, the most important contribution for China's soft power is to put the leadership in an agenda-setting role in Asian regionalization. For example at the April 2004 conference, the newly appointed Chinese President, Hu Jianto (2004), gave a five-point defence of China's contribution to 'Asian rejuvenation' and its commitment to the building of an Asian Community. Other Asian leaders such as Goh Chok Tong (2004) paid their appropriate rhetorical tribute, while a year later Malaysian Prime Minister Badawi (2005) elaborated on a seven-point roadmap for the establishment of an East Asian Community. For Prime Minister John Howard (2005) Boao was yet another forum to argue for Australia's right to be part of an East Asian Community by dint of its degree of economic integration with East Asia.

Yet despite the Boao Forum's ostensible role in Chinese agenda-setting, two major diplomatic events for the Chinese leadership in autumn 2006 demonstrated some of the complexities, and potential limitations, in Chinese capacity to take on a leadership role within a larger Asian entity. Despite a renewal of the commitment to establish a China–ASEAN FTA by 2011, the third China–ASEAN Business and Investment Summit was completely overshadowed three days later in Beijing by the grandiose China–Africa Cooperation Summit, involving the presence of over 40 heads of state.[19] These two meetings highlighted China's role as global player for whom regional solidarities in Asia are secondary to bilateral and multilateral modus operandi.

While both these summits were essentially about trade and investment and, above all, Chinese access to raw materials and energy sources, the language of the China–Africa summit in, for example, the opening speech by Hu Jintao (2006) harked back to the non-aligned, anti-colonial rhetoric of Bandung, however with a new twist. Chinese political leaders presented their country as a model for modern development, a fraternal exemplar, so to speak, as well as a trading partner within a community of interests dating from 1955. His speech referred to the same civilizational arguments, claims of common destiny and goals, found in Bandung ... and in much of the rhetoric of Asian regionalism. While it may be premature to talk in terms of a Beijing consensus (Ramo 2004) in ideological competition with a Washington consensus, the elements of such an ideological model can be gleaned in recent years. Yet the elaboration of a Chinese universal message remains work in progress.

These two meetings underlined the problem faced by China's leaders and public intellectuals in articulating a particularly Asian vision. This springs from the lack of a common shared experience with other neighbouring countries in attaining independence and, above all, economic development. As far as the neighbouring Asian countries are concerned a Chinese universal message is absent or, in the references to ties of kith and kin,[20] is extrapolated as referring to the past. Other than a concern with mutual enrichment, there would appear to be no sense of an Asian 'ideal' projected into the future. At this juncture the Chinese political leadership would appear to be unwilling and/or unable to articulate a vision of a future Asian Community. How can this be explained? A realist view would underline the unwillingness of other Asian elites to accept Chinese leadership. More importantly a concern with Asia is subsidiary to the Chinese leadership's concern with its international objectives (Foot 2005). However, a fuller explanation would require looking at internal dynamics within Chinese society itself to tease out the links between foreign (and regional) relations and domestic considerations (Bhalla 2005). For some writers, such as Wang Gungwu (2004), Chinese cultural exceptionalism and the reinvention of values linked to China's peaceful rise prevents it from acting as an exemplar within the region. For other writers (Jian 2006), using the language of Jürgen Habermas, constitutional patriotism will need to replace primitive nationalism through a process of democratization within China and the strengthening of its civil society in order for China to share values, norms and procedures in developing an East Asian identity.

Neighbours at the club's doorstep

A third development, one which it is perhaps too early to measure in terms of its impact on Asian regional integration, needs to be addressed, namely Central Asia's burgeoning importance to all other Asian countries and in particular to China. The Shanghai Five grouping founded in April 1996, later transformed in June 2001 into the Shanghai Cooperation Organization,[21] may well be considered as one of the most important initiatives of post-Maoist regimes in restructuring the global order. Initially the Organization had a confidence-building and security agenda, with both internal aspects, related to concerns about separatist tendencies amongst the non-Han minorities on the borderlands, and to more classic geopolitical considerations on stability within China's immediate neighbourhood (Swanström 2005). At the beginning of the twenty-first century, the competition for energy resources and raw materials has strengthened Central Asia's importance in relation to China's international positioning. Indeed, within the Beijing policy community the Shanghai Cooperation Organization – as both a Chinese initiative, and one in which Beijing controls the agenda (and the secretariat) – is of far greater importance than other organizations in which it is merely a participant. Yet cultivating relations with Central Asia has complicated the Chinese regionalization agenda. Seen from a realist perspective, Central Asia can be considered, like Southeast Asia (Economy 2005), as a sub-region in which Chinese leadership would appear legitimate. However, as in Southeast Asia, such a role is contested both by political leaderships in Russia and India and by a reluctance amongst elites in Central Asia to return to a vassal state status of the past.

To turn to a fourth point, namely, India's return to Asia, during the Cold War period successive Indian governments did not choose the export-oriented developmental model of East Asia, but rather chose a model of import substitution. Moreover, border tensions with China, an alliance with the Soviet Union and estrangement from all Southeast Asian countries, except Vietnam, meant that, for Delhi, the idea of the greater Asia of Bandung was abandoned. A balance of payments crisis in 1991 persuaded the then Indian Finance Minister, and present Prime Minister, Manmohan Singh, to liberalize the economy under IMF guidance. East Asia was to be seen both as a source of investment and as providing a model for rapid economic development. India's 'look east' policy, like that of Mahathir in the 1980s, sought to bring together both process and ideology. Successive Indian governments embarked on serious diplomatic initiatives which saw India admitted as a dialogue partner with ASEAN and a member of the ASEAN Regional Forum.

Linked to its own internal economic transformation, India was able to attract investment, not only from Japan and Korea, but also from Malaysia and Singapore, both of whom possess minority populations of Indian origin. The culmination of these initiatives – changing economic models and trade flows – was that by 2003 Indian politicians and members of the Delhi policy community were reclaiming India's 'historic birthright' as a member of the Asian Community (Kumar 2004). While there was an appeal to an underlying cultural affinity rhetoric in this pleading, it was above all the positive economic advantages of Indian membership that were stressed (Singh 2006a; Asher and Sen 2005). Moreover, taking into account the concerns of Southeast Asian countries in relation to China, Indian officials have not hesitated to insist upon a convergence on security issues (Devare 2006).

Other actors in Asia provided logistical and ideological support for India's 'return to Asia'. As mentioned, Japanese quasi-governmental organizations provided significant help. Korean involvement is more difficult to measure even though Korea has become a major investor in India. India has also benefited from support in Thailand and Singapore. It was after all the then Thai Prime Minister, Thaksin Shinawatra, who in 2001 initiated yet another informal sub-regional economic grouping, BIMSTEC, involving the Bay of Bengal countries.[22] The Singaporean government by organizing the first conferences of overseas Indians, through its own FDI in India, and through the support provided by Singaporean think-tanks enhanced India's Asian credentials (Kumar 2004; Lee 2005). Such new-found support reflects modifications in the regionalization processes where India is now factored in and, on the level of regionalism, an attempt to balance Chinese influence.

The Kuala Lumpur and Cebu summits; keeping ASEAN in the 'drivers seat'?

'One Vision, One Identity, One Community': the banners adorning the streets of Kuala Lumpur revealed the grandiose ambitions of the Malaysian hosts for the East Asia Summit.[23] They also revealed a great many of the ambiguities alluded to previously – for was the intergovernmental meeting announced that of the ten ASEAN governments? Or that extended into ASEAN+3 (with China, Japan and Korea)? Or the inaugural meeting held on 14 December of an East Asia Summit, an ASEAN+3… +1 +2 with the invitation to India, Australia and New Zealand? Behind the tedious international relations mathematics lie three issues of importance: Southeast Asia's cohesiveness and centrality in the construction of an East Asian Community; coping with an increasingly economically powerful and diplomatically assertive China; and the 'return' of India to Asia. The two latter concerns having been already dealt with, in this section the problem of ASEAN centrality will be addressed.

The first two days of the ASEAN Summit saw the Association having finally recovered from the economic crisis of 1997 to return to its own internal consolidation. By expressing demands for tangible political reforms in Burma/Myanmar the Association broke with its sacrosanct principle of non-interference. Moreover, the appointment of an Eminent Persons Group to draft an ASEAN Charter demonstrated that the Association had finally come to grips with establishing rules for club membership.[24] Perhaps the greatest success for Badawi was to ensure ASEAN's centrality in the process of regional construction. To use the shorthand language of the summit, ASEAN would remain in the 'drivers seat', and future annual East Asia Summits would be held in ASEAN countries 'back-to-back' with the Association's annual meetings. Given Sino-Japanese rivalry, and the unwillingness of the governments of either country to accept the leadership of the other, by default, ASEAN remains the least unacceptable alternative as regional coordinator, a view ostensibly also held by the new invitees, India, Australia and New Zealand. In the diplomatic formula decided upon in the summit, a compromise was reached with the East Asian Community being defined in terms of ASEAN+3, with the three new partners seen as sharing common interests. However, at the same time, in the jargon of 'inclusiveness' and 'openness' the Asian Community could extend to embrace them as well as Russia. Regions, as Katzenstein (2005) has suggested, are porous entities indeed.

Nevertheless, concerns over China remained and have engendered competing strategies. The summit demonstrated divisions within ASEAN as a regional organization, with the Singaporean, Thai and Indonesian support for enlargement from the ASEAN+3 formula being at odds with the more closed membership proposed by Malaysia, Cambodia and Vietnam. These cleavages, reiterated in think-tank and other meetings since the summit (Matsubara 2006, *Nikkei Weekly* 29 May 2006), reflect not only geopolitical considerations, but also internal political factors, with some domestic groups in ASEAN countries being more favourable to a broader Asia including the three new democratic invitees. Moreover, different Asian actors have rather different expectations for an Asian Community. For example, documents emanating from major pro-governmental think-tanks in Korea and Singapore advocate a putative East Asian Community essentially as being an exercise in confidence-building concerned primarily with security questions (Kwon and Hong 2005; See and Emmers 2005).

Developments in the year following the Kuala Lumpur summit and in the second summit just over a year later, would seem to underline the tensions already present there. The Annual Meeting of the Asian Development Bank (ADB) held in Hyderabad in early May 2006 was revealing in this regard. For the first time a multilateral body was called upon by some participants, including the Chinese representative, Jin Renqing, to encourage Asian regional integration through developing local bond markets, for example, and to 'help Asia find its voice' (*International Herald Tribune* 2 May 2006). Manmohan Singh in particular sought ADB aid in creating a pan-Asian FTA (Singh 2006b). In developing an Asian Currency Unit, based on a basket of hard and soft East Asian currencies, the ADB is building on the monetary regionalization that involves swap agreements and cooperation between Asian central banks (Dieter and Higgott 2003). The negotiation of an India–ASEAN FTA, like that between China and ASEAN due to come into force in 2011, would seem to be an element in a larger pan-Asian FTA, but it is juxtaposed with the bilateral FTAs signed with individual ASEAN countries such as Singapore and Thailand. While the Chinese are pushing for an ASEAN–China FTA, the Japanese, through the Ministry of Economy Trade and Industry, are favourable to cooperation among the 13 participants in Kuala Lumpur (*Japan Times* 8 May 2006). In practice this involves concentrating on bilateral agreements and downplaying ASEAN as an interlocutor.[25]

By the time of the second summit in Cebu there had been two contingent developments. The first, it would appear, was an acceptance by the Chinese leadership that it would need to accept the virtual enlargement of an Asian Community to include India (as well as Australia and New Zealand) and, therefore, in order to limit its impact, to complete the negotiations for an East Asian inner circle (i.e. ASEAN+3), in which China would be the main player through the signing of a China–ASEAN PTA. The second was to relegate this meso (i.e. regional) level compact as subordinate to a number of bilateral initiatives, for example, in securing energy supplies in Africa or Australia and, as mentioned, in reinforcing relations in Central Asia. At the same time, on the multilateral level, the Chinese leadership, albeit with a deal of reluctance, demonstrated a willingness to readjust the value of the yuan and thus to contribute to a readjustment of global trade balances.

The second East Asia Summit held in the Filipino island of Cebu was postponed from the original December 2006 dates to mid-January 2007, ostensibly because of the weather, but also – or because of – concerns with terrorist threats. The Cebu summit was dominated by a further step towards the promulgation of an ASEAN Charter and specific bilateral initiatives with both China and India. Yet in its very low key banality, Cebu confirmed that the Sino-Indic conceptualization of an Asian Community of Bandung had re-established itself as a central, if not uncontested, imagining of a twenty-first century Asia. A return to the future, so to speak.

Conclusions

Writing about the time of Bandung on another region – or was it a country? – of significance Edmundo O'Gorman wrote 'America, as such, literally does not exist, even though a mass of land exists which, in due course, will be endowed with that meaning' (O'Gorman 1959: 73). A similar comment could be made concerning Asia, with the proviso that the endowment of meaning is an ongoing process. Within these processes the disparities in capacity amongst both state and non-state actors have become apparent (Hamilton-Hart 2003). In this focus on two emblematic events – the Bandung meeting of 1955 and the first two, much lower profile, East Asia Summits a half-century later – an attempt has been made to demonstrate that, when looking at phenomena of regionalism, an inclusive conceptualization of Asia is more rooted historically than the concentration on East Asia proffered by most studies. Furthermore, when factors other than purely economic ones are clearly given their place in the equation, then a Greater Asia embracing India as a central element in both regionalization and regionalism becomes more salient.

The preceding analysis of developments toward an Asian Community would suggest that the three initial postulates are, perhaps, helpful in understanding phenomena of Asian regional integration. By giving a much broader historically grounded 'brush stroke' to our perspectives on Asian integration it is possible to factor in normative and culturalist perspectives of Asia as embracing in an overarching way, in the words of a number of actors, the great civilizations of China and India. Second, by bringing into play inter- and intra-disciplinary insights it is possible to tease out the various competing, contradictory and complimentary discourses on an Asian Community. Finally, by providing as a heuristic device a distinction between 'regionalization' and 'regionalism', it is possible, on the one hand, to explain a certain number of tensions and contradictions in the phenomena of Asian regional integration, and, on the other, to provide a framework for reintegrating a more nuanced analysis of the role of the state in the future.

Acknowledgments

A preliminary version of this chapter was presented at the conference on *Regionalisation and the Taming of Globalisation? Economic, Political, Security, Social and Governance Issues* at the University of Warwick, 26–28 October 2005 and published in *The Pacific Review*. The comments then of Heribert Dieter, T.J. Pempel and Richard Stubbs were most helpful. My gratitude also to Lee Chung Min for his insights and to the Director and staff of the Lee Kuan Yew School of Public Policy at the National University of Singapore where I undertook research in December 2005. Serena Han Bing, Yukari Akeda and Marylène Gervais, Park Sung-Hoon and Irina Kolotouchkina very kindly provided help and translation for documents respectively in Chinese, Japanese, Korean and Russian. Finally, thanks to Shaun Breslin and the two anonymous reviewers for their suggestions and encouragements. The usual caveats apply.

Notes

1 Björn Hettne and Fredrik Söderbaum's (2002) proposal for a concept of 'regionness' as a kind of yardstick of regional construction is an attempt also to deal with this problem.
2 Few studies offer such an historical perspective. The exceptions are provided by Arrighi *et al.* (2003) and Stubbs (2005) which, while not per se studies of regional integration, do provide a series of historical reference points as does He's (2004) analysis of the normative aspects of Asian regionalism.
3 In this and related sections space has not permitted an examination of the Korean role in Asian regional integration. For a rather rich recent edited volume devoted to the subject see Armstrong *et al.* (2006).
4 For example one protagonist/scholar of India's entry in an Asian Economic Community has claimed that 'in the light of the historical context … it can be argued that the 200-year colonial period was but an interregnum and that traditional links can be revived in the current context' (Shanker 2004: 15).
5 Rizal returned a century later as an emblematic figure for proponents of an Asian Renaissance such as Anwar Ibrahim (see Anwar 1996b).
6 The above relies on Deshingkar (1999) and Jaffrelot (2003).
7 Thanks to Amitav Acharya for discussing with me his research on Bandung. His forthcoming study with Stanford University Press should represent a significant rewriting of its history.
8 Bandung is seen, correctly, as leading to the creation of the non-aligned movement including important African as well as other non-Asian countries. However the participation in the conference itself was overwhelmingly Asian.
9 I owe this point to Richard Stubbs.
10 While the Ministry of International Trade and Industry was generally supportive of the proposal, the Foreign Ministry was largely opposed, despite its in-house China lobby.

11   For an example of some of the debates provoked in the two track policy community see Tay *et al.* (2002).
12   The study cited is part of a joint research project of the Singapore Institute of International Affairs and the Institute of International Relations, a think-tank close to the Taiwanese government. A development worthy of further study is the public diplomacy of the Taiwanese in Southeast Asia. These political initiatives parallel the role of Taiwanese companies in the sub-region. Taiwan has become an objective ally of ASEAN in attempting to balance the increasing preponderance of the PRC in Asian regionalization.
13   Quoted in the *Nikkei Net Interactive* (www.nikkei.co.jp), 25 May 2005.
14   This theme was taken up at the first Northeast Asia Trilateral Forum held in Seoul in February 2006 in which Nakasone stressed the need for Northeast Asian Cooperation to be within the East Asian Community (*Nikkei Weekly* 20 February 2006). Other Japanese voices however have overtly called for a Sino-Japanese leadership (Kohara 2005).
15   The Trilateral Security Dialogue involving the foreign ministers of the United States, Japan and Australia inaugurated in 2001 and which held its first ministerial meeting in Sydney in March 2006 is a further, if minor, institutional expression of the way the Japanese leadership balances the conflicting demands of its East Asian and Asia-Pacific regional memberships and its attempt to contain China.
16   This barbarism implies a twofold approach of 'containment' and 'engagement'.
17   An example of this is the Asia Leadership Programme financed by the Japan Foundation and the International House of Japan since 1996 (see, for example, the results of some of its meetings in Bolasco *et al.* 2006)
18   My reference to these two Chinese authors close to the Chinese Foreign Ministry relies on the synthesis provided by Michal Meidan in *China Analysis* 2 December 2005: 15–16.
19   Of course form does not outweigh content and the $50 billion of trade with the African continent in 2005 is overshadowed by the $130 billion in trade with Southeast Asia. However, trade with Africa has grown more rapidly, rising from $10 billion in 2000 (Wen 2006). Trade with Southeast Asia is predicted to rise to $200 billion in 2010.
20   The presence of large communities of Chinese origin in much of Southeast Asia has always been problematical. While overseas Chinese business networks have been essential in Asian de facto economic regionalization, their role in contributing to national identities is a source of controversy. This impacts on their place in civil society in contributing to a pan-Asian identity.
21   The original five, China, Kazakhstan, Kyryzstan, Russia and Tajikistan, were joined in 2001 by Uzbekistan. Turkmenistan is the only one of China's neighbours not to be a member.
22   Bangladesh, India, Myanmar (Burma), Sri Lanka and Thailand.
23   For an overview of the issues at the summit see Lee *et al.* (2006) and for the summit itself see Malik (2006).
24   Initial proposals, namely those compiled by a former ASEAN Secretary General, suggested that the charter would be liberal in tone (Severino 2005). Nevertheless, ASEAN NGOs have objected that the Charter was being drafted without any civil society consultation (*Independent Press Service* 2 November 2006)
25   Continuing disagreements over membership of a putative Asian Community remained apparent at the 12th International Conference on the 'Future of Asia' held in Tokyo in late May 2006 (*Nikkei Weekly* 29 May 2006).

References

Acharya, Amitav (2004), 'How Norms Spread: Whose Norms Matter? Norm Localization and Institutional Change in Asian Regionalism', *International Organization*, 58 (Spring): 239–275.

Aggarwal, Vinod and Kwei, Elaine (2006), 'Asia-Pacific Economic cooperation (APEC): Transregionalism with a New Cause?' in Heiner Hänggi, Ralf Roloff and Jürgen Rüland (eds), *Interregionalism and International Relations*, London: Routledge, pp. 67–84.

Amrith, Sunil (2005), 'Asian internationalism: Bandung's Echo in a Colonial Metropolis', *Inter-Asia Cultural Studies*, 6(4): 557–569.

Anwar Ibrahim (1996a), *The Asian Renaissance*, Singapore: Times Books International.

Anwar Ibrahim (1996b), 'Jose Rizal: The discourse on the Asian Renaissance' in M. Rajaretnam (ed.), *Jose Rizal and the Asian Renaissance*, Kuala Lumpur: Institut Kajian Dasar/Manila: Solidaridad Publishing House, pp. 38–42.

Armstrong, Charles, Rozman, Gilbert, Kim, Samuel and Kotkin, Stephen (eds) (2006), *Korea at the Center: Dynamics of Regionalism in Northeast Asia*, Armonk NY: M.E. Sharpe.

Arrighi, Giovanni, Hamashita Takeshi and Selden, Mark (eds) (2003) *The Resurgence of East Asia: 500, 150 and 50 Year Perspectives*, London: Routledge.

Ash, Robert (2005), 'China's Regional Economies and the Asian Region: Building Interdependent Linkages' in David Shambaugh (ed.), *Power Shift: China and Asia's New Dynamics*, Berkeley CA: University of California Press.

Asher, Mukul and Sen, Rahul (2005), 'India–East Asia Integration: A Win-Win for Asia', *RIS Discussion Papers*, 91#2005 (www.ris.org.in).

Badawi Abdullah (2004), 'Towards an Integrated East Asia Community', Speech at a meeting organized by the Boao Forum for Asia, Kuala Lumpur, 6 December (domino. kln.gov.my).

Badawi Abdullah (2005), 'Statement at the Boao Forum for Asia', Hainan, 23 April.

Baldwin, Richard (2006), 'Managing the Noodle Bowl: The Fragility of East Asian Region-alism', *Centre for Economic Policy Research Discussion Paper Series*, no. 5561, (www.cepr.org/pubs/dps).

Beeson, Mark (2007), *Regionalism and Globalization in East Asia: Politics, Security and Economic Development*, Basingstoke: Palgrave Macmillan.

Bhalla, Madhu (2005), 'Domestic Roots of China's Foreign and Security Policy', *International Studies* 42(3–4): 205–225.

Bolasco, Karina, Butalia, Urvashi, Lee Jong Won & Ohashi Masaaki (eds) (2006), *The Community of Asia: Concept or Reality?*, Pasig City: Anvil Publishing/Japan Foundation.

Callahan, William (2006), *Cultural Governance and Resistance in Pacific Asia*, London: Routledge.

Ching, Leo (2001), 'Globalizing the Regional, Regionalizing the Global: Mass Culture and Asianism in the Age of Late Capital' in Arjun Appadurai (ed.), *Globalization*, Durham NC: Duke University Press, pp. 279–306.

Council on East Asian Community (2005), *The State of the Concept of (an) East Asian Community and Japan's Strategic Response Thereto*, August (www.ceac.jp).

Dent, Christopher (2006), *New Free Trade Agreements in the Asia-Pacific*, Basingstoke: Palgrave Macmillan.

Deshingkar, Giri (1999), 'The Construction of Asia in India', *Asian Studies Review*, 23(2): 173–180.

Desker, Barry (2004), 'In Defence of FTAs: From Purity to Pragmatism in East Asia', *The Pacific Review* 17(1): 3–26.

Devare, Sudhir (2006), *India & Southeast Asia: Towards Security Convergence*, Singapore: Institute of Southeast Asian Studies.

Dieter, Heribert & Higgott, Richard (2003), 'Exploring Alternative Theories of Economic Regionalism: From Trade to Finance in Asian Co-operation', *Review of International Political Economy*, 10(3): 430–454.

Dirlik, Arif (1998), 'The Asia-Pacific Idea: Reality and Representation in the Invention of a Regional Structure' in Arif Dirlik (ed.), *What's in a Rim?: Critical Perspectives on the Pacific Region Idea* (2nd edn), Lanham MA: Rowman & Littlefield, pp. 15–36.

Duara, Prasenjit (2003), *Sovereignty and Authenticity: Manchukuo and the East Asian Modern*, Lanham MA: Rowman & Littlefield.

East Asia Study Group (2002), *Final Report of the East Asia Study Group*. ASEAN+3 Summit, 4 November (www.aseansec.org).

East Asian Vision Group (2001), *Towards an East Asian Community: Region of Peace, Prosperity and Progress*, 31 October (www.aseansec.org).

Economy, Elizabeth (2005), 'China's Rise in Southeast Asia: Implications for the United States', *Journal of Contemporary China*, 14(44): 409–425.

Foot, Rosemary (2005), 'China's Regional Activism: Leadership, Leverage and Protection', *Global Change, Peace & Security*, 17(2): 141–153.

Gamble, Andrew and Payne, Anthony (eds) (1996), *Regionalism and World Order*, Basingstoke: Macmillan.

Goh Chok Tong (2004), 'Asia – Catalyst for Global Integration', *Asia Europe Journal*, 2(1): 1–5.

Hamilton-Hart, Natasha (2003), 'Asia's New Regionalism: Government Capacity and Cooperation in the Western Pacific', *Review of International Political Economy*, 10(2): 222–245.

Hay, Stephen (1970), *Asian Ideas of East and West: Tagore and his Critics in Japan, China and India*, Cambridge MA: Harvard University Press.

He Baogang (2004), 'East Asian Ideas of Regionalism: A Normative Critique', *Australian Journal of International Affairs*, 58(1): 105–125.

Hemmer, Christopher and Katzenstein, Peter (2002), 'Why Is There No Nato in Asia? Collective Identity, Regionalism and the Origins of Multilateralism', *International Organization*, 56(3): 575–607.

Hettne, Björn & Söderbaum, Fredrik (2002), 'Theorising the Rise of Regionness' in Shaun Breslin, Christopher Hughes, Nicola Phillips and Ben Rosamond (eds), *New Regionalisms in the Global Political Economy*, London: Routledge, pp. 33–47.

Higgott, Richard and Stubbs, Richard (1995), 'Competing Conceptions of Economic Regionalism: APEC versus EAEC in the Asia-Pacific', *Review of International Political Economy*, 2(3): 516–535.

Howard, John (2005), 'Transcript of the Address to the Boao Forum, China', 23 April (www.pm.gov.au/news/speeches).

Hu Jintao (2004), 'China's Development is an Opportunity for Asia', Speech at the Opening Ceremony of the Boao Forum for Asia 2004 Annual Conference 23 April 2004 (www.chinaembassy.org.au).

Hu Jintao (2006), 'Full text of President Hu's speech at China–Africa Summit', *China View*, 4 November (www.chinaview.cn).

Huang Shan (2005), 'Perspectives on the East Asian Summit', *Caijing*, (148) 12 December (in Chinese).

Hund, Markus (2003), 'ASEAN Plus Three: Towards a New Age of Pan-East Asian Regionalism? A Skeptics Appraisal', *The Pacific Review*, 16(3): 383–418.

Ingleson, John (1997) 'The Post-Colonial Construction of Asia: Regionalism in Historical Perspective' in John Ingleson (ed.), *Regionalism, Subregionalism and APEC*, Melbourne: Monash Asia Institute, pp. 20–36.

Iwabuchi Koichi, Muecke, Stephen & Thomas, Mandy eds) (2004), *Rogue Flows: Trans-Asian Cultural Traffic*, Hong Kong: Hong Kong University Press.

Jaffrelot, Christophe (2003), 'India's Look East Policy: An Asianist Strategy in Perspective', *India Review*, 2(2): 35–68.

Japan Forum on International Relations (2003), *Japan's Initiative for Economic Community in East Asia*, Tokyo: JFIR.

Jayasuriya, Kanishka (2006), 'Beyond New Imperialism: State and Transnational Regulatory Governance in East Asia' in Vedi Hadiz (ed.), *Empire and Neoliberalism in Asia*, London: Routledge, pp. 38–51.

Jian Junbo (2006), ' Identity and Integrity of East Asia' in He Peiqun and Yu Yixuan (eds), *International Relations and Politics of Identity,* (*Fudan International Studies Review*, 5: 80–101 (in Chinese).

Kahin, George McTurnan (1956*), The Asian–African Conference: Bandung, Indonesia, 1955*, Ithaca NY: Cornell University Press.

Kalla, Jusuf (2006), 'Indonesia's Role on (the) Road to (an) Asian Community', *Jakarta Post*, 1 June (www.thejakartapost.com).

Karl, Rebecca (2002), *Staging the World: Chinese Nationalism at the Turn of the Twentieth Century*, Durham NC: Duke University Press.

Katzenstein, Peter (2005), *A World of Regions: Asia and Europe in the American Imperium*, Ithaca NY: Cornell University Press.

Katzenstein, Peter and Shiraishi, Takashi (eds) (2006), *Beyond Japan: The Dynamics of East Asian Regionalism*, Ithaca NY: Cornell University Press.

Khoo Boo Teik (1999), 'The Value(s) of a Miracle: Malaysian and Singaporean Elite Constructions of Asia', *Asian Studies Review*, 23(2): 181–192.

Kim, Samuel (2004), 'Regionalization and Regionalism in East Asia', *Journal of East Asian Studies*, 4(1): 39–67.

Kitamura Toshiaki (2006), 'Japan's New Deal for Asia', *Far Eastern Economic Review*, 169(7): 41–44.

Kohara Mashahiro (2005), *East Asian Community*, Tokyo: Nihon Keizai Shimbun (in Japanese).

Koizumi Junichiro (2002), *Japan and ASEAN in East Asia: A Sincere and Open Partnership*, Singapore: ISEAS.

Korhonen, Pekka (1997), 'Monopolizing Asia: The Politics of a Metaphor', *The Pacific Review*, 10(3): 347–365.

Kumar, Nagesh (2004), 'A Vision of an Asian Economic Community' in Nagesh Kumar (ed.), *Towards an Asian Economic Community: Vision of a New Asia*, New Delhi: RIS/Singapore: ISEAS, pp. 1–12.

Kwon Yul & Hong Sooyeon (2005), 'Challenges and Prospects for East Asian Summit', *Korean Institute for International Economic Policy*, 5(1) (in Korean).

Lee Kuan Yew (2005), 'India in an Asian Renaissance', *The Straits Times*, 21 November.

Lee Poh Ping, Tham Siew Yean & Yu, George T. (eds) (2006), *The Emerging East Asian Community: Security and Economic Issues*, Bangi: Penerbit Universiti Kebangsaan Malaysia.

Lim, Hank and Lee Chyungly (eds) (2004), *The Emerging North–South Divide in East Asia: A Reappraisal of Asian Regionalism*, Singapore: Eastern Universities Press.

Mackie, Jamie (2005), *Bandung 1955: Non-Alignment and Afro-Asian Solidarity*, Singapore: Editions Didier Millet.

Mahathir Mohamad (1999), *A New Deal for Asia*, Subang Jaya: Pelanduk Publications.

Mahbubani Kishore (2002), *Can Asians Think?* (2nd edn), Singapore: Times Book International.

Malik, Mohan (2006), 'The East Asia Summit', *Australian Journal of International Affairs*, 60(2): 207–211

Martin Jones, David and Smith, M.L.R. (2006), *ASEAN and East Asian International Relations: Regional Delusion*, Cheltenham: Edward Elgar.

Matsubara Hiroshi (2006) 'Asia/Asian Community Remains Distant Goal', *Asahi Shimbun*, 8 March (www.asahi.com/english).

Milner, Anthony and Johnson, Deborah (1997), 'The Idea of Asia' in John Ingleson (ed.), *Regionalism, Subregionalism and APEC*, Melbourne: Monash Asia Institute, pp. 1–19.

Morris-Suzuki, Tessa (1998), 'Invisible Countries: Japan and the Asian Dream', *Asian Studies Review*, 22(1): 5–22.

O'Gorman, Edmundo (1959), *The Invention of America*, Bloomington: Indiana University Press.

Pang Zhongying (2005), 'The Chinese Role in the Transformation of the Asian Regional Order', *Waijiao pinglun (Foreign Affairs Review)*, 83 (August): 41–49 (in Chinese).

Pempel, T.J. (ed.) (2005), *Remapping East Asia: The Construction of a Region*, Ithaca NY: Cornell University Press.

Poon, Jessie (2001), 'Regionalism in the Asia Pacific: Is Geography Destiny?', *Area*, 33(3): 252–269.

Ramo, Joshua (2004), *The Beijing Consensus*, London: Foreign Policy Centre.

Ravenhill, John (2001), *APEC and the Construction of Pacific Rim Regionalism*, Cambridge: Cambridge University Press.

Richardson, Lloyd (2002), 'Now, Play the India Card', *Policy Review*, October (www.policyreview.org).

Richardson, Michael (2005), 'Australia–Southeast Asia Relations and the East Asian Summit', *Australian Journal of International Affairs*, 59(3): 351–365.

Robison, Richard (2006), 'The Reordering of Pax American: How Does Southeast Asia Fit in' in Vedi Hadiz (ed.), *Empire and Neoliberalism in Asia*, London: Routledge, pp. 52–68.

Samarani, Guido (2005), 'Shaping the Future of Asia: Chiang Kai-shek, Nehru and China–India Relations During the Second World War Period', *Working Paper in Contemporary Asian Studies*, 11, Centre for East and South-East Asian Studies, Lund University (www.ace.lu.se).

See Seng Tan & Emmers, Ralf (eds) (2005), *An Agenda for the East Asia Summit*, Singapore: Institute of Defence and Strategic Studies.

Severino, Rodolfo (ed.) (2005), *Framing the ASEAN Charter: An ISEAS Perspective*, Singapore: ISEAS.

Shambaugh, David (2005), 'Introduction: The Rise of China and Asia's New Dynamics' in David Shambaugh (ed.), *Power Shift: China and Asia's New Dynamics*, Berkeley CA, University of California Press.

Shanker, Vincenta (2004), 'Towards an Asian Economic Community: Exploring the Past' in Nagesh Kumar (ed.), *Towards an Asian Economic Community: Vision of a New Asia*, New Delhi: RIS/Singapore: ISEAS, pp. 13–40.

Shiraishi Takashi (2006), 'The Third Wave: Southeast Asia and Middle-Class Formation in the Making of a Region' in Peter Katzenstein and Takashi Shiraishi (eds), *Beyond Japan: The Dynamics of East Asian Regionalism*, Ithaca NY: Cornell University Press, pp. 237–271.

Singh, Manmohan (2006a), 'Prime Minister's Address at 16th Asian Corporate Conference Driving Global Business: India's New Priorities, Asia's New Realities', 18 March (http://pib.nic.in).

Singh, Manmohan (2006b), 'Prime Minister's Address at 39th Annual General meeting of the Asian Development Bank', Hyderabad, 5 May (http://pib.nic.in).

Söderbaum, Fredrik and Shaw, Timothy (eds) (2004), *Theories of New Regionalism: A Palgrave Reader*, Basingstoke: Palgrave Macmillan.

Sopiee, Nordin (1995), 'The Development of an East Asian Consciousness' in Greg Sheridan (ed.), *Living with Dragons: Australia Confronts Its Asian Destiny*, Sydney: Allen & Unwin, pp. 180–193.

Stubbs, Richard (2005), *Rethinking Asia's Economic Miracle*, Basingstoke: Palgrave Macmillan.

Suettinger, Robert (2005), 'The Rise and Descent of "Peaceful Rise"', *China Leadership Monitor*, no. 12.

Sun Yat Sen [1924] (1941), 'China and Japan: Natural Friends – Unnatural Enemies', Shanghai: China United Press. Translation of 'Da Yaxiyazhuyi' ('Greater Asianism'), *Xinyaxiya*, 1(5): 2–7.

Swanström, Niklas (2005), 'China and Central Asia: A New Great Game or Traditional Vassal Relations?', *Journal of Contemporary China*, 14(45): 569–584.

Tay, Simon, Estanislao, Jesus and Soesatro, Hadi (eds) (2002), *Reinventing ASEAN*, Singapore: ISEAS.

Terada, Takashi (1998), 'The Origins of Japan's APEC Policy: Foreign Minister Takeo Miki's Asia-Pacific Policy and Current Implications', *The Pacific Review*, 11(3): 337–363.

Terada, Takashi (2003), 'Constructing an 'East Asian' Concept and Growing Regional Identity: From EAEC to ASEAN+3', *The Pacific Review*, 16(2): 251–277.

Wang Gungwu (2004), 'The Fourth Rise of China: Cultural Implications', *China: An International Journal*, 2(2): 311–322.

Wen Jiabao (2006), 'Work Together to Usher in a New Era of China–ASEAN Economic Cooperation and Trade', Speech at the Third China–ASEAN Business and Investment Summit, Nanning, 31 October, *Peoples Daily Online* (http://english.people.com.cn).

Woods, Lawrence (1993), *Asia-Pacific Diplomacy: Nongovernmental Organizations and International Relations*, Vancouver: University of British Columbia Press.

Young, Louise (1999), *Japan's Total Empire: Manchuria and the Culture of Wartime Imperialism*, Berkeley CA: University of California Press.

Zhang Yunlin & Tang Shiping (2005), 'China's Regional Strategy' in David Shambaugh (ed.), *Power Shift: China and Asia's New Dynamics*, Berkeley CA, University of California Press.

3 China's rise in Asia

Regional cooperation and grand strategy

Thomas G. Moore

One of the defining features of Chinese foreign policy over the past decade has been the country's increased participation in multilateralism, a remarkable development given Beijing's longstanding skepticism of – and, at times, hostility toward – institutionalized forms of international cooperation (Medeiros and Fravel 2003; Wang 2005).[1] While Chinese activity in global-level multilateralism is now well documented, fewer studies have focused on the increasingly important regional dimension of Chinese multilateralism. For example, although China's accession to the World Trade Organization (WTO) has received detailed attention from policy makers, scholars, and journalists, Beijing's growing participation in the emerging economic regionalism of East Asia remains a less-studied phenomenon. This chapter attempts to complement the existing literature by examining how Beijing has sought to use regionalism in managing various foreign policy challenges, including challenges associated with globalization.

The chapter begins by providing a brief overview of China's so-called new multilateralism, with an emphasis on Beijing's participation in East Asian regionalism. In so doing, the chapter raises the critical question of whether China is undergoing a fundamental shift in foreign policy orientation from realist internationalism toward liberal internationalism. Long regarded as a bastion of realpolitik, China's foreign policy orientation during the second half of the twentieth century is perhaps best characterized as one of deepening realist internationalism. Especially as China became a less inward-looking country with the passing of the Mao Zedong and Deng Xiaoping eras, the national interest was increasingly seen as requiring active engagement in world affairs. From this perspective, unlike that of realist isolationism, it is not enough to secure one's own borders and pursue internally focused development given the existence of a potentially hostile outside world that impinges on Chinese interests.[2] According to realist internationalism, multilateral processes are no substitute for coercive power in managing conflicts of interest among states. Institutions may be a useful tool in pursuing certain foreign policy objectives, but they cannot be relied upon to protect Chinese interests. Consequently, realist internationalism privileges the development of political-diplomatic clout and coercive power (especially, but not only, military power) in order to safeguard China's interests.

According to John Ikenberry, liberal internationalism is distinguished by its 'reliance on inter-governmental mechanisms to institutionalize international cooperation'. In terms of specific pursuits, liberal internationalism combines a fundamental 'commitment to open trade' with acceptance of a 'social bargain' that allows 'domestic protections and the creation of a social safety net'. Another crucial component of liberal internationalism is the pursuit of 'cooperative security' in which states bind themselves together in networks of security partnerships (Ikenberry 2005).[3] In contrast to idealism, which in some variants sees force as largely obsolete, liberal internationalism acknowledges that military power still plays a prominent role in deterring aggression and otherwise supporting the institutions that safeguard peace and security. That said, the use of force is governed by multilateral processes. To say that China's foreign policy orientation is shifting toward liberal internationalism suggests that China's beliefs have changed, not just about how best to achieve its goals but also about what goals it should pursue. Specifically, the pursuit of institutionalized cooperation becomes identified with the national interest, not simply as a means for pursuing foreign policy objectives but as an end in itself, even to the point where it takes precedence over the accretion of national power (especially military power) when the two objectives find themselves at cross-purposes. In resolving conflicts of interest among states, from economic strife to security disputes, reliance on the independent exercise of national coercive power is replaced by multilateral processes. Specifically, national interests are protected through such mechanisms as arms control institutions, collective security organizations and international trade regimes (Rhodes 1999).

According to the liberal view, which the chapter considers first, China's pursuit of institutionalized cooperation signifies a growing commitment to a rules-based, norm-driven international order. Responding to incentives for cooperation provided by international institutions and the challenges associated with multidimensional globalization, so the liberal argument would go, China's leaders have made a strategic choice to pursue an order based more on rules than power. Consistent with liberal precepts, China can be seen as increasingly employing multilateralism to pursue freer trade, cooperative security, and what it calls the 'democratization of international relations', all as part of its bid to be a 'responsible power' that helps build a more 'harmonious world'. Even Beijing's persistent diplomatic emphasis on respecting the diversity of civilizations in world politics and the need to establish a fairer international economic system to ensure that the benefits of globalization are shared more evenly can be seen as dovetailing with Ikenberry's notion that a social bargain is embedded, à la John Ruggie, in liberal internationalism (Ruggie 1982).

With respect to Asian regionalism, Beijing is seen as having become a major catalyst for institutionalized cooperation despite its traditional adherence to realist precepts. Indeed, the liberal position would argue that China's policy toward Asia should be characterized as 'racing to integrate' (or, alternatively, 'competing to cooperate') given its leadership in the promotion of free trade agreements (FTAs), security dialogues, and other regional initiatives. From this perspective,

China is driving the process of regional cooperation by inducing similar initiatives from, among others, Japan, the United States, and India, especially but not only in their relations with the Association of Southeast Asian Nations (ASEAN).

The chapter next explores the view that China's pursuit of institutionalized cooperation can be reconciled quite satisfactorily with realist thinking. From this perspective, the pattern of China's behavior in Asia reveals that Beijing is actually 'cooperating to compete' (or, alternatively, 'integrating to compete') with the likes of Japan, the United States, and India. For example, China is seen as using FTAs and other mechanisms of enhanced regional cooperation – including security initiatives – primarily to compete for political influence in Asia. This analysis suggests a zero-sum dynamic, rooted in a struggle for relative power, in which countries vie over the strength of ties with various partners. Seen in this light, FTAs are instruments of economic statecraft. For example, what Beijing seeks through the ASEAN–China FTA (ACFTA) is not greater interdependence for its own sake, as the liberal interpretation would contend, but institutionalized cooperation with ASEAN as a means to advance the interests of the Chinese state, interests still best understood primarily in terms of coercive power, political influence and national security. The concluding sections of the chapter discuss various implications of this analysis for the study of Chinese foreign policy and for the evolving shape of Asian regionalism.

Before proceeding, a few definitional clarifications are required. In political science, multilateralism is typically defined as the 'practice of co-ordinating national policies in groups of three or more states, through ad hoc arrangements or by means of institutions' (Keohane 1990: 731).[4] In economics, by contrast, multilateralism typically refers only to global-level processes such as the WTO. Indeed, the WTO considers cooperation among smaller groups of countries, including regional groups, to be plurilateral rather than multilateral. Another approach is to distinguish among four modes of governance: unilateralism, bilateralism, minilateralism, and multilateralism, where minilateralism is synonymous with what the WTO calls plurilateralism (Aggarwal 2006). As distinct from bilateralism, minilateralism involves more than two countries.

As used in this chapter, multilateralism refers to actions taken by three or more states; it thus combines minilateralism/plurilateralism and multilateralism as outlined above. Depending on the specific case, therefore, multilateralism can be global, regional or transregional. What, then, is regionalism? As used here, regionalism refers to the process whereby two or more states within a particular geographical area construct collaborative agreements or otherwise coordinate activities. (The term thus encompasses what might be called regional bilateralism and regional minilateralism, which is useful since China's regional initiatives in Asia overlap bilateralism and minilateralism/multilateralism.) Most importantly, regionalism is associated with the conscious policy choices of states rather than the uncoordinated activities of non-state actors such as multinational corporations. In this respect, regionalism is distinct from regionalization, the process whereby economic interaction, such as flows of goods and capital, increases faster among countries within a particular geographical area than between those countries and others outside the area. As such, regionalism is a political process whereas regionalization is an economic process (Mansfield and Milner 1999: 591, Ravenhill 2001: 6–7).

China's new multilateralism

By all accounts, multilateralism has enjoyed an unprecedentedly high profile in China's foreign policy discourse and behaviour in recent years. In one of his annual statements to the United Nations General Assembly, Foreign Minister Li Zhaoxing declared that 'multilateral cooperation … should become the principal vehicle in the handling of international affairs', identifying multilateralism as central to the 'future well-being of mankind' (Li 2003). On another occasion, Li opined that:

> multilateralism is an effective way to deal with the common challenges of humanity. It is an important means to resolve international disputes. It is a forceful promotion and guarantee for the benign development of globalization. It is also the best way to promote democratic and law-based international relationships.
>
> (Li 2004)

In keeping with this growing rhetorical emphasis on multilateralism, terms such as common security, interdependence, and cooperative development have become commonplace in China's foreign policy lexicon. Security and prosperity are increasingly identified as positive-sum objectives that cannot be achieved at the expense of other countries. From this perspective, the successful management of interstate relations through multilateralism is presented as a win–win proposition. Although much of the emphasis initially was placed on economic affairs, even China's perception of security institutions has, as David Shambaugh notes, evolved over the past decade 'from suspicion, to uncertainty, to supportiveness' (Shambaugh 2004–05: 69).

In a recent assessment of the prospects for security regionalism in Asia, with a focus on ASEAN, Sheldon Simon observed that 'in many ways, China appears to be more willing to support multilateral institutions in Southeast Asia than the United States – a remarkable reversal from only a few years ago' (Simon 2003–04: 282). After beginning as a consultative partner in 1991, China participated in the establishment of the ASEAN Regional Forum (ARF) in 1994, and became a full ASEAN dialogue partner in 1996. Subsequent highlights of ASEAN–China cooperation include the November 2002 signings of the *Declaration on the Conduct of the Parties in the South China Sea* and the *Joint Declaration on Cooperation in the Field of Nontraditional Security Issues*. Even more notable was China's October 2003 accession to ASEAN's *Treaty of Amity and Cooperation*, as well as the simultaneous signing of a *Joint Declaration on Strategic Partnership for Peace and Prosperity*. Among other things, the latter called for a security dialogue to be established between China and the ten members of

ASEAN. Beijing's separate proposal for, and subsequent hosting of, a first-ever ARF Security Policy Conference in 2004 broadened this initiative even further. China's unprecedented diplomatic activism also includes two events hosted in 2005: the Second Greater Mekong Subregion (GMS) Summit and an ARF seminar exploring cooperation on non-traditional security threats. In 2006 Beijing hosted a China–ASEAN workshop on regional security that examined issues ranging from maritime security cooperation and counter-terrorism exercises to peacekeeping operations and the role of the military in disaster relief efforts. That year also saw China reiterate its intention to accede to the Protocol to the Treaty on the Southwest Asia Nuclear-Weapon Free Zone. As this evidence suggests, China's engagement of ASEAN on security issues shows few signs of slowing down. Indeed, in a speech commemorating the fifteenth anniversary of official China–ASEAN dialogue in 2006, Premier Wen Jiabao expressed Beijing's hope that the two sides will continue to 'institutionalize defense cooperation' in the future (Wen 2006). Although much of Beijing's focus has been on its Southeast Asian neighbours, China's participation in security regionalism extends beyond ASEAN to initiatives such as the Shanghai Cooperation Organization (SCO) in Central Asia and the Six-Party Talks on North Korea's nuclear weapons program in Northeast Asia.[5]

A similar, and indeed even stronger, assessment would apply to economic regionalism, where Beijing has taken an especially active leadership role. Overall, China's integration into multilateral institutions (global as well as regional) seems to have proceeded even more quickly than many proponents of engagement policies had projected during the intense political debates in the United States and elsewhere during the 1990s. Today, Beijing holds membership in every significant global and regional economic forum for which it qualifies, including the WTO, International Monetary Fund (IMF), World Bank, Asia Pacific Economic Cooperation (APEC) forum, Asian Development Bank (ADB), Asia–Europe Meeting (ASEM) dialogue, East Asia Summit (EAS) and ASEAN Plus Three (APT) process.[6]

At a global level, the most salient development in China's economic multilateralism over the past decade is surely Beijing's long-sought WTO accession in 2001. To this point, however, the main significance of China's WTO membership has been its positive impact on domestic reform and China's incorporation into global commodity chains, not the WTO's emergence as a major new venue for Beijing's diplomatic activism. Indeed, China has maintained a low profile within the WTO, much to the frustration of observers who believe that Beijing's active involvement in the Doha Round might facilitate successful negotiations on liberalizing global trade.[7] Overall, China's reserved behaviour in the WTO is consistent with the pattern of its conduct in other institutions of global economic governance, such as the IMF.[8]

At a regional level, there have been several noteworthy developments, perhaps highlighted by China's pursuit of numerous FTAs – most notably, ACFTA – and its participation in various efforts at enhanced financial and monetary cooperation within APT. In the latter issue area, Beijing has been an active participant in the

Chiang Mai Initiative, which was created to provide emergency liquidity during regional currency crises, and the Asian Bond Market Initiative, which seeks to enhance the development of regional bond markets.[9]

In the area of FTAs, ACFTA has received the most attention, but China has in fact pursued FTAs with 28 countries or regions since 2001. All told, 11 FTAs covering one-quarter of China's total trade are currently either under official study, in negotiation, or have been concluded. Although China's FTA partners represent a wide geographic range (e.g. Iceland, Chile, Gulf Cooperation Council, Southern African Customs Union, Mercosur, Pakistan), much of China's focus has been in East Asia. Among its 15 EAS partners, for example, only Japan has not reached the stage of officially studying an FTA with China. (For its part, Beijing has expressed a willingness to discuss the issue of a bilateral FTA with Japan.) FTAs with ASEAN, Australia, New Zealand, India and South Korea are at various stages of study, negotiation or implementation. In addition, Beijing has periodically broached the idea of an FTA within APT, although this idea has not been pursued seriously by the group. Similarly, China proposed in 2003 that the six members of the SCO consider establishing an FTA. Although no feasibility study has yet been authorized by the group, Beijing remains ready to pursue an FTA in Central Asia if its SCO partners agree to proceed.

Cultivating rules-based, norm-driven interdependence: Chinese multilateralism as liberal internationalism

In general terms, China's increased emphasis on multilateralism would seem to violate the basic realist expectation that countries prefer to preserve flexibility in their foreign relations by pursuing relatively informal, ad hoc, non-binding commitments that carry low exit costs in the event that intergovernmental agreements prove to be disadvantageous.[10] From this perspective, Beijing's active pursuit of WTO membership, FTAs such as ACFTA, and enhanced financial and monetary cooperation in APT – not to mention its promotion of various economic and security initiatives in multilateral groupings such as SCO, ARF, ASEM, EAS and APEC – represents an analytical puzzle, in considerable measure because China consistently evinced strong skepticism of multilateralism until less than a decade ago.

Whereas realism generally expects states to regard the collective management of shared problems with suspicion because they wish to maximize independence, from the liberal perspective China's recent behavior indicates that Beijing is willing to tolerate – and may even be trying to cultivate – mutual dependence on certain issues.[11] Simply put, China seems to be consciously increasing levels of interdependence rather than avoiding deeper ties. In its relations with ASEAN and as a member of the SCO, for example, Beijing no longer insists upon the compartmentalization of economic and security dialogues. In fact, China has begun to link the economic and security arenas in ways that seemingly challenge the realist expectation that countries will seek to preserve their autonomy as a top priority.

Especially noteworthy is China's unprecedented embrace of institutionalized forms of cooperation. Consider ACFTA. In the words of Zha Daojiong, ACFTA 'will bind China to work with ASEAN under a set of negotiated rules' (Zha 2002: 55). Furthermore, the fact that China's leaders have pursued ACFTA, despite numerous studies predicting that ASEAN's material benefit from trade liberalization will outstrip China's, would seem to contradict realist expectations about the importance of relative gains.[12] In this respect, the favourable terms China granted ASEAN in their 2002 *Framework Agreement on Comprehensive Economic Cooperation*, to say nothing of subsequent 'early harvest' concessions it granted ASEAN during negotiations for the goods chapter of ACFTA, also require further explanation.

In keeping with this analysis, Justin Hempson-Jones argues that China has become 'strikingly liberal in its emphasis on the cooperative nature of state interaction', especially in its 'interactions with economic, political, and security intergovernmental organizations …' (Hempson-Jones 2005: 711, 703). More generally, Hempson-Jones observes that 'liberal patterns in the PRC's foreign policy are embodied in a more relaxed attitude toward interdependence' (Hempson-Jones 2005: 703). While Hempson-Jones acknowledges that China's liberal turn has been most pronounced in the economic realm, he also argues that 'liberal trends exist in Chinese foreign policy even in the fundamentally important area of state security – the stronghold of prudent realpolitik,' citing China's multifaceted engagement of ASEAN and its participation in ARF as evidence (Hempson-Jones 2005: 704).

Indeed, authors writing in this vein often focus on China's relations with ASEAN in arguing that China's recent behaviour represents a significant change in foreign policy orientation rather than simple pragmatism. To cite another example, Shambaugh argues that:

> China's efforts to improve its ties with ASEAN are not merely part of a larger 'charm offensive.' They represent, in some cases, fundamental compromises that China has chosen to make in limiting its own sovereign interests for the sake of engagement in multilateral frameworks and pursuit of greater regional interdependence.
>
> (Shambaugh 2004–05: 76)

Along similar lines, Hempson-Jones contends that by joining the WTO and otherwise increasing its participation in various multilateral economic, political and security forums, China has 'embarked on a course that has substantially compromised its autonomy'. Specifically, he cites Beijing's 'acceptance of conditionality' in interstate relations and its 'adherence to WTO requirements' as evidence that China's approach to international relations has undergone fundamental change (Hempson-Jones 2005: 711).

Not surprisingly, Shambaugh and Hempson-Jones both regard realism as a degraded tool for understanding Chinese foreign policy. Although Shambaugh recognizes the limitations of any single theoretical perspective for understanding China's engagement of Asia and the resulting transformation of regional order, he argues that 'realist theory seems particularly incapable of explaining such a complex and dynamic environment ...' (Shambaugh 2004–05: 99). Hempson-Jones agrees, concluding that Chinese behaviour is more consistent with neo-liberal institutionalism than realism. From its 'sovereignty-bending admission' to the WTO to its 'more pragmatic stance (on UN peacekeeping) that sanctions a certain level of interference into other states' affairs', Hempson-Jones argues that 'constraints on Chinese behaviour have been accepted in exchange for gains for the state' (Hempson-Jones 2005: 704). Whatever Beijing's original intentions were in interacting more extensively with the outside world, the benefits China has accrued have reinforced its cooperative orientation by continually pushing 'Chinese behaviour in a more liberal direction' (Hempson-Jones 2005: 711).

At a minimum, this perspective suggests that China's leaders regard growing interdependence as a fundamental condition of international politics that cannot be resisted in conducting state-to-state relations. More provocatively, Beijing can be seen as actually embracing liberal internationalism as a strategic choice in an era defined by globalization. According to this second position, interdependence has become valued for its own sake. Whereas interdependence used to be accepted rather narrowly as an economic means to China's developmental ends, in the new millennium Beijing can be seen as assigning independent weight to interdepend-ence as a broader political goal of Chinese foreign policy. From this perspective, China is a status-quo power that seeks to advance its interests through the exist-ing international system.

As a strategic context, globalization is seen as introducing – or at least accel-erating the emergence of – new sources of economic and security vulnerability such as unregulated capital flows, weapons proliferation, drug trafficking, transna-tional terrorist networks, cyber crime and the spread of infectious diseases. The fact that mainstream leaders, bureaucrats and scholars in China view such a wide range of issues in terms of globalization underscores the phenomenon's impor-tance as a lens through which elites view the challenges facing the country. Indeed, globalization figures more and more prominently in China's strategic thinking (Deng and Moore 2004). From the rising threat of non-state terrorism and the regional economic weaknesses highlighted by the 1997–98 Asian finan-cial crisis, to the outbreak of Severe Acute Respiratory Syndrome (SARS) and the transnational diffusion of lethal military technologies, forces associated with globalization are seen as providing significant challenges to Chinese interests. As a result, the liberal interpretation contends, Beijing now wishes for the world's great powers to move away from a traditional, zero-sum, unilateralist struggle for security and prosperity – which is increasingly self-defeating – in favour of positive-sum, multilateral efforts at what Chinese officials have called 'common security' and 'globalized cooperation'.[13]

Indeed, China's leaders have repeatedly acknowledged that globalization encourages broad participation in multilateral institutions at both the regional and global levels.[14] Although Beijing remains cautious about the implications of mul-tilateralism for national autonomy, institutionalized forms of cooperation are now seen as instruments by which China can pursue its interests both effectively and with international legitimacy. Notably, multilateralism allows China to assert a leadership role – especially in Central Asia and East Asia – without unnecessarily exacerbating fears that Beijing harbours revisionist intentions.

In one variant of this position, the emerging Chinese colossus can be seen as pursuing what John Ikenberry calls an 'institutional bargain'. In this bargain, the leading state 'agrees to tie itself to the commitments and obligations of an inter-state institution' so long as those 'institutional agreements ... lock in other countries into a relatively congenial and stable order' conducive to the leading state's long-term interests (Ikenberry 2002: 124). In this way, multilateral agreements can enhance the exercise of what Joseph Nye calls 'co-optive behavioral power – getting others to want what you want' (Nye 1990: 88). In what Ikenberry calls a 'free-floating' (i.e. uninstitutionalized) order, the leading state must resort to the 'constant and costly exercise of power to get its way' (Ikenberry 2002: 124). Even though China must accept some measure of reduced policy autonomy as a demonstration of self-restraint, this tradeoff is more efficient than repeated reliance on coercive power. Especially as power resources become 'less fungible, less coercive, and less tangible' over time, institutionalized cooperation becomes an increasingly attractive tool for rising powers such as China (Nye 1990: 188).

Finally, the liberal trend in Chinese thinking is also arguably reflected in the increasing emphasis Beijing places on multilateralism over multipolarity. Whereas the promotion of multipolarity suggests that China seeks explicitly to balance against US power, Beijing's increasing diplomatic focus on multilateralism 'reflects a preference for a more democratic world order that emphasizes proper management of state-to-state relations over the redistribution of power' (Deng and Moore 2004: 122). According to a liberal interpretation, through its diplomacy at the UN and its advocacy of initiatives such as the New Security Concept,[15] China is increasingly eschewing realist great-power struggle, as characterized by internal military mobilization and hostile external alliances, in favour of a more cooperative, multilateral approach to development and security.

Cooperating to compete: Chinese multilateralism as realist internationalism

Although Chinese behaviour seems to be at odds with certain general realist expectations, many of Beijing's actions can also be reconciled quite satisfactorily with specific lines of realist thought. For example, China's engagement of ASEAN countries fits well with the classic realist explanation of Germany's trading relations with its smaller European neighbours between the First and Second World Wars, as set forth by Albert Hirschman in his landmark book *National Power and the Structure of Foreign Trade* (Hirschman 1945). In Hirschman's account, Germany sought to increase its political leverage by offering favourable trade arrangements to its smaller neighbours. Rather than try to dominate by extracting economic concessions from weaker parties, Germany sought to increase its political influence by purposely accepting asymmetric economic relations. From this perspective, contemporary China would be seen as cultivating interdependence with smaller countries such as its ASEAN partners, not as a separate end or primarily for economic purposes, but as a means of enhancing its political power. If analogous arguments are made about China's participation in the SCO, or even its ongoing, multifaceted bilateral engagement of countries such as South Korea, Australia, New Zealand and Pakistan, each of which are engaged in FTA discussions with China, one could identify a realist-oriented strategy in which Beijing is trying to increase its regional political influence through economic statecraft.

It remains to be seen whether ASEAN or China will benefit more from ACFTA in the long run. Even if ASEAN countries enjoy higher rates of economic growth from ACFTA, China will still accrue critical benefits such as newly expanded export markets and improved access to raw materials and other inputs vital to its economic well-being. In this way, ACFTA could enhance China's long-term autonomy in world economic affairs vis-à-vis dominant players such as the United States, the European Union and Japan, thereby enhancing its security.

Similarly, for all the wealth creation that ASEAN countries might enjoy as a result of ACFTA, this would come at the expense of greater dependence on China. As the importance of trade with China grows for ASEAN countries, so too does Beijing's political leverage. In this way, Hirschman argued that 'commerce can become an alternative to war ... by providing a method of coercion of its own', namely through the potential disruption of economic ties (Hirschman 1945: 15). To be sure, any interruption in commerce can be expected to hurt both sides, but the adjustment costs are likely to be far greater for the smaller partner. It is in this respect that Hirschman's analysis was quintessentially realist: he focused on the use of foreign trade to create 'relationships of dependence and influence between nations' that increase coercive power (Hirschman 1945: 15).

In fact, China may not even need to twist arms or threaten punitive action to ensure that ASEAN acts in accord with Beijing's interests. As the International Political Economy literature has repeatedly noted, small states often perceive their interests as converging with those of larger neighbours as the result of FTAs and other agreements that institutionalize cooperation. More broadly, domestic politics has long been understood as being significantly shaped by the structure of a country's international economic relations (Berger and Dore 1996; Keohane and Milner 1996; Kirshner 2003; Rogowski 1989). Specifically, the beneficiaries of trade liberalization in the smaller countries (e.g. ASEAN) have an interest in defending and even advancing relations with the larger partner (e.g. China). From this perspective, economic restructuring associated with ACFTA should strengthen those sectors, firms and factors of production in ASEAN that are advantaged by trade liberalization with China. Indeed, new political interests and coalitions could be expected to emerge that favour the articulation of domestic and foreign policies beneficial to China.[16]

From this perspective, China's more active participation in multilateralism signifies not a commitment to liberal internationalism but a realist-oriented willingness to use institutionalized cooperation in managing relations with certain countries. Consistent with Hegemonic Stability Theory, a leading realist explanation of US behaviour in the post-Second World War era, China can be seen as a large regional power trying to lock smaller countries into 'enduring policy positions' by providing public goods or other benefits to smaller countries on favourable terms (Ikenberry 2001: 41). To this point, it should be noted, China's multilateral agreements with partners such as ASEAN and SCO have not been very costly in terms of reduced policy autonomy. In this sense, the opportunity cost of institutionalized cooperation has been low compared to the gains China stands to accrue by building long-term commitments that other states will find difficult to retract (Ikenberry 2002: 127).

While Beijing's longstanding aversion to institutionalized cooperation has weakened substantially, China's leaders remain cautious about the obligations they accept, often still preferring codes of conduct and statements of principle in favour of legalized agreements with robust enforcement mechanisms. For example, Beijing maintains a preference for pacts, such as ASEAN's *Treaty of Amity and Cooperation*, which reinforce principles of sovereignty, territorial integrity and non-interference in domestic affairs.[17] Similarly, Beijing is most enthusiastic about agreements that emphasize consultation and consensus on key issues such as dispute management. The SCO is defined by the so-called Shanghai Spirit, just as China's expanding relations with ASEAN extend and strengthen the much-ballyhooed ASEAN Way. Although the SCO is a formal organization, it is based on voluntary principles that reinforce Westphalian notions of sovereignty.

Indeed, a point often missed by observers who emphasize a liberal trend in Chinese foreign policy is that the regional groups in which China holds membership have largely eschewed any movement toward supranationality. For its part, China has sought to promote (or at least reinforce) the norm of sovereignty. For example, Beijing has skilfully used Asian regionalism to further ostracize Taiwan. Not only is Taiwan excluded from the likes of APT, ARF and EAS, but China has used these groups and other forums to socialize its neighbours – especially ASEAN – to accept Beijing's views on matters such as Taiwan's status. This example shows that socialization is a two-way street. For analysts who see China's participation in multilateralism as pushing Chinese foreign policy in a liberal direction, discussion is too often restricted to how China will become socialized by its interlocutors rather than the other way around.

In many respects, China seems to be engaged in a balancing act. On the one hand, growing economic and security interdependence in world affairs has increased China's interest in the kind of stable, rule-governed environment associated with deepening multilateralism. At the same time, Beijing's traditional resistance to shared sovereignty and the constrained policy autonomy that accompanies collective decision-making militate against greater acceptance of formal institutionalization. To this point, Beijing has coped with these conflicting pressures in two central ways. First, China has sought to ensure that it belongs to a sufficiently wide range of groups to allow for the kind of forum shopping that enables states to avoid (or at least minimize) outcomes deleterious to their interests. By virtue of its size and power, China wields leverage not only in raising or lowering the profiles of various forums but also in setting their agendas and in cutting deals consistent with its interests. By participating in myriad dialogues and processes – to say nothing of contributing to the proliferation of forums in Asian regionalism – China affords itself strategic flexibility in pursuing international cooperation.

Second, China pursues institutionalized cooperation on a distinctly selective basis. In recognition that small numbers can be a source of vulnerability, Beijing seems to prefer larger groups except when China is the most powerful participant. Thus, Chinese leaders have pursued institutionalized cooperation most enthusiastically either in global settings (e.g. WTO and UN) or regionally with weaker partners (e.g. ASEAN and SCO). Consistent with realist concerns about the danger of entering into agreements with stronger partners who might find their leverage further enhanced, China favours trade liberalization in the WTO over APEC. Although its membership draws on 21 economies from both sides of the Pacific, APEC still lends itself to dominance by the United States (and its allies such as Japan). As a result, there has long been concern in Beijing that institutionalized cooperation in APEC would likely reflect US interests at China's expense. Whatever the risks of WTO entry, China's participation in a group with 150 members offers a more attractive alternative because its agenda is less easily dominated by the United States. To the extent that growing interdependence advances a Chinese interest in a stable, rule-oriented environment, the pursuit of institutionalized cooperation in large groups such as the WTO represents a more desirable choice.

China's differentiated approach to trade liberalization – vigorously pursuing FTAs with weaker actors such as ASEAN while actively discouraging a broader agreement in APEC and exhibiting mild enthusiasm for WTO negotiations under the Doha Round – undermines not only the notion that China opposes institutionalized cooperation altogether but also the notion that Beijing uniformly supports institutionalized cooperation. As such, a realist interpretation would emphasize the selective, partial and generally uneven nature of China's turn toward multilateralism. In this sense, it is not so much institutionalized cooperation that China resists as the prospect that certain venues for institutionalized cooperation might produce outcomes adverse to Chinese interests.[18]

The fact that Beijing has pursued trade liberalization more actively through FTAs than through APEC, when the latter would yield greater welfare gains for China, supports the realist view that the goal of initiatives such as ACFTA has been more political than economic. If welfare gains were valued most, Chinese policy would likely follow one of two paths. First, Beijing could try to force its smaller partners to accept disadvantageous trade deals. Second, Beijing could pursue broader trade liberalization, as studies have shown that China stands to enjoy the greatest welfare gains – both absolutely and relative to its leading partners – through trade liberalization in the WTO, APEC and APT, respectively (Scollay and Gilbert 2001). In this respect, initiatives such as ACFTA are economically suboptimal.

China's new-found support for FTAs also reflects the powerful opportunity that FTAs provide to establish new rules, standards and procedures consistent with Chinese interests. As discussed earlier, FTAs such as ACFTA also stand to create regional trade structures that would make China's partners more dependent economically. This in turn would confer power on Beijing. As numerous studies have shown, China's deepening participation in the world economy – as symbolized and accelerated by Beijing's WTO accession – is already having a profound restructuring effect on global trade patterns (Rumbaugh and Blancher 2004; Wang 2003; Yang 2003). ACFTA and China's other FTA initiatives represent a regional intensification of this trend. Indeed, changing trade patterns have profound security externalities. Consistent with Hirschman's analysis of interwar Germany, the strategic use of economic multilateralism by contemporary China seems designed to cultivate interdependence with smaller countries as a means of enhancing its political power.

Consistent with this interpretation, another purpose of China's efforts at regionalism may be to balance against US power. In the absence of formal military alliances, it could be argued that China's approach is one of hedging or even soft balancing. Indeed, realists would argue that Beijing's promotion of 'partnerships without alliance' – an application of China's New Security Concept – in its relations with ASEAN and SCO countries is a thinly veiled effort to counter Washington's dominance. Whereas the liberal interpretation of China's foreign policy orientation would emphasize how Beijing's growing commitment to multilateral processes reflects its preference for a rules-based order, albeit one that arguably restrains the exercise of US power, the realist interpretation would be that Chinese multilateralism – pursued selectively and opportunistically rather than uniformly – is actually designed to enhance Chinese power at the expense of the United States by weakening the bilateral alliances that serve as the core of Washington's grand strategy in East Asia. In the long run, moreover, China seeks to position itself as the hub of a new network of regional relationships.

Multilateralism as China's strategic choice in an era of globalization and regionalism

This chapter does not address the role of domestic politics in China's foreign policy decision-making or how the choices that China makes are conditioned by the international environment with which it interacts. For example, Chinese initiatives in the area of economic cooperation may have been a response, at least in part, to factors such as the lessons of the Asian financial crisis and the spread of FTA fever that has gripped the international political economy in recent years. At a global level, China's epochal choice to join the WTO cannot be understood in isolation from the long-term commitment displayed by the advanced industrial democracies – and the United States in particular – to the commercial engagement of China. At a regional level, ASEAN's receptivity to Chinese initiatives such as ACFTA has of course also been critical in shaping Beijing's evolving position on multilateralism.

The point is simply to acknowledge that Chinese decision makers operate in a world marked by unipolarity, interdependence, globalization and regionalism, to cite just a few key characteristics. With respect to the last feature, for example, it is legitimate to ask whether it is China that is turning to regional multilateralism or whether it is Asia more broadly that is actually turning to regional multilateralism, with China primarily following this trend. This question raises the larger issue of whether China has a grand strategy that calls for the greater use of multilateralism as a means of pursuing specific objectives in its foreign policy. On this point, the liberal and realist interpretations presented in this chapter concur that China's more active participation in multilateralism reflects strategic choice rather than serendipity or simple pragmatism.

Although a case can be made that Beijing has 'crossed the river by feeling for stones' (*mozhe shitou guohe*) in its foreign policy as well as in its domestic economic reform, it would seem that China's increased use of multilateralism reflects more than a trial-and-error unfolding of events or the simple weakening over time of Beijing's principled opposition to multilateralism. Specifically, China's turn toward multilateralism seems to have coincided with high-level political decisions about the country's proper course domestically and internationally. Taken together, a series of major policy moves taken at the end of the 1990s and early in the new millennium suggest that China's turn toward multilateralism reflected the crystallization of a grand strategy, or at least a de facto grand strategy. For example, by the late 1990s Chinese leaders had come to the realization that unipolarity was likely to persist indefinitely. Indeed, it was also around this time that China lessened its official opposition to US alliances in East Asia, tacitly recognizing that American presence in the region benefits Chinese interests in certain respects. By electing not to openly oppose the United States, Beijing made it easier for neighbours such as ASEAN and South Korea to develop closer relations with China because they were not, in essence, forced to choose between Beijing and Washington. The timing of China's decision to join the WTO, followed by its comprehensive engagement of SCO, ASEAN and other countries on its periphery, further suggests that the rapid erosion of China's longstanding scepticism of multilateralism reflected strategic choice.

Even if there was no master plan with a blueprint detailing exactly what initiatives to take and how precisely these steps would fit into a formal grand strategy for making China rich and strong, the intensity and depth of China's forays into regionalism – from FTAs to security dialogues – seems hard to square with an argument that these developments were largely serendipitous and unconnected. Even if China's much-ballyhooed pragmatism played a role, it is difficult to see how, for example, the SCO evolved in unintended fashion as quickly as it did from a loose forum for the interstate coordination of border issues to a formal organization embodying aspects of a quasi-military alliance. Indeed, Beijing's active leadership role in the establishment of SCO further undermines the notion that little or no element of conscious strategy was involved. As Jianwei Wang has shown, China pushed to expand the SCO's agenda from security cooperation to economic cooperation in a self-conscious effort to maintain what Beijing regarded as the group's flagging momentum (Wang 2005). Similarly, the broadening of China's engagement of ASEAN since the late 1990s seems far too comprehensive to have unfolded in the absence of some strategic direction. All told, it is hard to fathom that China has unwittingly allowed its participation in multilateral cooperation to grow in ways that it actively resisted in the past.

The tale of the tape: A preliminary assessment

This chapter raises one central question: what is the ultimate goal of Beijing's more active participation in multilateralism, integration or domination? This dichotomy portrays the alternatives too starkly, to be sure, but the liberal interpretation does see China's increased pursuit of institutionalized cooperation as signifying a commitment to cultivate international interdependence for its own sake, with an explicit objective of advancing a rules-based, norm-driven order. By contrast, the realist interpretation sees China's growing participation in multilateralism primarily as a mechanism by which Beijing can increase its coercive power and political influence, with regional (or even global) primacy possibly as the ultimate objective. Although the evidence is mixed, recent developments in China's foreign relations seem, on balance, more consistent with the realist interpretation.

A multilateralism of its own?

As this chapter has emphasized, one striking characteristic of recent Chinese foreign policy is Beijing's determined pursuit of its own preferred multilateral mechanisms. In some cases, this has simply meant promoting existing forums that it favours, as exemplified by China's hosting of the Second GMS Summit in 2005, an event that further cemented China's growing influence in mainland Southeast Asia. Another existing forum Beijing seeks to strengthen is the SCO. Its limitations notwithstanding, the SCO is proving to be a useful diplomatic instrument in advancing China's foreign policy objectives. In July 2005, for example, the heads of state issued a joint statement at the annual SCO summit calling for the United States to establish a timetable for the withdrawal of American forces from Kyrgyzstan, Uzbekistan and Tajikistan.

Beyond its use of existing forums, China has also sought to promote new mechanisms for multilateral dialogue. For example, the ARF Security Policy Conference was widely interpreted as a Chinese effort to create an alternative to the annual Shangri-La Dialogue hosted by Singapore. Along the same lines, the Boao Forum is yet another case in which Beijing has sought to put its own stamp on Asian multilateralism, as is China's promotion of various security workshops and seminars with ASEAN. Chinese leaders have even broached the ambitious idea of linking SCO and ASEAN through FTA structures, a development that would clearly position China as the hub of a new network of regional relationships (Yan 2003).

China's desire for its own multilateralism is perhaps best seen in the vicissitudes of its policy toward the EAS. By all accounts, China was quite enthusiastic initially about the EAS, identifying the group as a means for advancing its preferred vision of an East Asian Community. As planning began for the first meeting, which was ultimately held in Malaysia in December 2005, Beijing offered to host the second annual meeting. Although this gesture could have been interpreted simply as evidence of China's commitment to deeper regional integration in East Asia, most observers – including many of its neighbours – believed that China saw the EAS as a way to seize regional leadership by diverting diplomatic focus away from the ASEAN-centred APT toward a new vehicle in which the 'plus three' countries would be on equal footing with ASEAN. Given South Korea's smaller size and Japan's historical baggage in the region, so the argument went, China would find itself in the driver's seat. Furthermore, China found the idea of EAS desirable because the group would feature Beijing's role while excluding both Washington and Taipei. In the words of one US government official, 'China wants the East Asia Summit because it's not APEC'.[19] As such, EAS was thought to represent an opportunity for Beijing to develop a China-centred East Asian Community. To that end, China reportedly sought to broaden the EAS agenda to include political and military cooperation as well as economic cooperation.

When ASEAN ultimately blanched at China's offer to host the second EAS meeting, however, Beijing denied any interest in raising its profile and vigorously reiterated its support of ASEAN's central role in East Asian regionalism. In fact, when China, Malaysia and other APT members who resisted the inclusion of Australia, India and New Zealand in EAS lost out to Japan, Indonesia, Singapore and others who favoured granting EAS membership to these non-East Asian countries, Beijing worked furiously to ensure that the EAS declaration would highlight the guiding role of APT in East Asian regionalism, effectively downgrading EAS to a vehicle by which APT could strengthen its dialogue with outside countries. (These outsiders would include not only Australia, India and New Zealand as full members of EAS but also several observer countries.) Indeed, China succeeded in eliminating from the EAS declaration any mention of building an East Asian Community. All indications suggest that China is continuing its efforts to marginalize EAS in favour of APT.

According to this interpretation, China's behaviour toward the EAS is consistent with its selective, strategic, partial embrace of regional multilateralism. While China may retain an interest in advancing regional integration, Beijing's strong preference is to pursue limited cooperation within the more manageable APT. Even then, its enthusiasm is likely to be tempered by the reality that ASEAN occupies the central role in East Asian regionalism. Unlike the SCO, where China is both the founder and the leading force today, in the APT China's ability to shape the agenda is likely to be more limited.

China's participation in Asian financial and monetary cooperation

Although Beijing's support for financial and monetary cooperation in East Asia has reached unprecedented heights in recent years, China's behaviour in this issue-area still falls short of what most government officials, policy analysts and scholars consider a genuine shift toward liberal internationalism.[20] For example,

Chinese officials accepted somewhat reluctantly the agreement struck at the May 2005 APT finance ministers' meeting to double both the reserve size of swap arrangements under the Chiang Mai Initiative (CMI) and the draw-down mechanism for disbursing funds without an IMF-supported program. More generally, Chinese officials reportedly remain sceptical about transforming the network of bilateral currency swaps under the CMI into a multilateral mechanism. In the opinion of most observers, China is particularly wary about developing the kind of intrusive surveillance processes, standard setting practices and regulatory capacity that would be necessary to 'multilateralize' the CMI. Especially as China is unlikely to be a beneficiary if the swap arrangements are ever activated, given its current set of economic policies and vast foreign exchange reserves, the prevailing view is that Beijing's priority is to guard its autonomy and sovereignty.[21]

At the same time, Beijing has acquiesced to APT and ADB plans to study the collective management of currency swaps, creation of local bond markets and development of an Asian Currency Unit. By some media accounts, in fact, China is an 'active supporter of the idea of an Asian Currency Unit (ACU) to help Asia cushion against a possible dollar shock' (Rowley 2006). According to officials from central banks and finance ministries in the region, however, there is sometimes a significant gap between Chinese rhetoric and Chinese behavior.[22] That said, financial and monetary cooperation in East Asia could never have progressed as far as it has in recent years without China's support and active participation. On issues related to the development of capital markets, such as the Asian Bond Market Initiative, Beijing appears to be genuinely enthusiastic. In other areas, where its power to shape the agenda is weak, China is clearly more cautious, preferring to wait for a consensus to develop and only then adopting the consensus position.

China's FTAs

The FTAs pursued by Beijing provide further support that Chinese behaviour reflects realist internationalism. As discussed earlier, China favours trade liberalization either regionally with weaker partners (e.g. ASEAN) or globally through the WTO, mainly for political reasons. Consistent with this analysis, Beijing continues to favour an East Asian FTA (APT membership) over the US-proposed Asia Pacific FTA (APEC membership) or the Japanese-proposed East Asia Partnership Agreement (EAS membership), although its preferred outcome apparently remains the establishment of a hub-and-spokes system of China-centred FTAs with ASEAN, SCO, South Korea, Australia, New Zealand, India and Pakistan.

In addition to the membership issue, the nature of the FTAs that Beijing has concluded (or is negotiating) also supports a realist interpretation. For example, there is little evidence that China has bargained hard to maximize the liberalizing impact of its FTAs. According to one government official in the region, China more or less says to its partners, 'you pick your areas of exclusion, and we'll pick our areas of exclusion'.[23] For some countries, this makes China an attractive partner with whom to pursue an FTA, especially compared to more 'demanding' countries such as the United States. In some cases, China has reportedly sought to reduce tariffs for products where it has little or no trade with a prospective partner, presumably to make the coverage of its FTA appear as wide as possible. By contrast, some of the most sensitive, highly protected areas of traded goods remain outside the purview of China's FTA discussions.

While China is certainly not alone in this behaviour, the consensus among government officials, policy analysts and scholars in the region is that China's FTAs are designed more to improve political ties and to pursue specific economic objectives than to liberalize trade per se. According to individuals privy to Beijing's negotiating positions, China's overriding economic objective is to expand strategic cooperation with its FTA partners by improving access to natural resources, securing conferral of market economy status and facilitating government-to-government plans to increase trade and investment in targeted areas.[24] Consequently, it would be more accurate to say that China pursues preferential trade agreements (or, perhaps less charitably, discriminatory trade agreements) rather than FTAs per se, since the primary goal is not to make trade freer in the conventional sense.

According to an official in Japan's Ministry of Economy, Trade, and Industry, China's FTA diplomacy demonstrates a significant capacity for strategic action.[25] As China is not a democracy, the country's leaders are not accountable in the same way that their counterparts in the United States, Japan and elsewhere are. Whatever the constraints of regional, sectoral, bureaucratic or intra-party politics in China, top leaders in Beijing can and do pursue politically advantageous deals more freely than American or Japanese leaders could. Particularly in its relations with ASEAN and as a member of the SCO, China is using economic statecraft to grasp the political agenda and thereby occupy strategic space. Even if China's FTAs prove to be relatively low-quality FTAs in an economic sense, they are likely to be effective political instruments.

Is China learning? And does it matter?

This chapter focuses on why China pursues regional cooperation in Asia. Some observers, particularly liberal thinkers (and some constructivists), might argue that the question of whether Chinese policy is informed by liberal internationalism or realist internationalism is much less important than the fact that China has become more active multilaterally. According to this position, China's interests (or at least the calculation of its interests) are likely to be fundamentally transformed by its participation in multilateralism – regardless of Beijing's initial intentions. From this perspective, participation in multilateralism is a slippery slope. What may begin as instrumental participation (adaptation) often leads to enmeshment (adaptive learning) as national interests are transformed over time through the experience of participating in multilateral cooperation. The point, in short, is that norms often follow behaviour. Cooperative behaviour socializes the participants, creates incentives to conform to multilateral principles and other-wise contributes to the genuine (i.e. cognitive) learning in which value change takes place.

The realist interpretation would caution, however, that this process is neither as seamless nor as irreversible as described here. From this perspective, China's current commitment to multilateralism is too shallow and opportunistic to dismiss the question of motivations so easily. As much as China's views of, and policies toward, multilateralism have evolved, the permanence of Beijing's commitment to institutionalized cooperation on the basis of generalized principles of conduct is by no means assured. Particularly given China's traditional scepticism of mul-tilateralism, realists (and some constructivists) would caution that Beijing's recog-nition that multilateralism has utility in advancing Chinese interests should not be mistaken for value change.

While the liberal and realist interpretations differ markedly on a wide variety of issues, perhaps the most significant issue is whether Beijing is likely to con-tinue down the 'multilateral path' in the future, and, if so, how far. According to the liberal view, China can be expected to broaden and deepen its participation in multilateral groups, especially as the process of globalization continues to unfold. As such, growing interdependence in world affairs is likely to serve as an impor-tant stimulus in China's foreign policy learning. By contrast, the realist view would expect China's commitment to multilateralism to remain decidedly uneven. Participation in multilateral groups might broaden in order to pursue specific objectives with certain partners or to facilitate forum shopping. On the other hand, prospects for learning would be seen as weak. Indeed, realist analysis would anticipate a possible re-evaluation of current multilateral arrangements as the costs of constrained autonomy rise. As China becomes more powerful rela-tive to its partners, the opportunity cost of constrained autonomy will grow, even if neither the scope nor the depth of existing cooperative arrangements increases. Consequently, it is unclear – and even doubtful – from a realist perspective whether Beijing will be willing to take the next step in regionalism by sharing governance in any meaningful way. More generally, realists would caution against any assumption that a more 'multilateral' China will necessarily be more altruistic or civic-minded, as multilateral institutions have proved to be tools of domination in the past.

Concluding thoughts

There is no doubt that China's foreign policy has become more consistent with liberal internationalism in certain respects. At the same time, the literature needs to acknowledge the extent to which Beijing's participation in Asian regionalism still reflects a desire to control outcomes (in realist fashion) more than a wide-ranging commitment to a rules-based, norm-driven interdependence (in liberal fashion). Given its rapidly rising power, particularly as manifested in its market power, China is now in a position to exert increasing influence in East Asia. That Beijing often seeks to do so through institutionalized cooperation does not mean its behaviour is inconsistent with realism. In fundamental ways, China is cooperating to compete.

As this chapter documents, China's enthusiasm for institutionalized cooperation varies significantly across issue-areas and partners. What is more, Beijing has hardly eschewed unilateralism or threats to use force, as one can see from its exploitation of seabed resources in the East China Sea and frequent statements reserving the right to use military might to prevent Taiwan's independence. Indeed, China continues to build up its military capabilities at a robust pace in spite of its increased participation in multilateralism. In much the same way, it appears, Beijing seeks to enhance its capabilities economically and politically through both the establishment of regional FTAs and its participation in the likes of APT, SCO and ARF.

At the very least, China appears determined to render itself indispensable so others must take its interests into account before acting (Foot 2005). For all of Beijing's increased emphasis on multilateralism, there is also evidence of resurgent bilateralism (e.g. the establishment of the Strategic Economic Dialogue with the United States) as well as persistent unilateralism (e.g. Beijing's policy on Hong Kong, Chinese testing of anti-satellite missiles in space). As this suggests, China's foreign relations remain multifaceted. In this respect, the biggest story may not be Beijing's increased use of regional and global multilateralism as much as the larger, more active role China is playing in international affairs more generally. Contrary to Deng Xiaoping's belief that China should avoid a leading role in world affairs (*bu chu tou*), choosing instead to bide its time while building up capabilities (*taoguang yanghui*), Beijing has pursued a more activist foreign policy over the past decade under both the Jiang Zemin/Zhu Rongji leadership and the Hu Jintao/Wen Jiabao leadership. For reasons that the liberal and realist positions interpret differently, China has expanded its use of multilateralism in recent years. Especially for the realist interpretation, but also for the liberal interpretation, this increasing reliance on multilateralism is only one aspect of a broader, even more significant phenomenon.

Notes

1   Portions of this chapter first appeared in Moore (2007).
2   For an illuminating discussion of realist internationalism versus realist isolationism, see Rhodes (1999).
3   It should be noted that this institutionalist use of the term 'liberal internationalism' is quite different from the theoretical tradition, often closely associated with the philosopher Immanuel Kant, which emphasizes the so-called liberal peace among democracies.
4   In a slight variation, Ruggie (1993: 11) defines multilateralism as 'an institutional form that coordinates relations among three or more states on the basis of generalized principles of conduct'.
5   The members of the SCO are China, Kazakhstan, Kyrgyzstan, Russia, Tajikistan and Uzbekistan. The Six-Party Talks are comprised of China, Japan, North Korea, Russia, South Korea and the United States.
6   For present purposes, the most important forums are APT, EAS, and APEC. APT consists of the ten members of ASEAN plus China, Japan and South Korea. EAS comprises APT plus Australia, India and New Zealand. APEC's 21 members include the United States, Canada, Mexico, Chile and Peru, in addition to most of the EAS, plus Russia, Taiwan, and Hong Kong.

7   For an excellent overview of China's behaviour as a member of the WTO, see Pearson (2006).
8   Here, it is worth noting that China's approach to membership in the IMF has not yet changed markedly as a result of the 2006 changes in IMF voting rights, which saw China's voting share increase 25 per cent to a level almost two-thirds of Japan's share.
9   For a recent overview of these initiatives, see Grimes (2006).
10 For an excellent primer on the different expectations of realism and liberalism as applied to comparative regionalism, see Chan (2001). On the preference for flexibility, see p. 10.
11 For a classic realist statement on interdependence, see Chapter 7 of Waltz (1979).
12 See, for example, *Forging Closer ASEAN–China Economic Relations in the Twenty-first Century*, October 2001. Online. Available at: www.aseansec.org/newdata/asean_chi.pdf (accessed 22 March 2007). This report, submitted by the ASEAN–China Expert Group on Economic Cooperation in October 2001, predicted that percentage growth in gross domestic product would favour ASEAN. The 'early harvest' provisions added later would seem to make that outcome even more likely.
13 On common security, see Wu (2003). On globalized cooperation, see Li (2003).
14 On economic affairs, see Jiang (2000). On security affairs, see Tang (2002).
15 In place of traditional alliance structures, such as those associated with the Cold War, the New Security Concept promotes the creation of a more 'progressive' security order in which bilateral relations and multilateral institutions are characterized by mutual trust and benefit, equality and cooperation.
16 For a more general argument along these lines, see Kirshner (2003: 277).
17 For the text of the *Treaty of Amity and Cooperation*, see www.aseansec.org/1217.htm (accessed 22 November 2004).
18 The China-specific argument presented here is consistent with the more general analysis of Asia-Pacific institutionalization provided in Kahler (2000).
19 August 2005 interview with an official at a US embassy in Asia.
20 June 2004, December 2004, August 2005 and December 2005 interviews.
21 Ibid. For a further discussion see Dieter's contribution on financial cooperation (Chapter 7 of this book).
22 June 2004 and August 2005 interviews.
23 August 2005 interview.
24 June 2004, December 2004, August 2005 and December 2005 interviews.
25 August 2005 interview.

References

Aggarwal, V.K. (2006) 'Bilateral Trade Agreements in the Asia-Pacific' in V.K. Aggarwal and S. Urata (eds) *Bilateral Trade Agreements in the Asia-Pacific*, New York: Routledge, pp. 3–26.

Berger, S. and Dore, R. (eds) (1996) *National Diversity and Global Capitalism*, Ithaca, NY: Cornell University Press.

Chan, S. (2001) 'Liberalism, Realism, and Regional Trade: Differentiating APEC from EU and NAFTA' *Pacific Focus* 16(1): 5–34.

Deng, Y. and Moore, T.G. (2004) 'China Views Globalization: Towards a New Great Power Politics?' *Washington Quarterly* 27(3): 117–136.

Foot, R. (2005) 'China's Regional Activism: Leadership, Leverage, and Protection' *Global Change, Peace & Security* 17(2): 141–153.

Grimes, W. (2006) 'East Asian Financial Regionalism in Support of the Global Financial Architecture? The Political Economy of Regional Nesting' *Journal of East Asian Studies* 6: 353–380.

Hempson-Jones, J.S. (2005) 'The Evolution of China's Engagement with Intergovernmental Organizations: Toward a Liberal Foreign Policy?' *Asian Survey* 45(5): 702–721.

Hirschman, A.O. (1945) *National Power and the Structure of Foreign Trade*, Berkeley, CA: University of California Press.

Ikenberry, G.J. (2001) *After Victory,* Princeton, NJ: Princeton University Press.

Ikenberry, G.J. (2002) 'Multilateralism and US Grand Strategy' in S. Patrick and S. Forman (eds) *Multilateralism and US Foreign Policy,* Boulder, CO: Lynne Rienner, pp. 121–140.

Ikenberry, G.J. (2005) 'The Future of Liberal Internationalism'. Online. Available at: www.tpmcafe.com/story/2005/10/10/181851/23 (accessed 28 February 2007).

Jiang, Z. (2000) 'Speech at the Eighth APEC Informal Leadership Meeting, 16 November 2000'. Online. Available at: www.fmprc.gov/cn/eng/6004.html (accessed 11 March 2003).

Kahler, M. (2000) 'Legalization as Strategy: The Asia-Pacific Case' *International Organization* 54(3), 549–571.

Keohane, R. (1990) 'Multilateralism: An Agenda for Research' *International Journal* XLV: 731–764.

Keohane, R. and Milner, H. (eds) (1996) *Internationalization and Domestic Politics,* Cambridge: Cambridge University Press.

Kirshner, J. (2003) 'States, Markets, and Great Power Relations in the Pacific' in G.J. Ikenberry and M. Mastanduno (eds) *International Relations Theory and the Asia-Pacific*, New York: Columbia University Press.

Li, Z. (2003) Speech to UN General Assembly, 23 September 2003. Online. Available at: www.un.org/webcast/ga/58/statements/chinaeng030924.htm (accessed 9 October 2003).

Li, Z. (2004) 'Full Text of Chinese FM's Press Conference, 6 March 2004'. Online. Available at: http://english1.peopledaily.com.cn:80/200403/07/print20040307_136794. html (accessed 7 February 2005).

Mansfield, E.D. and Milner, H.V. (1999) 'The New Wave of Regionalism' *International Organization* 53(3): 589–627.

Medeiros, E.S. and Fravel, M.T. (2003) 'China's New Diplomacy' *Foreign Affairs* 82(6): 22–35.

Moore, T.G. (2007) 'Racing to Integrate, or Cooperating to Compete? Liberal and Realist Interpretations of China's New Multilateralism' in G. Wu, (ed.) *China Turns to Multilateralism: Foreign Policy and Regional Security*, London: Routledge.

Nye, J.S. (1990) *Bound to Lead*, New York: Basic Books.

Pearson, M.M. (2006) 'China in Geneva: Lessons from China's Early Years in the World Trade Organization' in A.I. Johnston and R.S. Ross (eds) *New Directions in the Study of China's Foreign Policy*, Stanford, CA: Stanford University Press, pp. 242–275.

Ravenhill, J. (2001) *APEC and the Construction of Pacific Rim Regionalism*, Cambridge: Cambridge University Press.

Rhodes, E. (1999) '...From the Sea and Back Again: Naval Power in the Second American Century' *Naval War College Review* 52(2): 13–54.

Rogowski, R. (1989) *Commerce and Coalitions*, Princeton, NJ: Princeton University Press.

Rowley, A. (2006) 'More Support for Asian Currency Index,' *Business Times* (Singapore), 26 May 2006. Online. Available at: http://ytlcommunity.com/commnews/shownews. asp?newsid=23358 (accessed 22 March 2007).

Ruggie, J.G. (1982) 'International Regimes, Transactions, and Change: Embedded Liberalism in the Postwar Economic Order' *International Organization* 36(2): 379–415.

Ruggie, J.G. (1993) 'Multilateralism: The Anatomy of an Institution' in Ruggie (ed.) *Multilateralism Matters*, New York: Columbia University Press, pp. 3–50.

Rumbaugh, T. and Blancher, N. (2004) 'China: International Trade and WTO Accession', *IMF Working Paper*, WP/04/36.

Scollay, R. and Gilbert, J. (2001), *'New Regional Trading Arrangements in the Asia Pacific?'*, Washington, DC: Institute for International Economics.

Shambaugh, D. (2004–05) 'China Engages Asia: Reshaping the Regional Order' *International Security* 29(3): 64–99.

Simon, S. W. (2003–04) 'Southeast Asia: Wither Security Regionalism?' in R.J. Ellings and A.L. Friedberg (ed.) *Strategic Asia 2003–04*, Seattle: National Bureau of Asian Research, pp. 269–289.

Tang, J. (2002) 'Speech at the Ninth ASEAN Regional Forum Foreign Ministers' Meeting, Brunei, 31 July 2002'. Online. Available at: http://fmprc.gov.cn/eng/33228.html (accessed on 11 March 2003).

Waltz, K. (1979) *Theory of International Politics*, Reading, MA: Addison-Wesley.

Wang, J. (2005) 'China Multilateral Diplomacy in the New Millennium' in Y. Deng and F.L. Wang (eds) *China Rising: Power and Motivation in Chinese Foreign Policy*, Lanham, MD: Rowman and Littlefield, pp. 159–200.

Wang, Z. (2003) 'The Impact of China's WTO Accession on Patterns of World Trade' *Journal of Policy Modeling* 25: 1–41.

Wen, J. (2006) 'Join Hands to Create a Better Future for China-ASEAN Relations'. Online. Available at: http://english.people.com.cn/200610/30/print20061030_316510.html (accessed 31 October 2006).

Wu, B. (2003) 'Create a Hundred Years of Peace in Asia, Jointly Build Sustained Development of Asia', 1 September 2003, in Foreign Broadcast Information Service, CPP2003–0901000066, Online. Available at (subscription only): http://wnc.fedworld.gov/.

Yan, M. (2003) 'Free Trade Zone Proposed' *China Daily*, 24 September 2003. Online. Available at: http://www.chinadaily.com.cn/chinagate/doc/2003-09/24/content_267127.htm (accessed 22 March 2007).

Yang, Y. (2003) 'China's Integration into the World Economy: Implications for Developing Countries' *IMF Working Paper* WP/03/245.

Zha, D. (2002) 'The Politics of China–ASEAN Economic Relations: Assessing the Move Toward A Free Trade Area' *Asian Perspective* 26(4): 53–82.

4 Japan and the evolution of Asian regionalism

Responsible for three normative transformations

Takashi Terada

Introduction

Regional institutions have established themselves as some of the key phenomena of contemporary world politics, as illustrated by the emergence of the European Union (EU) as a powerful actor able to emulate American hegemony in international economic affairs such as trade liberalization talks in the World Trade Organization (WTO). One of the conspicuous natures of those regional institutions, defined here as a forum where three or more participants from a certain geographical space gather for the purpose of forming common policies approaches and priorities, is the tendency for regional consciousness among members to be expressed by perceiving boundaries that differentiate insiders (members) from outsiders (non-members). A regional concept that identifies its geographical boundaries is necessary for any regional grouping including regional institutions. Without clear and agreed-upon boundaries, there can be no demarcation of the region based on which regional institutions are created. Here a 'regional concept' is defined as a geographical framework constructed and shared by human beings responsible for political decision, specifying the potential members of a certain regional institution.

There are many regional institutions based on their own regional concepts, such as the EU based on the European regional concept and the North America Free Trade Agreement (NAFTA) based on that of North America. Unlike Europe where almost all relevant regional institutions have evolved around the single regional concept, despite the concept being expanded by absorbing new member countries over the decades, the establishment of regional economic institutions in Asia has developed on the basis of different regional concepts. The 1960s saw the establishment of the Asian Development Bank (ADB), the Ministerial Conference on Southeast Asian Development (MCSEAD) (disbanded in mid-1970), Pacific Trade and Development (PAFTAD) conferences and the Pacific Basin Economic Council (PBEC), while the Pacific Economic Cooperation Council (PECC) and Asia-Pacific Economic Cooperation (APEC) forum were formed in 1980 and 1989, respectively. Subsequently, the Asian financial crisis urged East Asian countries to gather together to discuss regional economic and political issues, leading to the 1997 establishment of ASEAN+3 (Association of Southeast Asian Nations Plus Three), now regarded as an actual regional institution in East Asia through being associated with the East Asia Summit (EAS), established in 2005 in Kuala Lumpur. These institutions commonly provide occasions where participants, whether government officials, business leaders or academics, can strengthen their commitment to policy cooperation on economic issues in Asia by exchanging policy information, ideas and opinions, and they can be linked in the common purposes such as further regional prosperity. These distinctive regional concepts have emerged in Asia as a basis for establishing different regional economic institutions over the decades and this chapter aims to shed a light on the implications of this feature of Asian regionalism from a longer-term research standpoint. Camirelli (2004: 25) stresses the appropriateness of using this long-term perspective for the analysis of regionalism:

> the way regions organize themselves, set their boundaries and develop their identities is necessarily subject to periodic change. The analysis of regionalism must therefore adopt an evolutionary perspective which takes account of the changing structural conditions ... to which institutions must adapt as well as of the changing perceptions and self-understanding of relevant actors.

The evolutionary approach allows us to identify three normative transformations in regional institutions in Asia, which present themselves as its unique characteristics, compared with other regions: (1) the gradual involvement of governments and the employment of a legally binding force of decisions; (2) the shift of the initial purpose of development cooperation to trade liberalization; and (3) continuous efforts to accommodate the rising significance of Asian economies, culminating in the formation of Asian-only regional institutions such as ASEAN+3 and EAS.

There is no other country that has been as committed as Japan to conceiving ideas for, and taking a leadership role in, the establishment of various kinds of regional institutions in Asia (see Table 4.1). Academics, business people, politicians and officials in Japan were central to establishing these regional economic institutions by forging partnerships from time to time with their counterparts from other regional countries, such as Australia. Their consciousness of these regional concepts and commitment to creating a new regional institution was reflected at each formative stage. This chapter aims to demonstrate that Japan has taken a leading role in a variety of regional institutions in Asia with distinctive regional concepts, reflecting changes in Japan's interests in regional institutions in Asia. In other words, the aforementioned three normative transformations have derived mainly from Japan's leadership role and interest in regionalism and this chapter intends to clarify the relevance of these attributes of Japanese regional diplomacy for the evolution of various regional economic institutions in Asia.

Regions and regional concepts

A regional institution as an organizational body usually sets up clear criteria for membership and one of the major criteria is whether potential participants, be

Table 4.1 Regional concepts and institutions

Regional concepts	Institutions	Approaches	Main purposes
Asia or Southeast Asia (1957–)	ADB and MCSED	Inter-government	Development cooperation including the provision of funds
Pacific I (1967–)	PAFTAD and PBEC	Non-government	Interaction and socialization of policy ideas on regional cooperation
Pacific II (1977–)	PECC	Quasi-government (non-binding)	Policy discussions and advice on trade, investment and development cooperation
Asia-Pacific (1987–)	APEC	Inter-government (non-binding)	Implementations of • trade liberalisation (non-discriminatory: open regionalism) • trade facilitation • economic and technical cooperation
East Asia (1997–)	ASEAN+3	Inter-government (non-binding?)	Implementations of • financial cooperation • trade liberalization (discriminatory: FTA) • development cooperation
Bilateralism in East Asia (1998–)	Bilateral FTAs	Inter-government (binding)	Implementations of trade liberalization (discriminatory)
Greater East Asia (2005–)	East Asia Summit (ASEAN+6)	Inter-government (non-binding?)	Trade liberalization (discriminatory: FTA)

they nation-states or individuals representing an organization such as a corporation, belong to a certain region. In other words, a regional institution needs to define its boundary in order to distinguish between members and non-members, an approach which allows only members to enjoy benefits of cooperation within the regional institution. Therefore, whether they are perceived to belong to the region or not is a significant political issue. In the past the term 'region' used to merely indicate a geographical locale without any political or policy relevance in the study of regionalism, but recent works have attached political dimensions to the definition. For instance, Katzenstein (2003: 105) states that regions are '… social and cognitive constructs that are rooted in political practice,' while Pempel (2005: 25) further argues: 'regions are fluid and complex mixtures of physical, psychological, and behavioral traits continually being re-created and redefined. They vary with the policy issues that confront a region.'

However, the term 'region' is not suitable as a dominant membership criterion, due to its ambiguity in examining political dynamics concerning regional institution-building, including the political process of distinguishing insiders from outsiders.

This is because the demarcations depicted by a region tend to be perceived differently by the various actors involved and a firm consensus cannot be formed as to who can be in or out of a certain region and why. For instance, Australia sometimes declares itself a nation of East Asia, such as when former Foreign Minister Gareth Evans (1995) tried to insist that Australia was a nation of the 'East Asian Hemisphere' in his strong push for an 'engagement with Asia' policy. Yet the claim that Australia was a part of it found little support in the region, mainly due to a general lack of shared understanding about the demarcation of the East Asian region. Australia was widely perceived to be a nation not belonging to the East Asian region, geographically and, more symbolically, culturally, as former Australian diplomat Dalrymple (2003: 150) declared. Japanese Prime Minister Koizumi (2002), however, advocated in January 2002 that Australia should be a core member of an East Asian community. Koizumi's regional concept of East Asia was, in turn, constructed as a result of his political calculations to check, together with Australia, China's growing influence in East Asia, as argued later. Japan's claim helped to accelerate other regional countries' acceptance of Australia as an East Asian nation. Koizumi's claim culminated in Australia's eventual participation in the inaugural 2005 East Asia Summit, an actual regional institution in East Asia. Here the regional concepts are set to be defined and constructed strictly in association with the actual regional institution, with clear political purposes, so the demarcation decided by the regional concepts can be much more clearly shared by the participating actors.

Normative transformation (1): Gradual involvement of the government

The first feature of the evolution of Asian regional institutions is that regional economic institutions have evolved progressively from non-governmental to intergovernmental via quasi-governmental institutions, an approach which stands in sharp contrast to Europe, North America, Latin America, Africa and Southeast Asia, where governments were involved directly in the initial stage of building regional economic institutions. Asia chose a 'cautious' approach through the gradual involvement of governments to promoting regional economic cooperation and this process is reflected in the leadership style Japan took, directional leadership by incorporating followers' interests. Features of directional leadership converge on leaders' efforts to adjust the different interests of potential participants and in persuading them to join new regional institutions by setting up common goals, which can be legitimated by followers who perceive the benefits of complying with those goals (Terada 2001). Given their recent emergence from the status of colonies occupied by powerful imperial countries, ASEAN countries tended to be cautious about involvement in intergovernmental regional institutions that might intrude on their sovereignty and include some of the former imperial powers, especially Japan, which had resorted to war to create a regional sphere of influence for itself. Japan's militarism had occurred only three or four decades before and Japan's image as an aggressor still remained. The non-aligned policy of Malaysia and Indonesia also contributed to ASEAN's negative attitude to intergovernmental regional economic cooperation. Japan was aware of these factors, which contributed to Japan's directional leadership in institution-building.

While the ideas of Japanese policy intellectuals such as Kiyoshi Kojima, Saburo Okita and Shigeo Nagano, who played a key role in the era of Pacific I of non-government approach to regional cooperation such as PAFTAD and PBEC, were intended to include the promotion of a regional trade expansion approach, the Asian developing countries were not as willing to be committed to regional trade cooperation as the people involved in the formation of PBEC and PAFTAD. Gordon (1966: 141–61), surveying the opinions of Asian leaders, notes that they were not attracted to trade-oriented regional cooperation but had began to focus on other means of strengthening economic interaction in Southeast Asia through harmonization of their separate development plans. The interests of Asian developing countries did not necessarily converge with those of the founders of PAFTAD and PBEC, whose top priorities included the promotion of regional trade. Mainly because of this reason, the participants of the first PAFTAD and PBEC were only from Pacific developed countries, namely, the United States, Canada, Australia, New Zealand and Japan. This meant that it was premature for those developing countries in Asia to participate in a regional institution in which trade liberalization would have been expected to be discussed. Japanese leaders came to be aware of this trend and had to wait for another decade to create another regional economic institution to promote regional trade cooperation.

The era of Pacific II, which saw the establishment of PECC, was not represented by an intergovernmental regional economic institution. PECC emerged as a quasi-government regional institution where government officials have participated in a private capacity. Although increasing interdependence was a major driving force behind the support of leaders in Japan as well as Australia for the Pacific Community idea, which was premised with the intergovernmental cooperation approach, ASEAN leaders were not yet ready to support it. This reflected on difficulties with ASEAN countries' understanding of the necessity for the Pacific Concept and the reluctance of some of their governments to make a commitment to it. Then Malaysian Deputy Prime Minister, Mahathir, for example, (1980) said:

> interdependence is still very much an economic concept that has no reality for a lot of poor nations. True interdependence must mean not just being mutually dependent on each other but some degree of equality of strength to support each other.

In Mahathir's view, a main function in a regional institution like PECC was to overcome 'the paucity of knowledge among the Pacific region countries of each other' and to share their similar views on regional economics and politics. Clearly, the value of greater interdependence, a fundamental driving force behind the claim by Japanese leaders such as Prime Minister Masayoshi Ohira and Foreign Minister Okita about the necessity for a new economic regional institution, was not shared by some ASEAN leaders. In essence, the summit meeting between Ohira and his Australian counterpart, Malcolm Fraser, in January 1980 saw their agreement that ASEAN countries which were preoccupied with their own political and economic matters could not afford to allocate much energy and time to a wider Pacific cooperation issue and that serious institutionalization should not occur until ASEAN was well established. Given national differences of size, history, culture and economic development, Ohira and Fraser thought it necessary to take the time to increase mutual understanding to overcome problems. Accordingly, they agreed that a non-government seminar was the proper initial step for exploring the Concept, which led to the organization of the Canberra Seminar (Fraser 1994: 321). This had been recognized in the era of 'Pacific I' and it was reconfirmed at the Pacific Community Seminar, the first PECC meeting, held in Canberra in 1980 (Crawford and Seow 1981: 28): 'there was still a major need for Pacific countries to "get to know each other" better before steps were taken towards creation of new, formal inter-governmental institutions for regional cooperation'. This acknowledgment of the need to create a consensus for the establishment of an intergovernmental institution contributed to making PECC's status quasi-governmental. Yet, the ten years of policy-oriented discussions within the PECC framework during the 1980s since its inception were invaluable in terms of socialization of the idea of regional economic cooperation which was instrumental in building the sense of shared interests and mutual trust, necessary for establishing an intergovernmental regional body such as APEC.

APEC, established in 1989, emerged as the first intergovernmental regional economic institution in Asia to gather foreign and trade ministers from regional countries. The actual creation and the circumstances of the announcement of the initiative were at the instigation of Australian Prime Minister Bob Hawke and his advisers and officials in the Australian government. Yet Japan's Ministry of International Trade and Industry (MITI) had floated a proposal for economic ministers' regional meetings in mid-1988 and Australia then expressed strong interest in MITI's idea, which led to coordination between Japan and Australia (Funabashi 1995; Terada 1999). Inclusion of Asia into the Pacific which had been a predominant regional concept for economic regional institutions in the 1960s–1980s was due in part to the continuing growth of Asian countries. This, in turn, led to confidence about their economies and greater interdependence in the 'Asia Pacific' region and was a major factor that promoted a common regional interest, including Japan's, in forming a consensus on the desirability of an intergovernmental regional institution. This provided the foundation for establishing APEC. The 'Asia-Pacific' regional concept was an indication that Asian countries were recognized as a core group in regional cooperation for the first time, thanks to their substantial growth, in which Japan had played a substantial role through its direct investment. This awareness was especially strongly held by Japan.

The appreciation of the yen was so steep (from 260 yen per US dollar in 1985 to 140 yen by late 1989) that Japanese exporters had difficulty exporting labour-intensive products made in Japan. As a result, exporters procured more of their parts and materials from overseas suppliers, and began to establish production facilities outside Japan. This contributed to the rise of Japanese direct investment in ASEAN and the NIEs, giving a strong boost to local industries that supplied materials and parts. This resulted in a flow of products from such facilities into Japanese markets, and Asian nations established closer economic relations with Japan through trade and direct investment, contributing to Japan increasing its imports from NIEs and ASEAN from less than 14.2 per cent of total imports in 1985 to almost 20 per cent three years later (Watanabe 1991). Strengthening those economic ties with East Asian countries and sustaining their growth was an important rationale for Japan to promote regional cooperation and propose a ministerial-level regional meeting. MITI then launched a report in 1988 (MITI 1988) which was distributed to regional countries, as a way to explore the possibility of a ministerial meeting on Asia-Pacific regional economic cooperation.

However, even after an intergovernmental APEC was established, regionalism in Asia did not rush into employing legally binding force in its policy decision; APEC's decision does not stipulate any legal compulsion or binding force, another element distinctive from regional institutions in Western countries. Among the members, for example, it was only the United States that sought to insist, unsuccessfully, on the necessity of the binding force being incorporated into the APEC Investment Code, discussed at the 1994 APEC Indonesia Meeting. Voluntary commitment to agreements reached in APEC based on consensus among members is an important criterion which Japan embedded at APEC's inception, as it took into account the preferences of developing countries in the region. The APEC norms do not necessarily conform to the approach usually associated with the United States and tend to follow the preferences of Japan, taking into account opinions of other APEC members, especially those ASEAN countries that had hoped APEC would remain a loose institution.

Some studies (Crone 1993; Higgott 1993; Aggarwal 1994; Kahler 1995) in applying international regime theory to APEC suggest that APEC is at best a weak regime, due to its non-binding character. For instance, although the APEC Bogor Declaration commits developing APEC economies to achieving free trade and investment in the Asia-Pacific region by no later than 2020, it does not stipulate any legal compulsion or binding force to achieve this objective. In the same vein, non- and quasi-governmental institutions such as PBEC, PAFTAD and PECC have proposed a number of policy recommendations, but it has been left to participating states to decide whether or not to follow these recommendations. The criticisms against APEC due to the non-existence of binding force were, however, controversial. It is true that APEC is not necessarily the same institution as that within Kahler's image of institutions, which are 'top down, contractual, and inter-governmental in form', a form which is likely to stem from Western institutions where the objectives are generally economic integration involving legally binding force. Given the differences in values, rules, economic and political systems, social understandings and national aspirations in the Asia-Pacific region, cooperative processes and institutions encompass a broader range of cooperative activities than those in Europe and North America which have a legal institutional base. For instance, Harris (1994: 260) criticizes the application of a concept that is more applicable to Western Europe than to the Asia Pacific region:

> the existing international relations and economic literature concerned with cooperation has been predominantly focused on global and western European economic institutions. This literature suggests that there is a need not just for common rules and understandings, but also for ways to limit free-riding and defection. But the relevance of this literature for cooperation in the Asia Pacific region is questionable.

Higgott (2005: 23) also supports this view by concluding that 'the less institutionalised approach that emerged in Asia in the early 1990s represented a deliberate choice to avoid the perceived "Cartesian" legal formalism of the EU'.

In sum, it was in the late-1990s when Asian regionalism started introducing legal binding force for their economic cooperation approach through signing a constellation of bilateral FTAs, an initial step for attaining regional integration in Asia. These arrangements, with their legally binding provisions for the reciprocal exchange of preferences that discriminate against non-partner countries, constitute a distinct departure from the non-discriminatory, less institutionalized and non-binding approaches that Asian countries once firmly supported in regional economic institutions such as APEC. The proliferation of these arrangements in East Asia, representing Asia's employment of a 'standard' approach to regional integration mainly developed in Europe, is a consequence of governmental response to demands of corporations involved in the expanding FTA network in Asia, as discussed later.

Normative transformation (2): Gradual shift of purpose from economic cooperation to trade liberalization

The initial regional economic institutions in Asia focused purely on the promotion of development cooperation to help the economic growth of developing countries in the region. This was symbolized by the phrasing of the solution of the North–South problem to which Japanese policy leaders often referred in the 1970s and 80s, but the principal focus was shifted gradually to trade liberalization in the subsequent regional institutions. This is the second normative transformation in the evolution of Asian regionalism. It is true that some Japanese proposals on regionalism in the 1960s and 70s, like Kiyoshi Kojima's Pacific Free Trade Area (PAFTA), entailed an agenda of regional trade liberalization, with a premise of inter-governmental approach, but Japan ended up with disregarding those ideas mainly because of the opposition it faced from the Asian developing countries, as mentioned earlier.

A self-awareness of Japan's position as a leader in 'Asia', which was synonymous with 'Southeast Asia' as there were no diplomatic relations with Northeast Asian countries such as China and South Korea around that time, urged Japanese political leaders to help growth in developing countries in Southeast Asia; this was a major rationale behind the ideas of regional institutions during this period. In April 1966, Japan hosted the Ministerial Conference on Southeast Asian Development in Tokyo, the first international conference that the Japanese government convened in the post-war period, and at the time it had a strong commitment to the establishment of the ADB. Those regional institutions provided the starting point for Japan's initiatives in the region.[1]

Japan's initial idea on economic cooperation in Asia/Southeast Asia, developed in the 1960s, appeared even after 'Asia Pacific' economic cooperation began to flourish through the activities of APEC. This implies that Japan's interest was not strongly linked to trade liberalization, and it instead emphasized more economic and technical cooperation. For instance, Australia, together with the United States, was to become eager to set a trade liberalization agenda. Japan's MITI's more serious consideration of ASEAN's view distinguished its approaches to APEC from those of Australia's. MITI emphasized economic and technical cooperation as well as trade liberalization. Masakazu Toyoda, a senior official of MITI in charge of setting up APEC in Japan, (cited in Funabashi 1995: 66) said:

> Australians were very eager to set specific agenda items, which clearly aimed at trade liberalization . . . we also had that in our mind, but here we believed that we had to handle it very carefully. You would scare away ASEAN countries if you talked about liberalization from the start . . . Australia did not have any viable policy instrument for [economic and technical] cooperation.

This implies that Japan was responsible for not highlighting trade liberalization in the Canberra Meeting and instead underscored the significance of development cooperation (Funabashi 1995: 192). MITI was also concerned about Australia's proposal for an Asian OECD, because this would have involved policy coordination, but it was too early for APEC to undertake this role, given ASEAN's certain opposition (*Nihon Keizai Shimbun*, 6 March 1989). MITI's more careful consideration of ASEAN's view, consistent with Japan's traditional approach to regional economic cooperation, upheld Australia's leadership role, leading to the successful establishment of APEC. In fact, APEC has placed emphasis on development and technical cooperation for developing countries, along with trade liberalization and Japan's high regard for development cooperation in APEC, epitomized by its launching of the concept of Partnership for Progress (PFP) in 1994 to promote human resource development, represents Japan's general and consistent approach in regional economic cooperation. Japan's consistent approach to development and technical cooperation in Asian regionalism has been well embedded in the APEC structure.

It was in the mid-1990s when the interest in trade liberalisation emerged as a serious and important agenda in APEC; this, however, failed to make any tangible progress due in the main to Japan's rejection of promoting agricultural liberalization in the APEC's Early Voluntary Sectoral Liberalization (EVSL) scheme. The inclusion of the trade liberalization programme in regional economic cooperation through APEC was a critical element in progress from the previous non- and quasi-governmental institutions, representing a major normative trans- formation in the development of regionalism in Asia. However Japan still saw open regionalism, promotion of trade liberalization on a *most favoured nation* or non-discriminatory basis, as the best way forward in its approach to regional trade liberalization, arguing that division of the world into inward-looking European, North American and East Asian blocs would be counter to Japan's interests.

Yet, Ravenhill (2001: 197) identifies APEC's open regionalism, with its empha- sis on non-discriminatory trade liberalization, concerted unilateral liberalization and peer pressure system as key weaknesses: 'the decision to adopt a voluntary, unilateral and flexible approach to integration has provided governments with an excellent excuse for inaction', suggesting that an enforcement mechanism is nec- essary for effective regional integration. Indeed, it might appear that Ravenhill's conclusions about the ineffectiveness of APEC's 'loose' form of regionalism have been borne out by the proliferation in recent times of proposals for, and the negotiation by some APEC members of, bilateral and regional preferential trade arrangements such as FTAs. These arrangements, as touched upon earlier, are a distinct departure from APEC's approach to non-discriminatory, globally oriented regional cooperation.

Changing external environments such as the frustrated attempt in trade liber- alization in APEC as well as the stagnated negotiation in the WTO, eventually encouraged Japan, like other regional countries, to utilize various forms of bilat- eral arrangements to realize the aim of trade liberalization with those countries in East Asia, as partly materialized in the 2002 Japan–Singapore Economic Partnership Agreement (JSEPA) (Terada 2006). Japan was labelled 'the staunchest multilater- alist' (*New York Times* 9 November 2001), due to its exclusive focus on global trade bodies such as the GATT and the WTO for the purposes of facilitating global trade liberalization, and Japan had long criticized FTAs as discriminatory against non-members and detrimental to the maintenance of the GATT/WTO-based inter- national trading system. Yet the establishment of JSEPA, the subsequent bilateral FTA negotiations with Mexico, South Korea, Malaysia, Thailand the Philippines, Brunei and Indonesia and proposals for the Japan–ASEAN FTA and an East Asian FTA represent Japan's determination to deviate from its solitary commitment to the multilateral trading system to a predilection of bilateral and regional FTAs in pursuit of trade liberalization in a discriminatory fashion. Those arrangements would be established on the basis of GATT Article 24 which permits signatories to discriminate against non-members, a feature which stands in sharp contrast with that of APEC in which trade liberalization was supposed to be executed on a non- discriminatory basis to avoid trade discrimination against third states by granting equal treatment to all. This has been called open regionalism, which Japan initially launched in 1955 (Terada 1998). This illustrates another normative transformation in regionalism in Asia, and Japan has played a significant role in the development of this new approach.

Japan saw JSEPA as a means for stimulating the liberalization movement in East Asia, which had fallen inert after the 1997 Asian financial crisis. In fact, China's interest in signing a FTA with ASEAN was spurred by Japan's interest in an FTA with South Korea and the announcement of JSEPA negotiations (Terada 2003). The movement by Japan led China to feel isolated in the FTA movement in East Asia. China ultimately joined it by proposing an FTA with ASEAN in October 2000, which was officially agreed on in November 2001. The establishment of a Japan–ASEAN Comprehensive Economic Partnership agreement was a response to the China–ASEAN FTA proposal. JSEPA also urged Malaysia and Indonesia, believed to be the least enthusiastic nations about bilateral FTAs in the region, to develop their FTA interests by studying all the pros and cons of JSEPA. China's and Japan's FTA approaches to ASEAN also contributed to South Korea developing an interest in pursuing the same path, as its Trade Minister, Hwang Doo-yun, showed in Brunei in September 2002, leading to the final agreement on the establishment of an FTA with ASEAN in 2004. These 'domino effects' of bilateralism in East Asia occurred mainly because of the exclusive nature of and major benefits accrued by FTAs, such as tariff eliminations at the expense of the third party countries.

One of the significant consequences flowing from Japan's pursuit of FTAs for its trade policy was that FTA policy contributed to creating an initial basis for the establishment of Japan's multilayered trade policy. This produced normative transformations in the relative importance of two issues of Japanese international trade policy. The first concerns multilateralism versus bilateralism: the absolute significance of non-discriminatory multilateralism was declining while its antithetic approach of bilateralism was gaining more importance. The second concerns the place of non-discriminatory APEC versus discriminatory regional arrangements in East Asia. APEC, in which Japan committed itself to open regionalism over years in line with the non-discriminatory GATT Article 1, had become ineffectual in terms of trade liberalization, as Japan committed itself to promoting discriminatory regionalism in lines with GATT Article 24 such as the Japan–ASEAN or East Asian FTA. In this context, Japan's decision not to dispatch both its foreign affairs and trade ministers to the 2002 Mexico APEC meetings is one indication of the doubts that have surrounded APEC's course in recent times. Meanwhile, Prime Minister Koizumi suggested making 'the best use of' ASEAN+3 'to secure prosperity and stability' in East Asia. ASEAN+3 became the institutional basis for the development of Japan–ASEAN and East Asian FTAs. It should be stressed, however, that Japan still places the highest priority on the maintenance and development of the WTO-based multilateralism, and a changing element in this context is that its longstanding strict observance of GATT Article 1, a basis for its conventional claim on the non-discriminatory trade policy priority, has been replaced by its determination to strictly abide by Article 24 instead. The strict observance of Article 24 in its involvement in FTAs has become a new normative basis for Japan's assertion of WTO-based multilateralism and its pursuit of bilateral FTAs with some East Asian countries.

The fact that Japan has signed FTAs with ASEAN countries is another indication of normative change on the part of Japanese regional policy in terms of equality with member countries. FTAs, as well as TAC, are international agreements that need the ratification of a Diet, and legal enforceability is also provided. Conventional Japan–ASEAN relations were developed, centred on forums that lacked such legal basis, and one of the major features was that there existed one-sided elements based on unilateral giving by Japan, including Official Development Assistance (ODA), foreign direct investments, preferential tariffs and technology transfers. Japan's FTAs with ASEAN countries adds afresh to Japan–ASEAN relations the element of the principle of reciprocity based on law, and they are a profitable strategy in building up a 'give-and-take' relationship where Japan can receive removed tariffs or equal national treatment in investments.

In short, the inclusion of bilateralism in the analysis of Asian regionalism can be justified from this longer historical perspective by arguing that the origins of Japan's interest in trade liberalization or market integration in Asia, an interest which Japan has finally decided to achieve more seriously through bilateral FTAs in the late 1990s, can be traced back to the mid-1960s when some Japanese leaders began to consider accomplishing it through a regionalism approach. The formation of bilateral FTAs is also relevant to the study of regionalism in the way in which any country has specific reasons to choose its FTA partners, as is the case with regionalism; the distinction of members and non-members (insiders and outsiders) is an important element in the establishment of both bilateral and regional arrangements.

Normative transformation (3): Open membership or not

The Japanese concept of open regionalism developed over the last five decades means 'open membership', and who should participate in the first meeting emerged as a major issue whenever Japan took an initiative in the establishment of regional institutions in Asia. In other words, which countries are supposed to belong to the regional concept, based on which a new regional institution is established, is an important political question to Japanese policy leaders. As a nation that long pursued the regional concept of 'Asia-Pacific' or 'Pacific' for promoting regional economic cooperation, Japan was not interested in joining regional institutions excluding 'Pacific' nations such as the United States and Australia. The involvement of the United States in any regional economic institution was especially significant to Japan, but the US global rather than regional interest in its trade policy in the 1960s and 70s was a consistent constraint on Japan's initiatives in Asian regionalism. For instance, Japanese business leaders worked hard to persuade its counterparts from the United States to participate in the first PBEC meeting, although American business leaders had difficulty finding a strong interest in an organization which appeared to have little impact on their overall trade (PBEC 1997: 6). According to Krause (1981: 10), the United States had initially responded sceptically to Japan's Concept on Pacific cooperation launched by Ohira because 'there was a belief that a Pacific organization is unnecessary and that if one were created, it might do more harm than good', as it was widely believed in the United States that a commitment to the Pacific Concept was inconsistent with the United States' globally oriented economic interests (*Far Eastern Economic Review* 21 December 1979). Japan continued to insist on its inclusion, despite Australia's hesitation, even in the 1989 establishment of APEC (Terada 1999).

In the 1990s, the concept of 'East Asia' developed through combining Northeast Asia and Southeast Asia in regional unity, serving as the formation and development of the ASEAN+3 meeting. Until the appearance of the abortive East Asian Economic Caucus (EAEC) idea, put forward by Prime Minister Mahathir of Malaysia in 1990, there was no strong conceptual framework for regionalism in East Asia as a whole. Mahathir explains what initially motivated his EAEC proposal:

> Suppose Malaysia goes alone to Brussels to lodge a complaint against European protectionism. Our voice would simply be too small. Nobody would listen. But if the whole of East Asia tells Europe that it must open up its markets, Europeans will know that access to the huge Asian market obliges them not to be protectionist. That was the reasoning behind the EAEC proposal.
>
> (Ishihara and Mahathir 1995: 44)

Given this rationale, Mahathir strongly urged Japan to be the linchpin of EAEC, in the belief that Japan was 'the only Asian country with the ability to help fellow Asian countries' (*Australian Financial Review* 24 October 1994). Yet its attitude to EAEC was lukewarm, and this was a major factor that prevented EAEC's realization. A reason behind Japan's unsupportive stance was that Japan did not view 'East Asia' as a concept for regional cooperation, and instead adhered to a concept of the 'Asia-Pacific' as a basis for promoting cooperation within APEC. The East Asian concept was not yet firmly enough established to gain the consensus among the relevant countries and Japan, seen as a leader in EAEC by Mahathir, did not take strong action towards realizing EAEC. Given America's overwhelming position in Japan's security and economic policies as Japan's ally and its major trading partner over years, it was rather difficult for Japan to accept Malaysia's request to take the lead in creating it.

Yet factors such as the Asian financial crisis and the development of regionalism in other regions such as Europe and North America helped to promote the self–other distinction more strongly, necessary for the gradual acceptance of the East Asian concept, especially in Japan. So, Japan's participation in the 1997 ASEAN+3 meeting was a milestone for East Asian regionalism, given its initial hesitancy to be involved in EAEC. Japan's Vice-Finance Minister, Eisuke Sakakibara, proposed the Asian Monetary Fund in September 1997 as an Asian financing facility with an initial capitalization of $100 billion; America and the IMF were staunchly opposed to it. The United States thought of it as eroding the significance of the US-dominated IMF. Sensitive to the view of the United States and the IMF, Japan, despite initial enthusiasm, began to heed the warnings from the United States and IMF officials. Other East Asian leaders also began to 'make speeches lauding the importance of the IMF. It quickly became clear that there was little appetite in Asia for a confrontation with the United States and the IMF amidst plummeting currencies and stock markets' (Altbach 1997: 10). One reason it was difficult to garner support from the region is that these countries wanted the United States to remain committed to the region in terms of economic links and security concerns. So, the establishment of ASEAN+3 forums and the East Asia Summit and Japan's strong commitment to this institution in East Asia, as was seen in its advocacy of an East Asian community by Prime Minister Koizumi, which encourages the self–other distinction among members like Japan and non-members such as the United States, represents the third normative transformation in regionalism in Asia.

However, until 1999, ASEAN was not sure if Japan would fully support ASEAN+3 because Japan had merely concentrated on Japan–ASEAN bilateral relations, Yet, since 1999, Japan's Ministry of Foreign Affairs had been using the term East Asia and described the ASEAN+3 meetings as 'an East Asian summit in a practical sense' (Terada 2003). At the 1999 ASEAN+3 Summit Meeting, Prime Minister Obuchi (1999) announced the Plan for Enhancing Human Resources Development and Human Resources Exchanges in East Asia, which Philippines President Estrada renamed the 'Obuchi Plan' to demonstrate the ASEAN countries' appreciation. Prime Minister Mori (2000) made a statement in Singapore on the three principles for enhancing open regional cooperation in East Asia, demonstrating Japan's political interests in ASEAN+3, and was followed by his successor, Koizumi (2002), who suggested making 'the best use of' ASEAN+3 'to secure prosperity and stability' in East Asia in his Singapore speech in January 2002. In contrast to Hashimoto (1997), who urged the need for closer ASEAN–Japan relations in the interests of stability and prosperity in the 'Asia-Pacific' region, the regional policy statements and initiatives launched by his successors symbolize Japan's growing interest in East Asia.

The fact that Japan has actively launched these policy initiatives within the ASEAN+3 framework is in sharp contrast with its lukewarm attitude to EAEC. One of the most significant reasons behind this change was Japan's realization that a consensus had developed that the time was ripe to create East Asian regionalism solely to tackle regional problems. The fact that the United States did not so palpably oppose the attempt, unlike the case of EAEC, was an important factor in Japan's changing approach to East Asian regionalism, as Japan felt less constrained about involving itself in the ASEAN+3 meetings. America's growing understanding of the need for Japan to provide the initiative for stability and prosperity in East Asia was a significant factor. In this sense, the existence of APEC, of which the United States is a member, has helped Japan to develop its further interest in ASEAN+3, since East Asian nations are able to maintain trade and investment dialogues with the United States through APEC.

A fully fledged East Asian organization in which member countries participate on an equal footing is yet to emerge. As long as the name ASEAN+3 remains, it will signify the activities of an ASEAN-sponsored regionalism, indicating that all member states do not fully acquire an East Asian identity. The ASEAN+3 meetings aim to launch two cooperation plans: the establishment of an East Asian FTA and an East Asian summit, as recommended by the East Asian Vision Group. This would suggest a more ambitious political connection of ASEAN and Northeast Asia, enabling East Asian leaders to identify common positions more easily and to articulate them more effectively in multilateral fora such as the WTO and the UN. In these arenas, the self–other distinction could be developed between East Asian and non-East Asian groups and a shared East Asian identity among members could eventually be more strongly entrenched by mobilizing the region more effectively and providing a quick response to further economic problems in the region through coordinating policies and setting cooperative directions collectively for the welfare of the region.

One symbolic question regarding the East Asian regional concept is whether Australia, as well as New Zealand, should be included in any activity associated with ASEAN+3. The membership of ASEAN+3 has been fixed, but Koizumi (2002) in his Singapore speech advocated that 'Australia should … become a core member of the [East Asian] community.' Australia, whose relations with ASEAN countries, especially Malaysia and Indonesia, were strained, had not been expected by many in the region to be a natural member of the community. Japan's interest in the inclusion of Australia in an East Asian regional arrangement has stemmed from its intention to involve more strategic elements in the Australia–Japan partnership in the face of the emergence of China. If China's interests in improving and strengthening the relations with ASEAN and its further commitment to the formation of an East Asian community were seen as a way of creating its own sphere of influence in East Asia, that would be counterproductive to America's regional interests. The role of the bilateral partnership between Japan and Australia, both key regional US allies, would function as an impediment to the realization of China's ambition to dominate the region. This sort of strategic consideration made it possible for Australia to participate in the first East Asia Summit in Malaysia in 2005 (Terada 2006), creating a different form of the East Asian regional concept through taking American interest into consideration.

The rise of China has influenced Japanese thinking of the way an East Asian community would develop. Japanese leaders such as Noboru Hatakeyama (2005), who played a pivotal role in prompting the Japanese free trade agreement policy, attribute the difficulty in forming a regional community in East Asia to the fact that some regional countries like China do not share universal values such as freedom, democracy or human rights with Japan. Prime Minister Shinzo Abe (2006) also stressed the importance of those values in Japan's regional policy and urged the need to strengthen relations with India and Australia, which, he believed, shared those values with Japan. Such a value-driven approach to an East Asian community-building by Japan pushed China to promote a regional framework which would help China keep its influence. For instance, during the first East Asia Summit held in December 2005 in Kuala Lumpur, China insisted that the

ASEAN+3, rather than the East Asia Summit, should be used as a forum for discussing community-building in East Asia, with membership of the community limited to ASEAN+3 nations. China's approach contrasted sharply with that of Japan, which advocated 'open regionalism' including Australia, India and New Zealand to reduce China's influence. Japan's open regionalism prevailed for the inaugural East Asia Summit, partly due to India's strong claim on the use of the East Asia Summit rather than ASEAN+3 as a vehicle for community-building in East Asia. An inclusion–exclusion element of regional institution-building in East Asia, based on two competing regional concepts of ASEAN+3 and ASEAN+6, has been highlighted by how to deal with the United States in the region, despite it being excluded from East Asian economic cooperation, representing its predominant presence in Japanese regional policy.

Conclusion

Nations usually possess a specific identity in international society and they (re)define foreign policy directions on the basis of this identity. Their citizens tend to accept their nations' international images, as they often represent the nation's role on the international stage. Foundations upon which Japan's identity has been shaped in the international society are geographical (Asia-Pacific or East Asian nation), economic status (developed nation), or strategic position (ally of the United States or member of the West). Japan's identity as the 'only' industrialized nation in Asia was a common phrase to most Japanese citizens, as their political leaders often referred to Japan as such in the 1960s, '70s and '80s. This identity also represented Japan's regional leadership role, as seen in its commitment to the promotion of the development of economic growth in developing Asian countries in the region, symbolized by the phrase, 'the solution of the North–South problem'.

   Yet, this identity has actually started weakening, since China has emerged as a potentially significant economic power in the region; for instance, if it were to develop its interest in a full membership at a G-8 summit. Japan has long considered its role to be a bridge between the Western developed countries and Asian developing countries. Japan's role as such would be substantially diminished and Japan's regional leadership identity would vanish with the rise of economic power in China. In other words, the rise of China has forced the Japanese people to realize that a leadership position in Asia, should not be taken for granted. In the past, Japan accepted the necessary burdens (mainly financial) of leadership as one of the few international obligations which it could fulfil, and took pride in being able to do so. But then the rise of China was juxtaposed with Japan's decade-long recession, which limited its capacity to flex its economic muscle, as it had done as the pre-eminent economic power in Asia, and many Japanese came to lose their confidence in Japan's continuing leadership position in Asia. This 'identity-crisis' was aggravated by the fact that China has also emerged as an aid giver, another identity which only Japan used to enjoy in Asia. China's way of distributing its aid is much more strategic than that of Japan in effectively realizing its national interests; for example, curtailing some nations' diplomatic ties with Taiwan or securing oil supplies. This has provided an opportunity for the Japanese to reflect on the wisdom of Japan's aid policy over the decades, and whether their taxes were used effectively for their nation. This sort of question forms the basis of the public demand for a decrease in the amount of Japan's overseas aid, narrowing the basis for Japan's leadership initiative.

Great diversities within Asia demanded a gradual approach to the eventual creation of an intergovernmental regional institution that aims to promote regional economic integration. Habit of cooperation in Asia over the last five decades can be conducive to strengthening shared beliefs in obtaining consensus and promoting cooperation, and to sustaining the solidarity necessary for increasing the understanding of cultural and social differences among members in regional institutions. The regional institutions can provide occasions where participants, including political leaders and government officials, can strengthen their commitment to cooperation by exchanging policy information regardless of cultural differences, a major feature in Asia. These functions may engender a growing sense of community and common identity among all policy individuals that are engaged in economic and political cooperation in a distinctive regional institution through the gradually expanding array of meetings, working groups and cooperative linkages within that institution.

Note

1 It should however be noted that the United States gave strong support to Japan's leadership in establishing the ADB and the Ministerial Conference at Southeast Asian Development. The United States was embroiled in the Vietnam War at that time and the US expectation of Japan's initiative was stated by Dean Rusk, then Secretary of State, in July 1967, when he said that to ensure security for free Asian countries, Japan would be expected to create a 'soft wall', a stability in the region through economic cooperation (*Mainichi Shimbun*, 8 December 1969).

References

Abe, Shinzo (2006) *Utukushii kuni-he* [Towards a Beautiful Country], Tokyo: Bungei Shunjyusha.

Aggarwal, Vinod (1994) 'Comparing Regional Cooperation Efforts in the Asia-Pacific and North America' in Andrew Mack and John Ravenhill (eds), *Pacific Cooperation: Building Economic and Security Regimes in the Asia-Pacific Region*, Sydney: Allen and Unwin.

Altbach, Eric (1997) 'The Asian Monetary Fund: A Case Study of Japanese Regional Leadership', *JEI Report* 47A, 19 December, 1–12

Camirelli, Joseph (2004) *Regionalism in the New Asia-Pacific Order: The Political Economy of the Asia-Pacific Region*, Volume II, Cheltenham: Edward Elger.

Crawford, John and G. Seow (1981) *Pacific Economic Cooperation: Suggestions for Action*, Kuala Lumpur: Heinemann.

Crone, Donald (1993) 'Does Hegemony Matter? The Reorganization of the Pacific Political Economy', *World Politics* 45 (4): 501–25

Dalrymple, Rawdon (2003) *Continental Drift: Australia's Search for a Regional Identity*, London: Ashgate.

Evans, Gareth (1995) 'Australia, ASEAN and the East Asian Hemisphere', speech to the ASEAN PMC 7+1 Session, Bandar Seri Bagawan, 2 August.

Fraser, Malcolm (1994) 'Taiheiyo Kyodotai Vijyon-no Doshi' [A Partner for a Pacific Community Vision] in S. Kumon *et al.* (eds), *Ohira Masayoshi: Seijiteki Isan* [Masayoshi Ohira: Political Legacy], Tokyo: Ohira Masayoshi Memorial Foundation.

Funabashi, Yoichi (1995) *Asia Pacific Fusion: Japan's Role in APEC*, Washington, DC: Institute for International Economics.

Gordon, Bernard (1966) *The Dimensions of Conflict in Southeast Asia*, (Upper Saddle River, NJ: Prentice-Hall)

Harris, Stuart (1994) 'Conclusion: The Theory and Practice of Regional Cooperation' in Andrew Mack and John Ravenhill (eds), *Pacific Cooperation: Building Economic and Security Regimes in the Asia Pacific Region*, Sydney: Allen & Unwin.

Hashimoto Ryutaro (1997) 'Reforms for the New Era of Japan and ASEAN: For a Broader and Deeper Partnership', speech delivered in Singapore, 14 January.

Hatakeyama, Noboru (2005) 'East Asian Community: Prospects and Problems Towards a Regional FTA', *Nihon Keizai Shimbun*, 25 November.

Higgott, Richard (1993) 'Competing Theoretical Approaches to International Cooperation: Implications for Asia-Pacific' in Richard Higgott, Richard Leaver and John Ravenhill (eds), *Pacific Economic Relations in the 1990s: Cooperation or Conflict?*, Sydney: Allen & Unwin, pp. 290–311.

Higgott, Richard, (2005) 'The Theory and Practice of Region: Changing Global Context', in Bertrand Fort and Douglas Webber (eds), *Regional Integration in East Asia and Europe: Convergence and Divergence*, New York: Routledge.

Ishihara Shintaro and Mahathir Mohamad (1995) *The Voice of Asia: Two Leaders Discuss the Coming Century*, Tokyo: Kodansha.

Kahler, Miles (1995) *International Institutions and the Political Economy of Integration*, Washington, DC: Brookings Institution.

Katzenstein, Peter (2003) 'Regionalism and Asia' in Shaun Breslin *et al.* (eds), *New Regionalisms in the Global Political Economy: Theories and Cases*, Routledge, New York.

Koizumi, Junichiro (2002) 'Japan and ASEAN in East Asia: A Sincere and Open Partnership', speech delivered in Singapore, 14 January.

Krause, Lawrence (1981) 'The Pacific Community Concept, Japan and the United States', *Round Table Report* No. 4, New York: East Asian Institute, Colombia University.

Mahathir, Mohamad (1980) 'Tak Kenal Maka Tak Cinta' in, *Asia Pacific in the 1980s: Toward Greater Symmetry in Economic Interdependence*, Jakarta: Centre for Strategic and International Studies) pp.12–22

Ministry of International Trade and Industry, Japan (1988) 'Aratanaru Ajia Taiheiyou Kyoryoku-wo Motomete' [Towards A New Asia Pacific Cooperation], Tokyo.

Mori, Yoshiro (2000) Press Statement, Singapore, 25 November.

Obuchi, Keizo (1999) Press Statement, Manila, 28 November.

Pacific Basin Economic Council (1997) *The History of the Pacific Basin Economic Council 1967–1997: Bridging the Pacific*, Wellington.

Pempel, T.J. (2005) 'Introduction: Emerging Webs of Regional Connectedness', in T.J. Pempel (ed.), *Remapping East Asia: The Construction of a Region*, Ithaca, NY Cornell University Press.

Ravenhill, John (2001) *APEC and the Construction of Pacific Rim Regionalism*, Cambridge: Cambridge University Press.

Terada, Takashi (1998) 'The Origins of Japan's APEC Policy: Foreign Minister Takeo Miki's Asia-Pacific Policy and Current Implications', *Pacific Review* 11(3): 337–363.

Terada, Takashi (1999) 'The Genesis of APEC: Australia–Japan Political Initiatives', *Pacific Economic Papers* No. 298, December.

Terada, Takashi, (2001) 'Directional Leadership in Institution-Building: Japan's Approaches to ASEAN in the Establishment of PECC and APEC', *Pacific Review* 14(2): 195–220.

Terada, Takashi, (2003) 'Constructing an "East Asian" Concept and Growing Regional Identity: From EAEC to ASEAN+3', *Pacific Review* 16(2): 251–/77.

Terada, Takashi, (2006) 'The Making of Asia's First Bilateral FTA: Origins and Regional Implications of the Japan–Singapore Economic Partnership Agreement (JSEPA)', *Pacific Economic Papers* No.354.

Watanabe, Toshio (1991) 'Nishi Taiheiyo Hatten-no Shinjidai' [A New Era of the Development in Western Pacific] in Watanabe Toshio (ed.), *Nishi Taiheiyo Shinjidai-to Nihon* [A New Era of Western Pacific and Japan], Tokyo: Japan Times.

Part II

Regionalism in trade, finance and production

5 Bilateral trade agreements in Asia

Wise or short-sighted policies?

Heribert Dieter

Introduction

In Asia, the governance of regional trade has been changing significantly. Whereas up to the turn of the century most countries in the region concentrated on participating in the multilateral trade regime, today there is a marked shift. Almost all countries in the Asia-Pacific have embarked on a new course for their trade policy. Bilateral trade agreements are mushrooming all over the world, but Asia, including the Asia-Pacific, is the region with the most prolific supporters of bilateralism (Lloyd 2002: 1282). Frustrated with the lacklustre development of APEC, and in view of the FTA networks of the European Union (EU) and the USA, Asian countries are following the bilateral trend (Hufbauer and Wong 2005: 3; Ziltener 2005: 279).

The implementation of discriminatory trade arrangements is arguably the most significant development in intergovernmental relations since the Asian crisis of 1997 (Ravenhill 2003: 300). The wave of bilateralism in trade has been fuelled by the weakness of existing regional organizations for economic integration, APEC and ASEAN in particular (Camroux 2001: 7).

In this chapter, I will analyse the utility of bilateral trade agreements. This requires understanding both the benefits as well as the costs of such agreements. Since both dimensions cannot be fully appreciated at an abstract theoretical level, I will examine the fine print of some trade agreements in Asia and the Asia-Pacific. When analysing trade relations, the inclusion of the Asia-Pacific is useful because many bilateral trade agreements involve an Asian as well as a Pacific country. Also, the continuing importance of the United States in economic affairs requires us to look at its bilateral agreements.

It has to be asked whether there is a large gap between the free trade rhetoric and the reality of such agreements. Of course, the rapid growth of the number of bilateral agreements requires a selection of cases that can be analysed within the limits of this chapter. I have selected three cases: First, the agreement between Australia and the United States will be considered. This is not only the first free trade agreement of Australia with another OECD-country apart from neighbouring New Zealand, but it is also the most important free trade agreement of the USA since the completion of the North American Free Trade Agreement (NAFTA) in the early 1990s. Although the United States have been negotiating a number of free trade agreements in recent years, the economies concerned are mostly relatively small, e.g. Jordan, Bahrain, Chile or Singapore.[1] By contrast, Australia is a relatively large, developed economy with 20 million inhabitants and a GDP of over US$600 billion (2004 figures). The importance of this agreement is comparable to the FTA between America and South Korea, on which agreement was reached in April 2007.[2]

In this chapter, I assume that the multilateral regime is superior to the bilateral regulation of trade. The World Trade Organization (WTO) provides central functions, not supplied by any other international organization, for the regulation of international trade of goods and services. It is an important cornerstone of what is known as 'global economic governance'. The WTO operates by consensus. Each country has a seat and can veto any proposal – at least in theory. In no other relevant organization do developing and emerging countries have such wide-reaching powers of obstruction. All 150 members of the WTO have a veto. This clearly makes the negotiation process more difficult, but at the same time it gives the organization's decisions a high level of legitimacy. The extremely important dispute resolution mechanism is a significant step forward in comparison to the regulations of the GATT (out of which the WTO was born in 1995); whereas in the GATT the introduction of a claim could be blocked by the affected party, this cannot be done in the WTO.

Of course, the WTO can be criticized for a range of negative developments. However, we have to differentiate between (unwarranted) consequences of free trade and the regulation of trade in the WTO. Even when considering all the shortcomings of the multilateral regime, it should not be overlooked that international trade of goods and services should preferably be regulated by a global regime that is the same for all regions of the world. Too many levels of regulation – national, bilateral, regional, global – make it more difficult for less efficient actors, in particular, to participate in possible welfare gains achieved through the international division of labour.[3]

In the following section, I will discuss advantages and disadvantages of bilateral trade agreements. Both the higher transaction costs – due to the need for certificates of origin – and the potential deterioration of dispute settlement have to be considered when these agreements are analysed. In the subsequent three sections the bilateral agreements of Australia, Singapore and Thailand will be discussed.

The debatable logic of bilateral trade agreements

In the Asia-Pacific, the financial crisis of 1997 and 1998 continues to be a watershed. Since that crisis, the strategies for shaping external economic relations have changed, both in trade and in finance. Before 1997, the emphasis was on multilateral organizations, i.e. on the International Monetary Fund and on the World Trade Organization. In economic relations, two trends are emerging – monetary regionalism in finance and bilateralism in trade, and the latter will be analysed in this chapter. In trade, the change is very obvious. Bilateral trade agreements are mushrooming all over Asia.

Of course, the current wave of bilateral and other preferential trade agreements is having severe repercussions for the WTO. In 2005, for the first time ever, more trade was carried out in preferential agreements than under the most-favoured-nation clause.[4] Article 1 of the General Agreement on Tariffs and Trade, the most-favoured-nation clause, has degenerated into the least-favoured-nation clause, as the American trade economist Jagdish Bhagwati has been proclaiming.

Today, there are more than 300 free trade agreements and a few customs unions either already implemented or being negotiated. Until a few years ago, Asian countries, with the exception of the ASEAN project, were not contributing to this trend. Countries like Japan and South Korea, but also Pacific economies such as Australia, were staunch supporters of the multilateral regime. This, however, has changed dramatically. Partly because there continues to be a momentum for bilateral agreements, partly because some countries in the region are using these agreements to fast-forward their economic and political position in the region, no country in Asia is willing to abstain from the current fashion.

An important reason for a sceptical evaluation of bilateral trade agreements is the risk of weaker dispute settlement. In many bilateral schemes there is an option – either bilateral dispute settlement or multilateral dispute settlement. It is obvious that the bilateral route offers many possibilities for the more powerful partners to promote their case. Hierarchy and power – never fully absent in international trade – have a more prominent role in bilateral trade agreements than in the multilateral regime. The existence of an alternative to the WTO dispute settlement mechanism provides the more powerful countries with an additional choice, but for weaker countries this is a drawback.[5] In the WTO countries can form coalitions in dispute settlement, which both reduces costs and increases the bargaining influence (Davis 2006: 7). The WTO dispute settlement mechanism continues to be superior to bilateral deals because of greater transparency and the ability to form coalitions of like-minded countries (Davis 2006: 39).

Another disadvantage of bilateral trade agreements is the administrative burden that rules of origin cause. In an entirely open world economy with no restrictions of the flow of goods, rules of origin would not matter because it would be irrelevant where goods originate. Today, however, the origin of a product matters, in particular in preferential agreements. All free trade areas including bilaterals require rules of origin to establish the 'nationality' of a product. The reason is that in FTAs participating countries continue to have diverging external tariffs. One country might have a high tariff on, say, cars in order to protect domestic producers, whilst the other might have a low or no tariff on that product. Since only goods produced within the free trade area qualify for duty-free trade, there have to be procedures that differentiate between goods produced within the FTA and goods from the rest of the world. The preferential system becomes complicated. And expensive: On average, the cost of issuing and administering certificates of origin is estimated to be 5 per cent of the value of a product (Dieter 2004: 281; Roberts and Wehrheim 2001: 317).[6]

In the past 40 years, the use of rules of origin has changed significantly. After decolonization, many developing countries used rules of origin as instruments to enhance their economic development. Rules of origin were used to increase the local content of manufactured products and to protect the infant industries in those economies against foreign protection. This function of rules of origin is of minor importance today. Rather, developed countries use strict rules of origin to protect their aging domestic industries.

When criticizing the negative consequences of rules of origin, there is a caveat. By paying the appropriate tariff, they can be easily overcome. Since peak tariffs continue to cause difficulties in some sectors, the protectionist effect of rules of origin should nevertheless not be underestimated. The combination of tariffs and stringent rules of origin can be an efficient instrument for the protection of a market. One example is the textile market in NAFTA, where rules of origin for certain products require the yarn to be spun in NAFTA (yarn-forward rule) or even the fibre to be produced in NAFTA (fibre-forward rule), which is used for many textiles containing cotton. The consequence is that Canadian or Mexican textile producers cannot source their cotton from, say African cotton producers, but instead have to buy cotton from US producers. Rules of origin are opaque protectionist instruments.

Methods for establishing origin

First, it is important to understand that there are two categories of certificates of origin, non-preferential and preferential ones. The former are used to differentiate between foreign and domestic products, for instance for statistical purposes, for anti-dumping or countervailing duties or for the application of labelling or marketing requirements (Jakob and Fiebinger 2003: 138). The second type is the one that can distort trade because it provides preferential access to a market.

To begin with, customs regulation does not permit multiple origin of a product. Current customs regulation requires that a single country of origin is established (Jakob and Fiebinger 2003: 138). There are four methods to establish the 'nationality' of a product in order to establish origin. There is natural origin and origin due to substantial transformation, this category being subdivided into three other forms: a change in the tariff heading, a minimum percentage of value added and specific production processes (Estvadeordal and Suominen 2003). Natural origin (wholly produced or obtained) is the least complicated approach. This applies to raw materials and non-processed agricultural products, i.e. to a relatively small part of international trade.

A change of tariff heading is already much more complicated. The Harmonized System (HS) is a set of regulations that has been agreed upon in the World Customs Organization (WCO). It consists of 1241 categories on the four-digit level and more than 5,000 categories on the six-digit level. If a product receives a different tariff heading after the production process, this can be used to qualify for origin. This method has considerable advantages. It is both transparent and easily established. Using the Harmonized System is simple, easy to implement and involves relatively little cost. The necessary documentation is undemanding. The trouble is that a change of tariff heading does not necessarily constitute a significant step in the production process. Minor changes to a product can lead to a change of tariff heading. Furthermore, if a final product consists of a large number of components, documenting origin becomes complicated, and therefore costly (Woolcock 1996: 200). Therefore, merely requiring a change of tariff heading to establish origin is the exception in FTAs.

The minimum value-added rule is probably the most complicated method to establish origin. Incidentally, it is also the most widely used scheme. A certain percentage of the value of the product has to be produced within the FTA to qualify for duty-free trade. The calculation of minimum value added is difficult and varies between different free trade areas. It also varies between product categories. Furthermore, technical details have to be considered. Which methods to calculate local content are accepted? For example, are capital costs counted as local content?[7] If yes, up to which percentage? In FTAs between developing and developed countries, the lower wages in the poorer countries ironically result in a disadvantage, because the minimum value added can be reached more easily if wages are higher.

Finally, specific production processes can be identified and agreed upon in order to establish origin. The trouble is that this method both requires complex negotiations on agreed production processes and continuous updating. Due to the changing patterns of production, new forms of production emerge that would constitute substantial transformation, but unless they are listed in the catalogue of agreed production processes, they would not qualify for duty-free trade.

Other free trade agreements have demonstrated how complex rules of origin can be. The NAFTA rules of origin cover more than 200 pages. There are byzantine regulations on local content, for instance a 62.5 per cent local content requirement for motor cars (for more details see Dieter 2004). NAFTA regulations are important because the USA uses them as a template for its trade agreements.[8] On balance, rules and certificates of origin create arbitrary incentives that contribute to the rise, not decline, of transaction costs in international trade (Garnaut and Vines 2006: 10).

For producers, these rules of origin result in an additional administrative effort rather than a facilitation of trade. An example where this is particularly obvious is the clothing industry in Asia. Today, state-of-the-art production chains need as little as three weeks from sample making to delivery. Production and sourcing processes are divided into up to 10 or 12 stages in various countries. By introducing rules of origin, this model will no longer be manageable due to the complexity of rules of origin (Dee 2005: 39). Of course, one might argue that slowing down the international division of labour is a useful development. But that is an entirely different debate: Preferential trade agreements are justified because they are supposed to facilitate trade, rather than obstruct it.

Rules of origin and their application have to be taken into consideration when evaluating the usefulness of free trade areas. They make transnational production processes more complicated, if not impossible. The inherent need for documentation of the production process is resulting in additional bureaucratic procedures. They may contribute to trade diversion, because manufacturers may use the cheapest supplier from within the free trade area rather than the cheapest supplier worldwide. Of course, there is considerable variation between free trade agreements with regard to the stringency of their rules of origin. But even when generous limits for establishing origin are chosen, the complex administration remains. Clearly, companies that are unwilling to meet the requirements of rules of origin can always opt out and simply pay the appropriate tariff, which in turn would reduce the economic utility of the free trade agreement to zero.

The limited benefits from the Australia–United States Free Trade Agreement

The Australian–United States Free Trade Agreement (AUSFTA) was agreed upon in February 2004. In 2003, Australia had been supporting the US invasion of Iraq, and Prime Minister John Howard wanted to benefit from the backing he had provided to George W. Bush's government. Australia got a free trade agreement, but surprisingly the deal is asymmetric in favour of America, not Australia. Rather than benefiting from the good political relationship between the two conservative governments, Australia got a lopsided deal. The richer country, the USA, got superior access to the Australian market, whilst Canberra accepted some important restrictions.

AUSFTA has been in force since 1 January 2005. In 2005, Australia experienced a rather dramatic increase of its goods exports: They grew by 20.8 per cent in the first eight months of 2005. However, Australian goods exports (excluding services) to the United States rose by only 2.1 per cent in nominal terms compared to the same period of 2004, a skimpy rate of export growth. Moreover, the rest of the world fared far better: American imports in the first eight months of 2005 grew to US$1015.2 billion, an increase of 10.3 per cent compared to the same period in 2004. America, by contrast, could increase the volume of exports to Australia: imports from America rose from US$9.9 billion in 2004 to US$10.9 billion in 2005, an increase of 10.7 per cent.[9] These developments are no coincidence: The asymmetric development – America benefiting more than Australia – can at least partly be explained by the agreement, which favours American producers. AUSFTA does not provide a level playing field.

Although Australia probably cannot determine the outcome of multilateral trade negotiations, it nevertheless has had an influence in the past. The Cairns Group, discussed in greater detail later, was driven by Australian initiative and had a major influence on the outcome of the Uruguay Round. Furthermore, by going bilateral Australia enables the United States to give the multilateral negotiations reduced relevance. As mentioned before, AUSFTA has been the greatest recent success of American trade policy: Australia is a significant OECD economy. AUSFTA has set a precedent for other countries. Therefore, it appears that Australia has both neglected its role in the Doha Round and provided an opportunity for the USA to defect from multilateralism.

Against this background, two questions have to be asked. First, is the agreement as bad as its critics suggest? Second, is this new strategy providing Australia with the appropriate trade regime for the twenty-first century?

Australia and the United States have agreed to eliminate most tariffs from day one of the commencement of the agreement. Tariffs on textiles and clothing, and some footwear, as well as some other items, will be phased out by 2015. Australia's tariffs have been reduced to a level of 5 per cent in general, with peaks of 15 per cent for textiles, 25 per cent for clothing and 15 per cent for passenger cars and 5 per cent for four-wheel-drive vehicles (Dee 2005: 4). US tariffs vary much more: Many tariffs are zero or very low, but tariff peaks result in substantial protectionism. On some textile clothing and footwear items, tariffs are as high as 37.5 per cent (Dee 2005: 4). The protection for cars is either very low or very high: Vehicles primarily designed for the transportation of people attract a negligible tariff of 2.5 per cent, whereas vehicles primarily designed for the transportation of goods attract a steep tariff of 25 per cent (Dieter 2005b: 176).[10]

The disadvantages for Australia are most visible in agriculture. Sugar, which can be produced competitively in Australia's tropical regions, is excluded from imports into the United States, apart from a quota of 87,402 tons per year which existed before the FTA. For beef and dairy products there are surprisingly long transitional periods of up to 18 years before Australian producers will have unrestricted access to the American market.

Australian trade negotiators apparently were unable to open up the US market for sugar. The Australian government, which had campaigned for the free trade agreement citing agriculture as a potential benefit for Australia, subsequently had to provide compensation to the domestic sugar producers who will receive AU$444 million, a rather hefty sum of AU$70,000 for each of the 6,500 sugar farmers in Australia (Capling 2004: 67; Weiss *et al.* 2004: 147).

Equally problematic is the deal on beef. The United States can stop Australian imports if American farmers are threatened by this competition. For more than 30 years, Australia fought a similar approach of the EU, only to accept it now in the case of the United States (Capling 2004: 82). Both the exclusion of sugar and the arbitrary regulation of beef imports are violations of the principles that Australian governments had been publicly supporting for decades. Garnaut and Vines have emphasized that the avoidance of liberalization in agriculture that would result in trade creation is a characteristic of the current wave of preferential agreements:

> An example ... is the complete exclusion of sugar and the gradualism to the point of imperceptibility in other major agricultural exports in the US–Australia FTA.
>
> (Garnaut and Vines 2006: 9).

The rules of origin in AUSFTA are as complex as those in many other FTAs. They can contribute to the circumscribing of market opening. The rules are tailor-made, tariff line item by tariff line item, and in general require significant transformation of a product (Dee 2005: 9). For the first time, Australia has accepted rules of origin that are complex and can be used as protectionist devices. Hitherto, Australia's FTAs used relative simple rules of origin based on regional value added (Dee 2005: 13).

In principle, a combination of methods is used. A change of tariff classification is needed for textiles and apparel or a list of products that are specified in Annex 5-A of the agreement (AUSFTA, Article 5.1.(i)). For products that require a minimum local content the thresholds are 35 per cent (build-up method), 45 per cent (built-down approach) and for some footwear the minimum percentage is 55 per cent (Dee 2005: 10). For cars the threshold is 50 per cent, the only permitted method being the so-called net cost method.[11] Particularly problematic – from an economic as well as from an ethical perspective – are the regulations on textiles and clothing, where all yarn must either come from Australia or the United States, the yarn-forward rule (Dee 2005: 10). Yarn produced in Asia cannot be used if the finished product shall be imported duty-free into the United States or Australia. But the more disturbing rule is the one on cotton and man-made fibres: There, the requirement is fibre-forward. This means that cotton from African producers cannot be used or duties have to be paid. The issue of American (and to a lesser degree European) cotton subsidies had been a major issue in the failed Ministerial Meeting of the WTO in Cancún in 2003.[12] Using rules of origin to exclude African producers from both the Australian and the American market is a less visible, but equally efficient method. It undermines decades of efforts of African producers to participate in the global division of labour. These are unfair practices in international trade that disadvantage the poorest.[13]

The complexity of the rules of origin in AUSFTA does not differ from NAFTA or other agreements with US participation. Rather than facilitating trade, these measures are making trade more complicated. Even if there is some reduction of costs due to lower tariffs, this cost-saving is probably more than cancelled out by an increase in administrative expenses.

Intellectual property rights are covered in Chapter 17 of AUSFTA. The provisions of the agreement are rather complex and cover 29 pages. Kim Weatherall has described them as 'breathtakingly long, detailed, and opaque' (Weatherall 2004: 19). The reason for this convoluted deal is not that intellectual property was previously badly protected in Australia. Rather, the USA had been unsuccessful with attempts to raise intellectual property rights through the WTO. Faced with opposition there, as well as in other multilateral fora dealing with intellectual property like UNESCO, the US has gone bilateral.[14] It has moved to impose its preferred standards through a template approach – the chapter on intellectual property is negotiated according to a template used in previous agreements, with the same provisions in all of them (Weatherall 2004: 19).

The downside of the new standards agreed upon with the United States is that the regime has become more complicated. Further, adopting US standards implies adopting an important element of US economic policy, which may not suit the interests of Australia. The tightening of intellectual property rights in Australia, which is a net importer of intellectual property, is resulting in additional costs to Australian consumers and producers alike (Weatherall 2004: 20).[15] America, by contrast, benefits. There will not be significant additional costs to American consumers, but American owners of intellectual property selling abroad will reap the reward. The copyright term has also been extended, resulting in a copyright term of the life of the author plus 70 years. This regulation is applicable to new and old literature. Again, as Australia is also a net importer in literature, this is an additional cost to Australia.

As mentioned in the introduction to this chapter, one of the most disturbing aspects of bilateral trade agreements is that they contribute to a weakening of the dispute settlement mechanism of the WTO. This applies to AUSFTA as well. Article 21.4 stipulates the following:

> 1) Where a dispute regarding any matter arises under this Agreement and under another trade agreement to which both Parties are party, including the WTO Agreement, the complaining Party may select the forum in which to settle the dispute.
> 2) Once the complaining Party has requested a panel under an agreement referred to in paragraph 1, the forum selected shall be used to the exclusion of the others.
>
> (AUSFTA, Article 21.4)

The consequences are far-reaching. There is a possibility that the bilateral dispute settlement will be used even for cases that affect the participation of the two countries in the multilateral regime. Although the weaker country has a choice of forum, in practice there will be considerable pressure by the more powerful country to use the bilateral mechanism.

In 1986 Australia and 13 other competitive producers of agricultural products, including Brazil and Canada, founded the Cairns Group. Ever since, this group has been able to increase awareness of the negative consequences of protectionism in agriculture (Capling 2004: 23). Moreover, the Cairns Group has been described as a model of group activity that smaller states can utilize to foster change in specific areas of the global economic order (Higgott and Cooper 1990: 592). But the Australian–American preferential trade agreement has resulted in severe damage for Australia's integrity. After all, if American protectionism with regard to sugar is acceptable to Australia, what should be wrong with Japanese protectionism in rice or European protectionism in cheese?

The bilateral agreement shows very few benefits for Australian commercial interests, but it has damaged the reputation of the country in international groupings. The Cairns Group is now relatively weak and major players within that organization, Brazil in particular, are today using other fora to promote their cases, e.g. the G-21 founded during the failed WTO ministerial round in Cancún. Bilateral trade agreements in general and the deal with the United States in particular are not in Australia's national (economic) interest. This conclusion is also drawn by Philippa Dee:

> It is often claimed that preferential trade agreements can achieve faster progress than multilateral negotiation in difficult areas. This appears not to be the case with AUSFTA. On a strict cost–benefit calculation, the agreement is of marginal benefit to Australia, and possibly of negative benefit

given some of the pernicious but unquantifiable elements of the intellectual property chapter

(Dee 2005: 38).

Australia, an exporter of raw materials and agricultural products, cannot benefit very much from free trade in manufactured products unless dynamic effects would lead to an increase in competitiveness of Australian manufacturers. The country would benefit from free trade in agriculture, but the agreement with the USA has set an unfavourable precedent for other FTAs.

Singapore's trade policy revisited

Singapore has been the most active proponent of bilateral free trade agreements in Asia. The country, a founding member of ASEAN, has been implementing a three-tiered trade policy in recent years: Bilateral, regional and multilateral. Singapore's bilateral free trade agreements have been presented as new generation, WTO-plus agreements. The scope of these agreements is more comprehensive than the approach of ASEAN. However, the traditional attempts to liberalize trade and investment in Southeast Asia have only shown modest improvements (Inama 2005: 561). Therefore, the question is why an approach that has not generated much progress at a regional, plurilateral level, i.e. the ASEAN group, is expected to perform so much better bilaterally.

Margaret Liang, who was Singapore's Deputy Permanent Representative to the WTO from 1998 to 2002, has suggested that bilateral agreements have advantages that are quite universal. First, she argues that FTAs provide impetus to multilateral liberalization, because FTAs allow countries to identify compatible partners with whom to implement faster and more comprehensive liberalization. This, in turn, would work as a catalyst for multilateral trade liberalization. Second, FTAs could be used as scapegoats in domestic policy processes. Resistance to reform is supposed to be overcome more easily if external pressure – by the other country in the FTA – is portrayed as a necessary condition for the conclusion of an agreement. Third, the competitiveness of businesses is believed to benefit because of improved market access (Liang 2005: 57f).

Considered in turn, none of these perceived advantages withstands scrutiny. The positive impetus of FTAs for the further development of the WTO is yet to be noticed. Rather, the Doha Round suffered from a lack of determination of WTO member countries because an alternative – bilateral agreements – exists. Although the Doha Round has not failed because of bilateral agreements, their availability has contributed to the (temporary?) collapse of multilateral negotiations. Using bilateral agreements as a scapegoat for reform processes that would otherwise not be accepted by democratic society is a risky strategy. Indeed, a deterioration of economic development could then be blamed on bilateral agreements. Finally, market access due to bilateral agreements is always somewhat limited. Regional or global improvements of market access are superior.

The Singaporean Linda Low praised the country's departure from the joint ASEAN approach and has suggested that the country has been embracing a strategy well suited for the twenty-first century:[16]

> Singapore has made no apologies with the fast and furious pace and ambition of its bilateral FTAs. It meant to stir ASEAN lethargy, especially since the Asian crisis, even circumvent mismanagement at the WTO multilateral level which is as painfully slow and bogged down and take Singapore into the new millennium economy.
>
> (Low 2003: 2).

This statement probably expresses the perception of bilateral agreements in Singapore's policy-making circles quite well. ASEAN had failed in the Asian crisis and therefore lost some of its appeal. The strategy of Singapore apparently is to complete many bilateral arrangements and to become a hub for the region. Margaret Liang has suggested that Singapore's trade policy aims at 'expanding its economic and political space' (Liang 2005: 53). Beyond the rhetoric, both dimensions are hardly promoted by bilateralism. The case is evident in the political domain, where bilateralism results in a departure from regionalism and consequently a reduction of the political space in which Singapore operates. Rather than building on deepening the integration in the ASEAN group, Singapore has decided to go it alone, which deprives the country of the additional backing of the other ASEAN countries. The economic benefits are similarly ambiguous. Bilateral agreements, even if they go beyond a preferential trade agreement, at best result in the deepening of the bilateral economic space. A regional approach, i.e. the development of regional regulation and a regional common market, is evidently the superior concept.

Singapore does not only want to liberalize its own trading relations, but the expectation is that it can transform its previous status as an entrepot trader. This concept is not received too well by Singapore's ASEAN partners, as there is an inherent hierarchy in Singapore's concept:

> Singapore ... seeks to forge as many bilateral trade arrangements as possible in an effort to maximise gains from freer trade by becoming a 'hub' country regardless of criticisms from other ASEAN member nations for violating its unanimous and collective approach to non-members. Other ASEAN members do not seem to be satisfied with the limited gains from freer trade as a 'spoke' country. They appear not to want to open their markets unilaterally to non-members who are indirectly coming from the hub country.
>
> (Lee and Park 2005: 23f)

This resentment of Singapore by its neighbours is understandable. If they had the intention to liberalize their import regime, they could do so without being aided by the small city-state. In particular, important ASEAN countries

(Malaysia, Indonesia, Thailand, the Philippines) have been negatively affected by the Asian crisis and are therefore reluctant to liberalize trade in services in general and financial services in particular (Thangavelu and Toh 2005: 1218). These countries fear that Singapore's FTA strategy will open their economies to foreign competition, and that assumption is dampening further integration in ASEAN.

But even the technical side of Singapore's hub-and-spoke concept does not work well. Singapore's bilateral FTAs with, say, the United States require substantial local content in order to qualify for duty-free trade. Products that have received most of the value added in other ASEAN countries do not qualify for duty-free access to the American market. Where there is no substantial American import duty there is no need to use the detour via Singapore.

Consequently, Singapore's concept of establishing itself as the free trade hub in the region is not convincing. The country has been trying to punch above its weight. In order to be attractive as a hub, an economy ought to have a sizable internal market, and Singapore does not have that. The USA or the EU can try to establish themselves as hubs, but that function differs sharply from the entrepot trader role that Singapore had in the past.

Singapore's partners in ASEAN were ostensibly not at all delighted by the change in trade policy. There have been concerns that the ASEAN Free Trade Area (AFTA) is severely weakened by Singapore's strategy. Malaysia's Foreign Minister remarked that although Singapore may not have done anything incorrect in legal terms, morally the country has undermined friendship in ASEAN (Daquila and Huy 2003: 914).

In 2007, the tensions between Singapore and its neighbours have erupted in a field that hitherto had been uncontroversial. Indonesia has prohibited the export of sand and certain types of gravel to Singapore, which has resulted in a tripling of the prices of these building materials since February 2007 (*Frankfurter Allgemeine Zeitung*, 19 April 2007: 13). Of course, the trade disputes are not the only cause of this conflict, but Singapore's diplomacy has probably been too short-sighted and placed too much emphasis on achieving certain goals for the country, rather than for the region.

In Singapore the agreement with the United States probably enjoyed most prominence in the debate on free trade agreements. The United States–Singapore Free Trade Agreement (USSFTA) has been in force since January 2004 and is reviewed annually. As in the FTA with Australia, the United States has insisted on some asymmetries. Whilst Singapore has been eliminating all import tariffs on American goods on entry into force, the United States has maintained some tariffs, which will be eliminated over a period of three to ten years (Thangavelu and Toh 2005: 1224). With regard to intellectual property rights, Singapore has had to change its regulations. In particular, copyright has been extended to the life of the author plus 70 years. Singapore also had to adopt measures against the circumvention of technologies that protect copyright works and change regulations on pharmaceutical products (Thangavelu and Toh 2005: 1226).

The rules of origin in the FTA are quite strict. Textiles and apparels qualify for duty-free trade if they meet the yarn-forward rule. This means the yarn can be sourced from two suppliers: either from Singapore or from the United States. Consequently, textile manufacturers in Singapore can no longer buy yarn in other parts of Asia if they want to export to the USA – they have to buy in America. This clear case of trade diversion is not a problem for supporters of the bilateral FTA. Linda Low suggests that 'the industry will work with US yarn suppliers, and restructure their manufacturing operations to benefit from the US–Singapore FTA' (Low 2003: 12).

Singapore's agreement with Japan probably is as important as the deal with the USA. The Japan–Singapore Economic Partnership Agreement (JSEPA) is hailed as a 'new age' partnership agreement. It not only covers trade in goods and services, but also the promotion of foreign direct investment as well as regulatory reform, facilitation of customs procedures, cooperation in science and technology, media and broadcasting, electronic commerce, movement of natural persons and human resource developments (Thangavelu and Toh 2005: 1211). Nevertheless, on scrutiny, there are several agreements that have received a joint label. The core continues to be the agreement on free trade in goods and services.

Empirical evidence suggests that trade has not dramatically increased since JSEPA came into force. In the first half of 2003, i.e. when the agreement was operational, bilateral trade actually shrank. This is hardly surprising, considering that Singapore reduced its tariffs to virtually zero unilaterally before the agreement became effective (Ziltener 2005: 294). The rules of origin are comparatively strict and require inter alia a local content of 60 per cent of the selling price (Daquila and Huy 2003: 917).[17] Thus, there could not be significant amounts of additional trade from Japan to Singapore. Conversely, the increase in exports from Singapore to Japan apparently has been at the expense of other countries. In particular, imports from Taiwan have been replaced by imports from Singapore because of tariff preferences (Ziltener 2005: 295). Although these could be exceptional cases, it is nevertheless evident that bilateral preferences can lead to trade diversion.

Overall, the benefits that Singapore can expect from bilateral FTAs are modest. Gains in merchandise trade can be expected to be limited because of the rules of origin issue and the unresolved problem of transnational production without cumulation of origin. Furthermore, not too much should be expected from services. For the time being, Singapore is primarily trading goods. Total merchandise trade in 2003 was S$473 billion; much larger than trade in services, which was S$105 billion (Liang 2005: 52f). More than half of the latter sum was due to transportation services and travel, and in those sectors no huge gains can be expected from bilateral agreements.

Singapore has embarked on a new trade policy that provides limited gains while undermining the country's credibility in the region. In particular, the lasting discord in ASEAN – a side-effect of Singapore's new policy – suggests that bilateralism is a rather short-sighted policy for a country of Singapore's size and political importance. Singapore has set a precedent which other ASEAN members feel compelled to follow. There is a danger that these countries draw the wrong lessons and create a messy patchwork of weak, market-distorting FTAs (Baldwin

2006: 1506; Sally and Sen 2005: 102). Furthermore, Singapore has lost the credibility it previously enjoyed as an honest broker in the WTO – not unlike the position Australia used to have.

Whilst ASEAN played an important role as a group in the Uruguay Round of trade negotiations, the recent emphasis on bilateralism has reduced the importance of ASEAN in the failed Doha Round. ASEAN cooperation in Geneva has all but broken down (Sally and Sen 2005: 111). Both the lack of cooperation in Geneva and the diverging trade policies in the region have resulted in several cracks within ASEAN. This is a short-sighted, even foolish approach. In the long run, each country in Southeast Asia needs an efficient and effective WTO, as Sally and Sen have stressed. The economies of the ASEAN countries are on a clear path towards further integration into the global economy, and this gives the region a stake in a liberal, non-discriminatory and rules-based multilateral trading system (Sally and Sen 2005: 111). Singapore may not have envisaged the grave consequences of its uncoordinated push for bilateralism, but the long-term consequences of neglecting the multilateral regime may put the entire ASEAN region at a disadvantage compared to the emerging hubs of global trade – the United States, the EU and China.

Thailand's preferential agreements and the strenuous negotiations with the USA

After Singapore had introduced its new emphasis on bilateral deals around the turn of the century, the Thai government followed soon after. This policy shift has had negative effects on cooperation in ASEAN, and at the same time has been providing only limited gains. Nevertheless, the early harvest program – part of the ASEAN-China FTA – received a lot of attention, primarily because it was the first bilateral trade measures that China implemented after joining the WTO. The Chinese immediately opened their market for Thai agricultural products, which in the first six months of 2004 resulted in an increase of vegetable exports to China of 38 per cent and of fruit exports of 80 per cent (Hufbauer and Wong 2005: 8).[18] Other agreements, however, show a great degree of protectionism.

On 1 September 2005, Thailand concluded a free trade agreement with Japan. This deal is another example of the lack of free trade in the bilateral agreements in Asia. Rather than liberalizing comprehensively, even if it is limited to bilateral trade, Japan and Thailand agreed not to hurt each other too badly. Thailand's automobile industry, which has been developing relatively well in recent years, continues to be protected against Japanese competition. For example, the tariff for cars with more than 3000 cc engine capacity has been reduced from 80 to 60 per cent, whereas the level of protection for cars with smaller engines, i.e. the majority of cars, remains unchanged. Japanese steel producers will not get duty-free access to the Thai market before 2015. As would be expected, Japan has wanted to protect its agricultural sector. Rice, beef, wheat, dairy products and fish are excluded from the free trade agreement.

Bilateral free trade agreements with such characteristics do not have much to do with the concept of free trade. Rather than increasing competition specifically in those areas where the producers in one country are less competitive than in the other, those sectors are excluded. Consequently, the potentially largest gains of the free trade agreement are left out. Furthermore, such agreements probably are a violation of Article 24 of the GATT, which permits free trade areas and customs unions only if they cover 'substantially all the trade'. Agreements that exclude agriculture, cars and steel violate this regulation. Pointing to very low levels of trade in these sectors prior to the creation of the FTA does not help, because the dynamic effects of trade liberalization ought to be considered.

Thailand and the United States have been negotiating a free trade agreement since 2004. Again, these negotiations demonstrate that free trade is not the main objective in many bilateral agreements. There are two main sectoral sensibilities, and both parties anxiously defend their respective industries. The negotiations also show both the weakness of America's traditional industries and the strength of American service industries. The two disputed industries are motor vehicles and financial services.

Today, Thailand is the world's second largest producers of light commercial vehicles (also called light trucks). Japanese and Korean manufacturers have been using Thailand's strong competitive position in manufacturing and export light trucks from Thailand to the rapidly expanding Asian markets as well as to OECD countries, such as Australia. However, there are virtually no exports of light trucks to the United States. The reason for that is the high tariff of 25 per cent that the United States is applying on light trucks ever since the German–American chicken war of 1962–63. Although this rather bizarre trade conflict between West Germany and the United States is virtually forgotten today, it resulted in an increase of the tariff for imported light trucks from 8.5 per cent to 25 per cent (Dieter 2005b: 174–182).

Unsurprisingly, the Thai government is asking for free trade in light trucks, but the American government is well aware of the fact that General Motors and Ford might become insolvent if competition were to increase dramatically. The Chief Economist of General Motors, Mustafa Mohatarem, has claimed that Thailand would become an 'aircraft carrier' for foreign producers if free trade were permitted between the two countries (*Financial Times*, 18 February 2005: 2). Consequently, there is very limited willingness of the US Trade Representative to yield concessions in this sector.

At the same time, the Thai government is trying to protect its financial sector. The country suffered a severe blow when the financial crisis hit Thailand and other countries in 1997. Ever since, the government has tried to strengthen the domestic financial sector. The American side is asking for a complete opening of the Thai market for financial services, which is understandable when considering the good competitive position of the American financial sectors.

The bottom line is simple: The American government fears Thai competition in trucks, and the Thai government fears American competition in financial services. If any of the two sides wished to increase competition in those sectors, they could do that unilaterally. Since both sides are apparently unwilling to make concessions, there will either be no agreement or the deal will be incomprehensive. More precisely, an agreement excluding both light trucks and services is a violation of both the letter and the spirit of the GATT, GATS and the WTO.

Whilst Thailand has not put as much emphasis on bilateral agreements as Singapore, the new priorities have resulted in weaker commitments to further development in the WTO. FTAs are today at the forefront of Thai trade policy, and the wisdom and effectiveness of shifting most resources to bilateral negotiations can be called into question (Sally and Sen 2005: 105). Two observers from Thailand's Ministry of Commerce admit the shift of resources quite openly, and they also suggest that Thailand fails in getting the desired results in bilateral FTAs:

> It is true that resources on international trade negotiations have been mobilized and redirected towards FTAs. Nevertheless, it is also apparent that Thailand is not getting anything she wants on the rule front under FTAs – no agricultural subsidies reduction, fragmented rules of origin, no reform on AD (Anti-Dumping).
>
> (Talerngsri and Vonkhorporn 2005: 73)

Thailand's quite sobering experience with FTAs may result in a reduced willingness for compromise in the WTO. Thailand may opt for tough positions on agricultural liberalization and the reform of Anti-Dumping measures, reject any far-reaching changes in intellectual property rights and oppose an agreement on labour standards (Talerngsri and Vonkhorporn 2005: 73). If that were to be the case, one could argue that in Thailand's case bilateralism has resulted at least in a clarification of strategic positions in trade policy. Whether this justifies the bilateral detour is a separate question.

Conclusion: The limited appeal of bilateral trade agreements

The trend for bilateral trade agreements in Asia and the Asia-Pacific is difficult to understand. These preferential agreements are often not liberalizing trade comprehensively, cause great administrative burden to producers and undermine the multilateral regime. Nevertheless, many countries are moving in that direction. What are their motivations?

The cases examined in this chapter offer a range of explanations. In Australia's case, a major motive probable was the desire to forge close links with the United States *and* use this allegedly close relationship in the 2004 election campaign. Singapore's leadership attempted to give the country the advantage of being the first economy in the region to establish bilateral agreements. Systemic consequences were ignored. Thailand is joining the bilateral wave, but it has not conceded many preferences in its existing bilateral agreement with Japan and is unlikely to allow extensive competition in the agreement currently negotiated with the USA.

Bilateral trade agreements can negatively affect the competitiveness of companies in a region. Companies have to spend resources on documenting origin, and these procedures are welfare reducing. The administrative burden of certificates of origin results in an increase of costs to producers. Overall, emphasis on these preferential agreements deters manufacturers from remaining competitive on world markets.

There is, however, one case in which bilateralism is a wise strategy. If the old multilateral trade regime is going to collapse – an unlikely event even after the collapse of the Doha Round but not entirely impossible – then a bilateral trade agreement would be a safeguard measure to avoid the breakdown of international trade. The irony is that bilateralism – despite many declarations that it is supposed to strengthen the WTO – actively contributes to the downfall of the multilateral order.

The bottom line is that bilateralism represents the third-best solution to a decisive problem of international economic relations. The multilateral regime – for all its failures and shortcomings – continues to be the first-best answer to the necessity of trade regulation. Regional approaches have some important benefits which make them a partially justifiable second-best approach. Bilateralism is – as has been demonstrated in this chapter – the least desirable position for the regulation of international trade. Ross Garnaut and David Vines have argued that the trend towards discriminatory bilateral agreements is '… an ill-thought-out early-twenty-first century response, and it is deeply disturbing' (Garnaut and Vines 2006: 2).

The trend towards bilateralism is often justified with the notion that simply relying on the WTO is like doing nothing. This is not the case. Multilateralism continues to function and to represent a superior form of regulation compared with bilateral regulation. The examination of the Singaporean approach has clearly shown that pushing bilateral agreements can negatively affect regional integration processes, in this case ASEAN. Bilateralism is neither a substitute for regional integration nor for the multilateral trade regime.

Notes

1 Gordon argues that Washington's turn to bilateralism is the major factor in explaining the change in trade policy in Asia (Gordon 2005: 9).
2 At the time of writing the US Congress had not voted on this agreement.
3 For a more detailed discussion of this issue see Dieter (2005a; 2005b: 171–222).
4 Whether the actual trade in the preferential agreements takes place utilizing the preferences or whether companies prefer paying the tariffs due to the complexity of rules of origin requires further analysis.
5 In the EU, disputes are conferred exclusively to the European Court of Justice and other EC bodies. By contrast, in NAFTA Chapter 20 there is a choice of forum for dispute settlement (Pauwelyn 2003: 1012).
6 In NAFTA, the costs of meeting rules of origin requirements have been estimated at 2 per cent of the value of *all* Mexican exports to the United States (Dee 2005: 22).
7 In NAFTA, the cost of capital for machinery can be included (Krueger 1995: 8).

8   But where the USA is not involved, rules of origin can be just as complex. For example, in the Japan–Singapore Economic Partnership Agreement, the Japanese government insisted on detailed, product-specific rules of origin which cover 200 out of the 360 pages of the agreement (Ravenhill 2003: 308).
9   IMF, Directions of Trade Statistics, January 2006, own calculations.
10 Tariff position 8703 is applied for cars, 8704 for light trucks. See the US customs database at http:// dataweb.usitc.gov/scripts/tariff2002.asp. The high tariff for light trucks has its origin in a curious trade dispute between Germany and the United States in the early 1960s. For details see Talbot (1978) and Dieter (2005b: 174–181).
11 For details see the agreement and explanations at http://www.dfat.gov.au/trade/negotiations/us_fta/guide/5.htm.
12 In 2002, the subsidies added up to $4,000 million in the United States and $700 million in the EU. *Frankfurter Allgemeine Zeitung* 10 September 2003: 3.
13 For details see Dieter 2005b: 192ff.
14 See, for instance, the speech of the US ambassador to UNESCO, Louise V. Oliver, on 17 October 2005, on the convention of UNESCO on Cultural Diversity, online http://www.amb-usa.fr/USUNESCO/texts/GenConf33_Amb_Intervention_CD_Amendments.pdf.
15 In 2002–03, Australia has spent AU$1.82 billion on royalties to foreign holders of intellectual property, but has only received AU$618 million from abroad (Weatherall 2004: 20).
16 Liang has argued similarly and thus provided an example of the extremely positive expectations prevailing amongst trade policy makers in Singapore: 'This web of interlocking economic and strategic interests help(s) contribute to regional stability, security, and prosperity' (Liang 2005: 58).
17 Note that all of Singapore's FTAs have diverging rules of origin. Even advocates of Singapore's bilateralism have been admitting that the complex rules of origin are not facilitating trade. Nevertheless, Linda Low hopes that the complexity of establishing origin increases innovation, creativity and flexibility (Low 2003: 19).
18 Trade in 188 agricultural products was liberalized as part of the early harvest program (Talerngsri and Vonkhorporn 2005: 69).

References

Baldwin, Richard E. (2006): 'Multilateralising Regionalism: Spaghetti Bowls as Building Blocs on the Path to Global Free Trade', *The World Economy*, 29(11): 1451–1518.
Camroux, David (2001): 'Die ASEAN vor dem Ende', *Le Monde Diplomatique*, February p. 7.
Capling, Ann (2004): *All the Way with the USA. Australia, the US and Free Trade*, Sydney: University of New South Wales Press.
Daquila, Teofilo C. and Huy, Le Huu (2003): Singapore and ASEAN in the Global Economy. The Case of Free Trade Agreements', *Asian Survey*, 43(6): 908–928.
Davis, Christina l. (2006): 'Do WTO Rules Creat a Level Playing Field? Lessons from the Experience of Peru and Vietnam', in: John Odell (ed.): *Developing Countries and the Trade Negotiation Process*, Cambridge: Cambridge University Press, pp. 219–256.
Dee, Philippa (2005): 'The Australia–US Free Trade Agreement: An Assessment', *Pacific Economic Papers*, No. 345. Online at http://apseg.anu.edu.au/pdf/pep/pep-345.pdf.
Dieter, Heribert (2004): 'Präferenzielle Ursprungsregeln in Freihandelszonen: Hemmnisse für den internationalen Handel?' *Aussenwirtschaft. Schweizerische Zeitschrift für internationale Wirtschaftsbeziehungen.* 59(III): 273–303.
Dieter, Heribert (2005a): 'Letzte Chance in Hongkong? Überwindbare Hindernisse auf dem Weg zum Abschluss der Doha-Runde', *SWP-Aktuell* 52, November.

Dieter, Heribert (2005b): *Die Zukunft der Globalisierung. Zwischen Krise und Neugestaltung*, Baden-Baden: Nomos-Verlagsgesellschaft.

Estevadeordal, Antoni Suominen, Kati (2003): 'Rules of Origin: A World Map and Trade Effects'. Paper prepared for the workshop: *The Origin of Goods: A Conceptual and Empirical Assessment of Origin in PTAs*, Paris, 23–24 May 2003. Online at www. inra.fr/Internet/Departments/ESR/UR/lea/actualites/ROO2003/articles/estevadeordal. pdf (accessed 17 November 2003).

Garnaut, Ross and Vines, David (2006): 'Sorting out the Spaghetti. On Reducing the Damage from the Proliferation of Discriminatory Regional Free Trade Areas', University of Columbia Business School, January 2006. at www0.gsb.columbia.edu/ipd/pub/ Vines_Reaction.pdf.

Gordon, Bernhard K. (2005): 'Asia's Trade Blocs Imperil the WTO', *Far Eastern Economic Review*, November: 5–10.

Higgott, Richard and Cooper, Andrew Fenton (1990): 'Middle Power Leadership and Coalition Building: Australia, the Cairns Group and the Uruguay Round of Trade Negotiations', *International Organization*, 44(4): 589–632.

Hufbauer, Gary Clyde and Wong, Yee (2005): 'Prospects for Regional Free Trade in Asia', Institute for International Economics, Working Paper Series, WP 05-12, October.

Inama, Stefan (2005): 'The Association of South East Asian Nations – People's Republic of China Free Trade Area: Negotiating Beyond Eternity With Little Trade Liberalization?', *Journal of World Trade*, 39(3): 559–579.

Jakob, Thinam and Fiebinger, Gernot (2003): 'Preferential Rules of Origin – A Conceptual Outline', *Intereconomics*, (May/June): 138–146.

Lee, Jong-Wha and Park, Innwon (2005): 'Free Trade Areas in East Asia: Discriminatory or Non-discriminatory?' *The World Economy*, 28(1): 21–48.

Liang, Margaret (2005): 'Singapore's Trade Policies. Priorities and Options', *ASEAN Economic Bulletin*, 22(1): 49–59.

Lloyd, Peter John (2002): 'New Bilateralism in the Asia-Pacific', *The World Economy*, 25(9): 1279–1296.

Low, Linda (2003): 'Singapore's Bilateral Free Trade Agreement: Institutional and Architectural Issues'. Paper prepared for PECC Trade Forum, 23 April 2003, Washington, DC. Online at http://www.pecc.org/publications/papers/trade-papers/5_ CP/3-low.pdf.

Pauwelyn, Joost (2003): 'How to Win a World Trade Organization Dispute Based on Non-World Trade Organization Law?', in: *Journal of World Trade*, 37(6): 997–1030.

Ravenhill, John (2003): 'The New Bilateralism in the Asia Pacific', *Third World Quarterly*, 24(2): 299–317.

Roberts, Michael and Wehrheim, Peter (2001): 'Regional Trade Agreements and WTO Accession of CIS Countries', *Intereconomics* (November/December): 315–323.

Sally, Razeen and Sen, Rahul (2005): 'Whither Trade Policies in Southeast Asia? The Wider Asian and Global Context', *ASEAN Economic Bulletin*, 22(1): 92–115.

Talbot, Ross B. (1978): *The Chicken War. An International Trade Conflict between the United States and the European Economic Community, 1961–64*, Ames, Iowa: Iowa State University Press.

Talerngsri, Pawin and Vonkhorpon, Pimchanok (2005): 'Trade Policy in Thailand: Pursuing a Dual Track Approach', *ASEAN Economic Bulletin*, 22(1): 60–74.

Thangavelu, S.M. and Toh, Muh-Heng (2005): 'Bilateral 'WTO-Plus' Free Trade Agreements: The WTO Trade Policy Review of Singapore 2004', *The World Economy*, 28(9):1 211–1228.

Weatherall, Kim (2004): 'Locked in. Australia Gets a Bad Intellectual Property Deal', *Policy*, 20(4): 18–24.

Weiss, Linda, Thurnbon, Elisabeth and Mathews, John (2004): *How to Kill a Country: Australia's Devastating Trade Deal with the United States*, Sydney: Allen & Unwin.

Woolcock, Stephen (1996): 'Rules of Origin', in: *Regionalism and its Place in the Multilateral Trading System*, Paris: OECD, pp. 195–212

Ziltener, Patrick (2005): 'Die Verhandlungen über bilaterale Wirtschaftsabkommen zwischen Japan und den ASEAN-Ländern, 2000-2005', *Aussenwirtschaft*, 60(III): 279–304.

6   Responses to regionalism

Corporate strategy in East Asia

Andrew Staples

Introduction

The globalization of economic activity has been a defining characteristic of recent years. Globalization is a much used and contested term but is employed here to describe the deepening integration of global economic activity facilitated by the rapid development of information and communications technology (ICT) and the underlying trend towards liberalization in trade and investment. The union of these two forces has resulted in global, if uneven, economic expansion. Globalization may also be understood as a continuation of the constant struggle between states and markets and although it has been claimed that states are increasingly losing out to other economic actors in this process, the multinational company (MNC) in particular, the growing trend towards regionalism appears to reaffirm the importance of the state as a critical unit of analysis. Indeed, regionalism, a defining feature of the late 1990s and early twenty-first century, is an exclusively state level process (Gamble and Payne 1996). At the same time, in East Asia[1] this political process has emerged as a response to globalization and the deepening regionalization of economic activity. This interaction between regionalization and regionalism, between private and state actors, is a key dynamic of the East Asian political economy today. Moreover, as regionalism may only be properly understood with reference to regionalization this in turn requires an investigation into the international division of labour as observed in East Asia.

The shock of the 1997/98 Asian financial crisis continues today to resonate throughout the region and beyond. In the same way that the 1985 Plaza Accord energized Japan's foreign direct investment (FDI) and boosted the rapid growth of the Association of Southeast Asian Nations (ASEAN) economies, the Asian financial crisis can be seen as a similarly seminal event, recasting fundamental aspects of the region's structure. This is taking place against a backdrop of stalled multilateralism, of deepening regional economic integration and the inexorable rise of the Chinese economy.

This chapter considers Japanese multinationals in East Asia in this era of regionalism. More specifically, it is suggested that in the post-crisis era the region's political economy has experienced and continues to experience a radical transformation and that this dynamic necessitates a re-evaluation of the way in which we can understand, or 'know', the complex interrelation between the regional political economy and international production. The central question of this chapter, then, is to what extent has the transformation of the East Asian political economy impacted on the strategies employed by Japanese multinationals in their East Asian operations? A secondary question asks whether the adoption of the twin-track (locating firm-level analysis in a broader or holistic political economy context) approach employed here is both appropriate and valid.

Transformation of the East Asian political economy

As noted above the underlying theme of this chapter is that since the mid- to late 1990s the East Asian political economy has experienced a radical transformation and that this transformation necessitates a broader (more holistic) approach to any investigation of MNC activity in the region. To facilitate such an investigation this section considers six trends and issues that collectively constitute key dynamics of the transformation: stalled multilateralism, deepening regional economic interdependence, responses to the Asian financial crisis in the fields of finance, politics and trade liberalization and, finally, the significance for the region of China's continuing economic ascent.

Stalled multilateralism

Multilateralism has defined the global economic environment within which MNCs operate and has held particular significance for East Asian economic development, premised as it has been largely on export-led industrialization within a liberal, global trading system. Given this, stalled multilateralism, defined here as failure to progress the WTO agenda, is an important contextual component of the transformation of East Asia's political economy. Indeed, stalled multilateralism is linked directly with the rapid growth of bilateral and regional free trade agreements observed in the world today and discussed below.

The late 1990s can to some extent be seen as the high water mark for WTO-led globalization. Until then trade liberalization had been progressing steadily under the GATT since 1947 and the Uruguay Round (1986–94) included many important agreements on trade liberalization in addition to the establishment of the WTO in 1995. Yet attempts to launch a new 'development' round of negotiations in Seattle (1999) failed, arguably as a result of deep resistance to the neoliberal agenda, the Washington consensus and globalization in general. It was only at Doha in 2001, where pressure was on for the global community to present something approaching a united front barely three months after the September 11 terrorist attacks, that the new round was launched. However, these talks progressed little and ultimately collapsed two years later at Cancún over the developed world's protection of agricultural sectors and the developing world's rejection of, among others, the Singapore issues.[2] In other words, in the nine years following the conclusion of the Uruguay Round the WTO failed to make any significant headway in promoting further trade liberalization and it is precisely in this period that the popularity of bilateral and regional free trade agreements

Table 6.1 Regional free trade agreements and the WTO

Period	Total	Asia-Pacific	WTO activity
1955–89	20	4	Successive rounds
1990–94	21	3	Conclusion of Uruguay Round
1995–2000	26	1	Seattle (1999), Doha (2001)
2001–2004	40	6	Cancun (2003)

Source: Compiled from WTO data.

Table 6.2 Intra-regional trade in the global triad

	Intra-regional trade as a percentage of global trade		Intra-regional exports as a percentage of region's total exports		Intra-regional imports as a percentage of region's total imports	
	1990	2003	1990	2003	1990	2003
East Asia	8.4	12.7	40.1	50.5	47.5	59.7
NAFTA	6.7	8.5	41.4	55.4	35.0	39.9
EU	29.1	23.3	66.0	61.4	66.6	63.5

Source: Compiled from *IMF Direction of Trade Statistics* 2004.

expanded. As shown above (Table 6.1) between 1955 and 1995 41 regional trade agreements (RTAs) were notified to the WTO, a rate of approximately one a year. This increased to an annual rate of approximately seven per year between 1995 and 2004 when a further 66 RTAs were notified.

Deepening regional economic interdependence

East Asian regionalism is based on the regionalization of production, trade and investment that has steadily proceeded over the past three decades and an increasing share of economic activity in the region is now accounted for by intra-regional flows. It appears, therefore, that the region is becoming more deeply integrated and interdependent and less reliant on traditional extra-regional markets. The sinews of this economic interdependence, intra-regional trade and investment, may be regarded as the building blocks of the emerging East Asian economic community. Table 6.2 documents intra-regional trade in the global triad. For East Asia between 1990 and 2003, intra-regional trade rose from 8.4 per cent to 12.7 per cent of global trade. In the same period, intra-regional trade as a percentage of the region's total exports rose by just over ten percentage points to 50.5 per cent while intra-regional imports rose by 12.2 per cent.

East Asia's growing share of world trade broadly reflects the export orientation of the region's industrialization. However, a rising percentage of this growth is accounted for by intra-regional trade within which intra-industry trade figures prominently. The share of total trade growth attributed to intra-industry trade rose from 42.5 per cent in 1986 to 75 per cent in 2000 (IMF, 2004). Intra-East Asian exports rose from approximately 20 per cent of the total in the 1970s to 40 per cent in 2002 (ibid.) while exports to the United States, the EU and Japan have declined (United States, Japan) or remained broadly stable (EU). However, as intra-regional trade is dominated by intra-industry trade in intermediate goods, these external export markets remain crucial for finished products. Therefore, demand in export markets (for manufactured products) is as important a driver of intra-regional trade as export-orientated growth policies and ASEAN Free Trade Area (AFTA) implementation.

While experience elsewhere (Europe) points to a positive correlation between FDI flows and integration, it is not clear that regionalism encourages FDI in the East Asian (ASEAN) experience. In contrast to the positive impact of AFTA on intra-regional trade, it appears that the agreement has had little impact on inward investment flows (Scally and Wickramanayake 2004: 60), although it should be noted that this assessment was based on data covering only the period between 1992 and 1997. However, as ASEAN implements the ASEAN Investment Area (AIA) it is anticipated that regional integration will be accelerated by increased investment and regionalized production as ASEAN's locational advantages are enhanced, encouraging a 'crowding in' of investment.

FDI has played a crucial role in the development of East Asia and this is particularly true for Southeast Asian nations (Ito and Krueger 2000; Freeman and Bartels 2004). Inward FDI increased rapidly in the 1980s and throughout the 1990s up to the crisis for the ASEAN 4 and China in particular. Moreover, the share of intra-regional investment has been increasing steadily relative to the share of inter-regional investment over the past two decades. Within this structure China is most dependent on intra-regional FDI, mainly from the Newly Industrialized Economies (NIEs) and Japan (68 per cent in 1995–97) while the ASEAN 4 received only 24 per cent of their inward investment in this way. The NIEs are even less dependent on intra-regional FDI which accounted for only 12 per cent in the same period. One conclusion to be drawn from these figures is that once FDI to China is omitted, East Asia is still largely dependent on FDI from outside of the region.

Responses to the Asian financial crisis – finance

In-depth analysis of the causes and immediate impact of the Asian financial crisis may be found elsewhere (Furman and Stiglitz 1998; Krugman 1999; Pempel 1999; Robison *et al*. 1999; Noble and Ravenhill 2000; Jomo 2003) and the debate continues as to where to apportion blame (crony capitalism or 'mad money'?). But it is the deeper trends emanating from the event that have specific relevance to the issues investigated in this chapter. The crisis brought home to East Asian policy makers the extent of their global and regional interdependence but, perhaps more importantly, it has served as a catalyst for subsequent closer regional cooperation. This trend is most clearly seen in the financial sector and it is to this that attention now turns.

The closing years of the 1990s witnessed a flurry of activity in East Asian financial sectors as governments attempted to first deal with the immediate crisis and, second, to take steps to prevent a further or future event. These measures can broadly be categorized as steps to develop regional financial facilities (bilateral swap agreements under the Chiang Mai Initiative), capacity for crisis management and prevention (economic monitoring, surveillance, information sharing and peer review) and the longer-term development of regional (and deeper) financial cooperation (Asian bond market, exchange rate mechanisms). It should also be noted that these developments are not exclusively in response to the crisis, as intensifying intra-regional economic activity provides a further rationale for a strengthened regional financial architecture.

Responses to the Asian financial crisis – institutionalism

A primary response to the crisis within East Asia has been the trend towards the institutionalization of regionalism. A proposal emerged from Malaysia in 1991 to establish an East Asian Economic Group (EAEG), subsequently renamed the East Asian Economic Caucus (EAEC), that articulated an attempt to create an exclusively East Asian (on racial grounds) economic and political entity. The EAEG should be viewed in the context of the then Prime Minister Mahatiar's 'Look East' (i.e. to Japan) initiative and growing concerns at the pace and depth of European and North American regional integration. Moreover it may also be seen as an attempt to respond to these developments by drawing the region out of the United States dominated Asia-Pacific vision promoted at APEC. While eventual acceptance of key objectives (economic cooperation, promoting free trade, accelerating economic growth and promoting open regionalism) was secured within ASEAN by the mid-1990s, Japan was unable to offer crucial support and the proposal ultimately languished (Hook *et al.* 2001).

Yet in 1997 the ASEAN+3 (APT) framework, which may accurately be described as the EAEC in all but name emerged. The APT framework became institutionalized in 1999 (Manila, 3rd Informal Summit) when the grouping issued the Joint Statement on East Asia Cooperation committing it to enhancing 'this dialogue process and strengthen[ing] cooperation with a view to advancing East Asian collaboration in priority areas of shared interest and concern' (ASEAN Secretariat, 1999).

However, the APT grouping lacked a dedicated secretariat despite a proposal from Malaysia in 2002 to instigate an ASEAN office to deal exclusively with Northeast Asian economic relations, and resistance to defining a stronger profile in this way emerged from some ASEAN members wary of duplicating existing responsibilities and thus undermining ASEAN itself. At the same time Japan remained somewhat ambivalent, reflecting the usual divergent views of its bureaucracy (Terada, 2004:18). This is an important issue as the APT process continues as the core of regionalism in East Asia; yet while it remains rootless (i.e. lacking its own secretariat) it also remains ostensibly an ASEAN and not an East Asian project. As something of a compromise, an ASEAN+3 Unit was established at the ASEAN Secretariat in December 2003 'to assist the ASEAN Plus Three Co-chairs to coordinate and monitor ASEAN Plus Three' (ASEAN Secretariat, 2004). Of central importance here was the decision of the APT group to follow the recommendation of the East Asian Study Group in 2002 to initiate an East Asia Summit (EAS) which, it was advertised and anticipated, would become the key vehicle for East Asian integration.

The inaugural EAS, duly held in Kuala Lumpur in December 2005, was supposed to mark a new stage in the evolution of East Asian regionalism. Yet due to competing visions of membership (whether or not to include India, Australia and New Zealand), status of that membership (as core members or peripheral observers) and the fundamentally competitive nature of Sino-Japanese relations, the reality was that little was achieved save for a commitment for further annual meetings to be retained within the ASEAN framework. At best, therefore, the inaugural summit defined the scope of the grouping and a commitment to future engagement which, given the anticipation of the event beforehand, fell well short of expectations. Among other agenda issues including energy, finance, education and avian flu, the second summit (set for December 2006 in Cebu, Philippines but postponed until January 2007 due to a typhoon) reaffirmed commitment to economic development and regional integration and to studying the Japanese proposal for the establishment of a Comprehensive Economic Partnership in East Asia (CEPEA).

The APT framework emerged in the midst of the region's financial crisis partly as an attempt to stabilize the region through greater political interaction, and cooperation thus remains the primary vehicle for East Asian regionalism. The establishment of the EAS by the APT was supposed to elevate East Asian regionalism to new heights but has so far failed to live up to expectations mainly due to a lack of clear distinction between the two groupings. The steady progress towards the establishment of an East Asian Community, as envisaged by the APT will not, therefore, be a linear process. The speed and depth of integration will continue to be challenged by domestic resistance to ever closer interdependence, continuing ambiguity on key 'directional' leadership and the search for a consensus on the aims and objectives of any future regional bloc. Moreover, this brief analysis has not referred to the perception of East Asian regionalism from outside of the region, most importantly from the United States, which, incidentally, has communicated a clear preference for the APEC vision and rejects any regional economic grouping in East Asian of which it is not a part. While the prognosis for East Asian integration might not be as rosy as anticipated in the first few years of the new millennium we can nevertheless and for the purposes of this chapter conclude that in the space of eight years East Asia has moved from a region characterized by the processes of private sector regionalization to one with a firm (if contested) and growing regionalist agenda.

Responses to the Asian financial crisis – growth of FTAs

As noted above, the increasing popularity and prevalence of FTAs in East Asia is part of a global trend that emerged in the 1990s (see Figure 6.1). The WTO

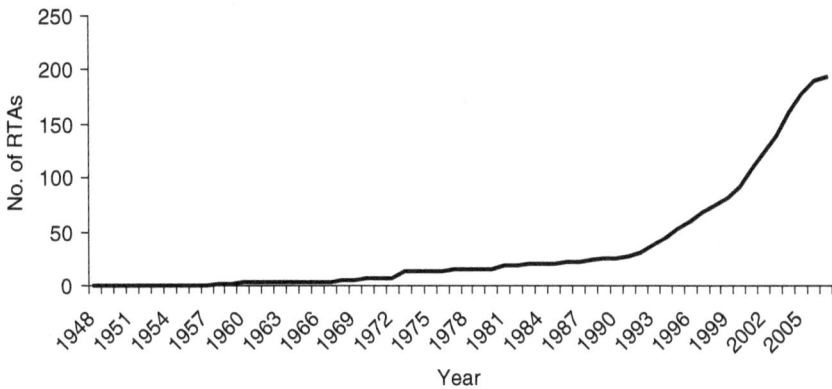

Figure 6.1 Global FTA growth (Source: WTO 2007)

confirms that 'sluggish progress in multilateral trade negotiations under the Doha Development Round appears to have accelerated further the rush to forge RTAs' (WTO 2005:1). While the EU and the United States forged their own regional FTAs in the early 1990s, East Asia has been a relative latecomer to the trend. However, the region has become an enthusiastic promoter of FTAs in the post-crisis period and the emerging network of agreements is a defining characteristic of 'lattice' regionalism (Dent 2003:1).

Yet, the recent and growing popularity of FTAs in East Asia should not simply be seen as a response to the Asian financial crisis. As indicated above, frustration at the lack of progress at the WTO is a strong motivator and a number of further, regional specific drivers are identified. Chief among these is the desire to create a seamless regional market and investment destination, particularly in ASEAN. At a broader level, FTAs are seen as a stepping stone towards the eventual establishment of an East Asian Community with all the accompanying status and bargaining power that this would confer vis-à-vis the world's most important regional economic entities: NAFTA and the EU. FTAs are also being woven into the fabric of East Asian developmentalism and are seen not only as a means to strengthen competitiveness but also to pull along, and lock-in, both emerging (CLMV[3] group) and more established economies (ASEAN 4, China).

A variety of agreements exist or are under negotiation in the region as demonstrated by Table 6.3. The Japan–Singapore economic partnership agreement is promoted as a 'WTO plus' or 'super' FTA in that it goes beyond trade liberalization to include non-trade issues (human resource development, services, investment). This form of comprehensive economic partnership is seen as a blueprint for the region and reaffirms the developmental intention of regional cooperation in contrast to trade liberalization between distant economies. The China–Hong Kong agreement on the other hand is a straight free trade agreement with no additional 'add-ons' and merely seems to confirm existing arrangements. Both

Table 6.3 Key free trade agreements in East Asia

In action	Under negotiation	Under study
AFTA (1992)	Australia–China	ASEAN-CER
Australia–Thailand (2005)	Australia–Japan	ASEAN-India
Bangkok treaty (1976)	India–Thailand[b]	ASEAN-EU
China–ASEAN[a] (2005)	Japan–Chile	ASEAN-US
China–Hong Kong (2004)	Japan–Korea	Australia-Chile
Japan–Malaysia (2005)	Japan–Thailand	Australia-Indonesia
Japan–Mexico (2005)	Korea–Singapore	Australia-Japan
Japan–Philippines (2006)	Singapore–Canada	Australia-Korea
Japan–Singapore (2002)	Singapore–Mexico	China-India
Korea–Chile (2004)	Singapore–India	Indonesia-New Zealand
Korea–ASEAN (2006)	Thailand–United States	Japan-ASEAN
Singapore–Australia (2003)	Thailand–Australia	Japan-Indonesia
Singapore–EFTA (2003)	Hong Kong–New Zealand	Korea-EU
Singapore–New Zealand (2001)		Korea-New Zealand
Singapore–United States (2004)		Malaysia-India
Taiwan–Panama (2004)		Singapore-Chile
		Singapore-Taiwan

Sources: Urata 2003; ASEAN Secretariat 2004; Bilaterals.org 2007.

Notes:
a Early harvest trade in goods programme. Trade in services negotiations ongoing.
b Agreement in principle, 2005.

bilateral and multilateral (regional) agreements are in place or at some stage of study or negotiation reflecting the complex nature of FTA strategies in the region. Moreover, inter-regional agreements with the United States, Australia and the EU can also be observed, indicating that an increasingly complex, if not 'spaghetti bowl', type network is emerging.

The trend towards FTAs in East Asia has been rapid and dramatic. This is driven by a range of global (stalled multilateralism), regional (responses to Asian financial crisis, leadership rivalry) and national dynamics. As discussed above, ASEAN has emerged as a 'hub' for FTA negotiations in the region through the APT framework, though it seems likely to concede this status to the anticipated East Asia Summit process.

The most important and only regional FTA to date is the AFTA launched in 1992. The timetable for implementation was accelerated in the wake of the crisis and has reduced tariffs between member states to between 0 and 5 per cent (CLMV member states excepted). Space limits any further investigation but, ultimately, AFTA by itself will not have a great impact on regionalism in East Asia, as the resulting market is still dwarfed by Japan and China and it is the inclusion of these two players that will confirm or otherwise the emergence of a more clearly defined and competitive regional economic entity. FTAs in East Asia, then, are a defining feature of and significant development within the region's contemporary political economy and inform any subsequent analysis of trade and investment structures in the region.

Significance of the rise of China for East Asia

The rapid growth of the Chinese economy presents perhaps the most challenging issue for individual East Asian nations and ASEAN in particular. This challenge extends across fundamental aspects of the region's political economy: politics, economics and security. Recent research by the ADB (Weiss and Shanwen 2003) indicates that China's expansion has resulted in increased competition with ASEAN in the key Japanese and US markets, in both labour-intensive and, less so, high-technology sectors. This increased competition was observed to be especially keen in the electrical and electronics sectors which is of particular concern for ASEAN given that these sectors account for approximately two-thirds of ASEAN's exports to the United States. It is inevitable that existing regional trade structures will be transformed as a result of China's growth and accession to the WTO, and this implies that ASEAN economies will lose, perhaps dramatically, their market share in a number of currently crucial industrial sectors. On the other hand, an expanding Chinese economy is expected to present fresh opportunities for ASEAN development of new industries, particularly in the service sector. From a modest starting point, trade between China and ASEAN in 2000 increased by 45 per cent over 1999 figures to reach approximately US$40 billion and ASEAN maintains a trade surplus with China. Moreover, some competition is to be welcomed as it can promote both mutual development and structural adjustment. WTO accession also locks China into a rules-based trading structure complete with an effective dispute settlement mechanism and offers further opportunities for ASEAN.

However, while the picture is mixed with regards to trading relations, it appears more clear-cut on the matter of FDI. As noted above, while FDI into East Asia is on an upward trend, China accounted for 66 per cent of the total in 2002 and 59 per cent in 2003 (China became the world's largest recipient of FDI in 2003) that directed to ASEAN is on a downward trend, dropping by 34.3 per cent in 2003. FDI to ASEAN fell from 51 per cent of total East Asian FDI in 1990 to 11 per cent in 2001, while China's share has rocketed from below 5 per cent to over 40 per cent in the same period. Japanese FDI also increasingly favours China over ASEAN. It has been argued that China does not receive a disproportionate level of investment given the size of its economy (Wu *et al.* 2002) and that FDI in East Asia is not a zero-sum game, but the fear of FDI diversion from Southeast Asia is not baseless and remains a key concern for ASEAN governments.

Summary

This section has surveyed a number of key trends and issues that, taken collectively, equate to a radical transformation of the East Asian political economy in the wake of the Asian financial crisis. By doing so, this section has sought to demonstrate the breadth and depth of the transformation and has been informed by an underlying suggestion that this not only sets the agenda for the coming decades but also necessitates a revised, holistic approach to our understanding of the activities of firms within the region and beyond. Set against a background of stalled multilateralism at the WTO, the deepening of intra-regional trade and investment relations, still evolving responses to the Asian financial crisis (finance, institutionalism, FTAs) and the rise of China, the region is now pursuing an overtly East Asian and regional vision in stark contrast to the previous Asia-Pacific norm under APEC. In the same way that AFTA forms the basis for expanded trade liberalization (and economic partnerships), the APT framework remains the foundation stone of East Asian regionalism. Thus, ASEAN is the hub for the ongoing development of East Asian regionalism. How far this will continue given the anticipated realization of the Asian Summit Meeting process is not yet clear and it is conceivable that within this framework the rivalry between China and Japan for directional leadership will intensify in a way that it could not under the APT framework.

Somewhat regardless of these political machinations, the implementation of an increasing number of FTAs signifies a 'ratcheting up' of economic relations and the continued deepening of regional interdependence. The impact of AFTA on corporate strategy is a key consideration of the case studies presented below but it is clear from the above that continuing efforts to create a regional and 'seamless' market in Southeast Asia point to a radically remodelled business environment within which firms can pursue their economic objectives.

Attention now shifts to consider the impact of this transformation on corporate strategy in the automotive sector. More specifically, the following sections offer analysis of empirical data gained through interviews with three leading Japanese auto manufacturers that took place between 2003 and 2004 in Japan, Singapore and Thailand. These were held with senior executives from those sections of the company concerned with strategy and/or regional operations. As noted above, this chapter posits that if we seek to better understand the international activities of firms a much more explicit role must be assigned to issues concerning the international political economy. The late Susan Strange was clear on this point:

> The explanation for the internationalization of production is not to be found within the firm but in the context, in the changing political economy within which the firm operates and competes with others in a global market for goods and services.

> (Strange 1993:104)

Accordingly, the questionnaire and interview survey sought to draw out the impact of changes in the political economy on the following areas of corporate activity: general strategy, regional strategy, investments, production and trade. A further question group elicited responses on specific issues concerned with scenarios for regional economic integration. Given the nature of this chapter however, a thematic approach is adopted below in an attempt to draw out key trends and issues from the case studies.

Responses to regionalism in the automotive sector

Japanese auto manufacturers maintain dominant positions in most national markets throughout East Asia, Southeast Asia in particular, and during the 1980s and 1990s Japanese automakers established, to greater or lesser degrees, an international division of labour in East Asia based on regional production networks (RPNs). The key trend to emerge from the survey is identified as the rationalization of these networks from the late 1990s and this has been accompanied by perhaps three further developments to be discussed below. These are; the establishment of regional management structures, the localization of production and models, and the emergence of Thailand as a regional hub.

Rationalization of production networks

MNCs regionalize production in pursuit of scale economies and the maximization of advantages afforded by national comparative advantage. Japanese multinationals, particularly in the automotive and electronics sectors, have been the most prolific regionalizers of production in East Asia. Additionally, automakers' strategy in the region prior to the Asian financial crisis was largely dictated by the fragmented nature of the market. Local content requirements in each country necessitated national organization and resulted in production for, and sales in, limited national markets.

RPNs, in addition to the IT revolution and globalization in general, have presented a serious challenge to the flying geese paradigm, which assumes the transference of 'full-set' industrial structures from lead to following economy (Bernard and Ravenhill 1995). By dividing up production regionally, Hatch and Yamamura (1996) charge that Japan has locked ASEAN economies into a structure of dependency. While this may be an overstatement it is clear that Japanese multinationals, by replicating to some degree their domestic *keiretsu* structures, have assumed dominant positions in key industrial sectors. Yet even this assessment is subject to change and more recent research suggests that abroad transactions are increasingly occurring outside of traditional *keiretsu* style relationships and are based more on cost (Charoenporn, 2001). RPNs have both contributed to regional economic interdependence (intra-regional trade and investment) and provided a rationale for deeper regional integration. The impact of the transformation of the East Asian political economy on these networks is now considered.

Toyota's regional production network is perhaps the most extensive of Japanese automakers in East Asia. Toyota has 16 manufacturing operations in seven regional countries excluding Japan. However, these production clusters were to a large degree autonomous with limited interaction between them. Toyota's ASEAN network in 1993 is described in Figure 6.2.

Figure 6.3 presents a more abstract representation of Toyota's networks in the region a decade later. The main points to note are the internal and external expansion of Toyota's Southeast Asian production network. Internally, Vietnam is included while production in the Philippines and Indonesia has been rationalized

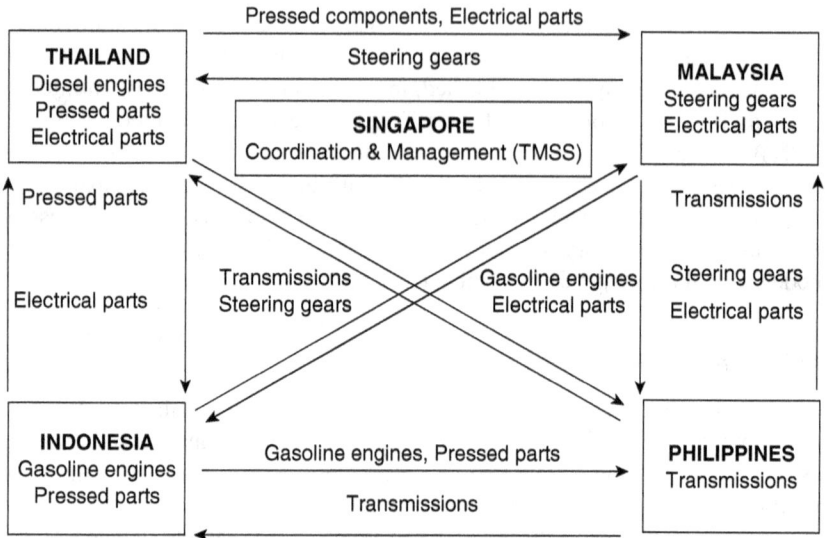

Pressed components, Electrical parts

THAILAND
Diesel engines
Pressed parts
Electrical parts

Steering gears

MALAYSIA
Steering gears
Electrical parts

SINGAPORE
Coordination & Management (TMSS)

Pressed parts

Transmissions

Electrical parts

Transmissions
Steering gears

Gasoline engines
Electrical parts

Steering gears

Electrical parts

INDONESIA
Gasoline engines
Pressed parts

Gasoline engines, Pressed parts

Transmissions

PHILIPPINES
Transmissions

Figure 6.2   Toyota's Asian regional production network, 1993 (Source: Petri 1993: 4)

to lend greater stress on Thailand as the regional hub. Externally, the IMV proj-
ect (Innovative International Multi-purpose Vehicle) links ASEAN, Thailand and
Indonesia in particular, with South America, South Africa and Europe, while the
Philippines exports transmissions to Japan and CBUs to Israel; CKDs from
Australia to ASEAN 4 countries are also noted.

Toyota's production network has developed both qualitatively and quantitatively by exploiting the advantages offered by AFTA and by seeking to position
ASEAN as a key producer, export base and market. In a sense, it is possible to
see Toyota's network as multilayered. The traditional model of regionalized production throughout the ASEAN 4 as described in Figure 6.3 persists and may be
seen as the base layer. A second layer describes the IMV project production network, while a third layer introduces both intra- and extra-regional players, including Vietnam, Australia, Taiwan and Japan, and has the potential to include China.

Rather than rationalizing regional operations around one or two countries,
Honda has in recent years expanded its production base among the four main
ASEAN auto producing countries. As noted above, this move is supported by significant use of the ASEAN Industrial Cooperation Scheme (AICO scheme) to
increase local sourcing and to make regional parts complementation more efficient. Honda believes that this strategy is consistent with the 'global regions'
approach[4] and that it will best utilize local characteristics. Essentially, Honda will
produce in, and export from, those countries where production is most cost effective for a given component or model. In this way, Thailand's more advanced
automotive industry can best support the production of latest models to high
quality and R&D, while Indonesia's skilled labour is able to produce the Stream

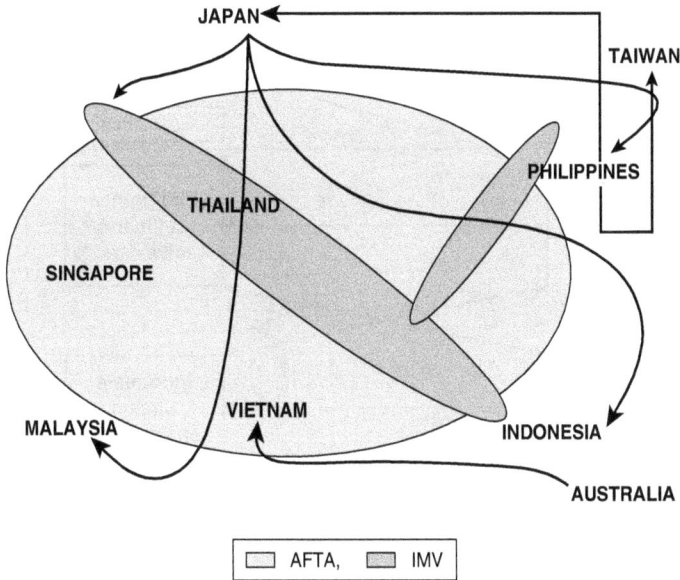

Figure 6.3   Toyota's Asian regional production network, 2004

MPV, the only other production of the model outside of Japan. The Philippines, with its labour cost advantages, has been designated as a hub for component production and export, particularly of transmissions. Additionally, this strategy is based on the global manufacturing system, which allows Honda to rapidly reorganize production on demand. Therefore, by investing in a regional production network in ASEAN (see Figure 6.4), Honda is not only well placed for regional growth but also fluctuations in global demand.

Of the four main Japanese auto assemblers, Mitsubishi had the least number (four) of approved AICO applications as of 2003. In accounting for this low uptake, interviewees cited difficulties in the implementation of the schemes and the implicit requirement to balance trade between participating countries as key issues. Additionally, the BBC scheme was seen as relatively unimportant. MMC did propose one BBC scheme but did not follow through as their ASEAN production network was not large enough to warrant it. Greater use has been made of AICO as illustrated by Figure 6.5 where Thailand's status as a regional hub is further demonstrated.

Establishment of regional management structures

The rising importance of East Asia as both market and production hub is reflected in the trend towards the establishment of regional management structures. Globally, this is not a new trend as operations in Europe and North America have been managed on a regional basis since the early 1990s. Yet regional

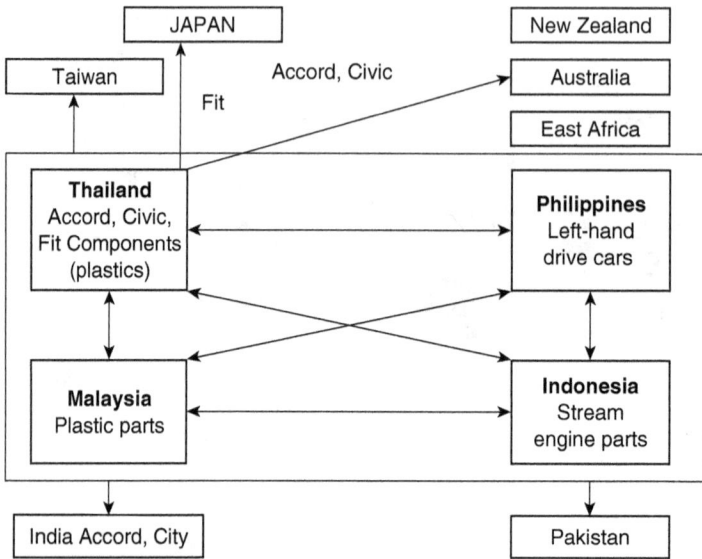

Figure 6.4   Honda's ASEAN production network

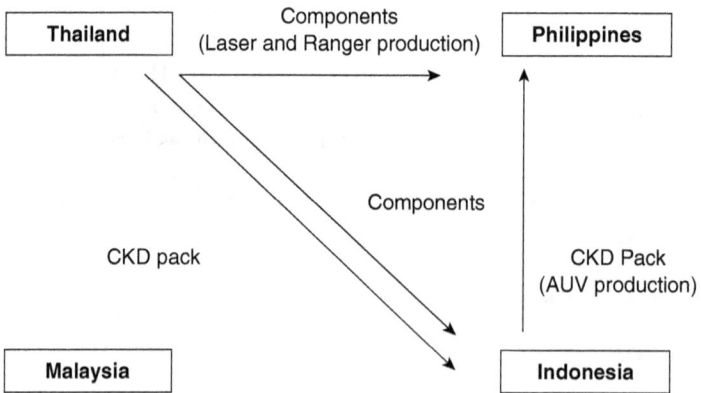

Figure 6.5   Intra-ASEAN production links under AICO

management in East Asia has only emerged in recent years and is still evolving, particularly with reference to China. The management of the three firms surveyed is reviewed below.

Toyota has organized its global operations into seven regions outside Japan: North America, Latin America and Caribbean, Europe, Africa, Middle East and

Southwest Asia, Asia and Oceania. Management in Asia (excluding Japan) was restructured to include China, hitherto a separate entity, in 2001 and is coordinated by Toyota Motor Asia-Pacific (TMAP) which is headquartered in Singapore and 100 per cent owned by TMC. TMAP emerged from Toyota Motor Management Services (TMMS), established in 1990, in recognition of a need for better coordination of activities, parts complementation in particular, in preparation for AFTA implementation. TMMS effectively oversaw production in the ASEAN 4 and thus became a natural entity for the coordination of business activities under AFTA. The key reported objective of TMAP is to manage component procurement to achieve the aim of a 100 per cent localization rate for ASEAN activities. A second objective is to strengthen sale and marketing capabilities and relevant divisions were established in 2001. In contrast to the more straightforward activities of regional management structures in North America and Europe, Toyota's organization in East Asia has emerged from an attempt to deal with the complex nature of the regional division of labour. It is anticipated that AFTA will facilitate smoother regional management.

Management of Honda's global operations has been organized on a regional basis since the 1990s. With the exception of Japan, each region is headed by a holding company wholly owned by HMC. In East Asia, Asian Honda Motor Co., Ltd. was established in 1996 to coordinate ASEAN operations and is based in Thailand, reflecting that country's dominant position as the largest manufacturing centre in Asia outside Japan. Asian Honda also 'supports and oversees the strategic development and operations of all Honda operations in the region' (Honda Annual Report 2003). As such, a key aim of Asian Honda as a management structure is to realize regional efficiencies through parts complementation and this office coordinates AICO applications between the ASEAN 4. Asian Honda coordinates all Honda activities across the three main product lines (automotive, motorcycles and power products). The latest addition to the regional structure was established in China in 2004. Honda Motor (China) Investment Co., Ltd (HMCI) a wholly owned subsidiary, plays a similar role to Asian Honda by coordinating strategy and operations throughout China, in addition to integrating these operations with the global network.

Mitsubishi's presence in East Asia includes vehicle manufacturing and/or assembly operations in China (six), Thailand (two), the Philippines (one) and Vietnam (one). Further parts manufacturing plants are located in Indonesia (one) and the Philippines (one). Vehicle production plants also exist in Malaysia (two) but these have been related to the Proton project from which Mitsubishi withdrew in 2004. East Asian operations are centrally managed by the North Asian and ASEAN offices under Group Headquarters but, in contrast to the North American and European experience, there are no regional holding companies in either location. Management structures at the time of survey were somewhat in flux due to the anticipated Turnaround Plan that was a result of Daimler Chrysler's effective termination of the strategic alliance that has existed between the two companies.

Unlike Mitsubishi, which is experiencing severe difficulties globally if less so in East Asia, both Toyota and Honda have established regional management structures to more effectively coordinate operations. Regional management has also been a key factor in the ongoing localization of production and emergence of regional models to which attention now turns.

Localization of production and models

Local content requirements in the early 1970s led Japanese automakers to encourage existing suppliers to undertake FDI in ASEAN, as local capability, where it existed, did not meet required quality standards. This is of course the point of a local content requirement policy; foreign assemblers enticed by locational advantages require concomitant development of supplier networks and this is where technology transfer can take place leading to the development of indigenous capability. Thailand has moved through perhaps four phases of localization policies: an initial phase from 1971–77, a more aggressive period that prohibited the establishment of new assembly plants and banned the import of CBUs between 1978 and 1986, rapid growth and partial liberalization into the 1990s and finally comprehensive liberalization and the lifting of local content requirements at the turn of the century. It is this latest development that is having considerable impact on the strategies of Japanese automakers.

Even though Toyota has been producing cars in Thailand for 40 years, local content rates are variable. Although exact figures were not available at the time of the interviews, media reports in 2002 indicated a 79 per cent localization rate for pickups, 74 per cent for the Corolla model, 55 per cent for the Soluna and 49 per cent for the Camry (AutoAsia, 2002). These generally compare favourably with Toyota operations in other parts of the world: 79 per cent for Camry in Australia, 80 per cent in the UK (European sourcing) and approximately 60 per cent in North America, although this is model dependent with higher rates achieved for certain models (Toyota 2003). Localization of production has been supported in Toyota's case by its policy of 'Thai-nization' or the localization of management.

Toyota's stated aim is to achieve 100 per cent localization in Thailand and throughout ASEAN, a level that appears achievable given that the localization rate for the Hilux has increased from 60 per cent to 96 per cent since the introduction of the IMV project – see below. Achieving 100 per cent localization within ASEAN under AFTA makes good business sense for Toyota on two fronts: components can be produced (and transported) more cost effectively in low-cost ASEAN countries than in Japan and the need for (expensive and tariff attracting) components sourced from outside the region (Japan) dissipates.

Toyota's regional product development structure is illustrated by Figure 6.6. Central technology will be retained and developed in Japan while research, design and development of products will be informed by local (regional) needs and knowledge. To this end, R&D facilities have been located in the United States (two), France and Belgium, and more recently (2003) linked centres in Thailand and Australia, further underlining the triadic nature of markets and production in the auto industry.

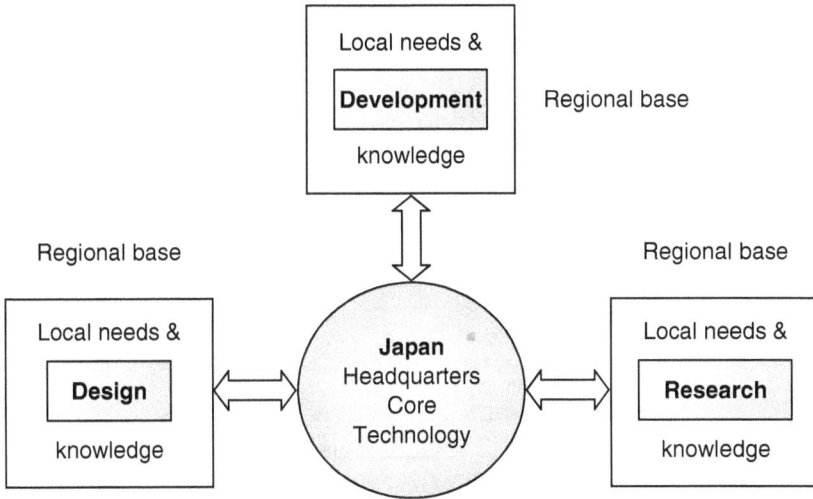

Figure 6.6   Toyota's regional product development strategy

The IMV project

Launched in 2002 and to some extent in response to the Asian financial crisis, the IMV project indicates a significant and strategic development. Mirroring general trends among Japanese automakers over the last three decades, global demand for Toyota models was initially met through domestic production and exports. A second phase (1980s onwards) of overseas expansion and localization followed, though Toyota was a relatively cautious overseas investor at first. This latest phase attempts to move a sizable proportion of Toyota production (500,000 units by 2006, approximately 11 per cent of Toyota's global production at 2002 figures) onto a truly global basis. ASEAN production bases (Thailand and Indonesia) are central to this strategy. Essentially the IMV project aims to 'realize global optimal production and supply networks' (Toyota 2003). In other words, Toyota is seeking to capitalize on the trend towards liberalization, exemplified by AFTA, by rationalizing production capacity to realize scale economies and linking global markets. It was suggested that the IMV project could realize cost savings of up to 30 per cent.

It is noteworthy that the project explicitly aims to link production in developing markets (Thailand, Philippines, South Africa and Argentina) to the 'advanced' market found in Europe. This may be taken as an indication of the advancements made in raising quality in these production centres. Figure 6.7 shows the IMV vehicle supply network. Thailand is the key player within this structure with an annual production capacity of 280,000 units of which 140,000 will be for export

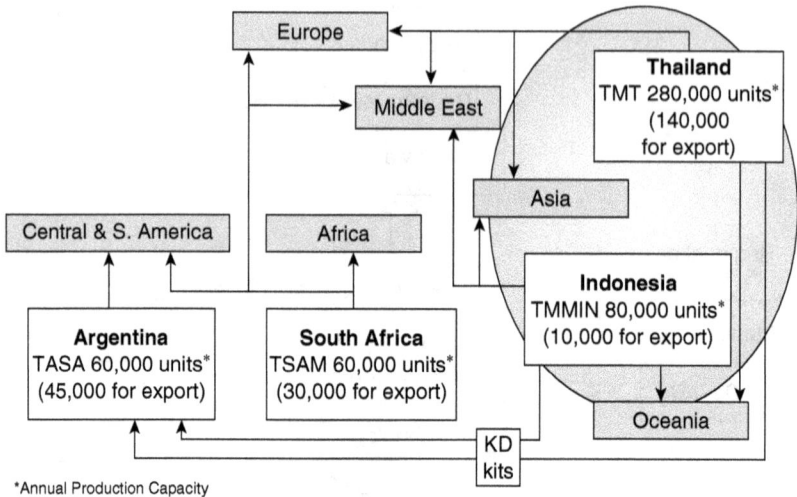

Figure 6.7   The IMV supply network

markets (Table 6.4). Production in Thailand of the first IMV vehicle, the Hilux VIGO pick-up, commenced in 2004 and the country will also produce diesel engines for export to other IMV production bases. The IMV project is to some extent premised on Toyota capitalizing on the low cost nature of production in Thailand and Indonesia.

As mentioned above, auto producing countries in ASEAN have relaxed local content requirements since the crisis in recognition of the 'cost penalties' that these incurred for assemblers. Mitsubishi echoed statements from Toyota regarding the current situation where localization is still the aim but now pursued by use of 'carrots' rather than 'sticks'.

Mitsubishi confirmed that localization of production is important to mitigate exchange rate risks and that they have pursued a policy of sourcing locally where possible. Additionally, the trend towards creating regional products, such as the Kuda, is better facilitated where components are sourced locally to reflect local requirements. However, it was also noted that volume is an important factor, as investment in new models must be justified by sales volume. In short, low potential sales volume equates to no incentive to develop a localized product. Localizing production has been retarded in ASEAN by national requirements but it was suggested that Mitsubishi will be able to increase localization rates regionally under AFTA. That is, a relaxation of local content requirements and virtually tariff-free intra-regional trade for components will allow Mitsubishi to consolidate component production based on competitive advantage. This appears to be happening in Thailand, the Philippines and China (engines). In this way, local content rates for

Table 6.4 IMV production in Southeast Asia

Country	Affiliate	Production vehicle	Start of production	Annual production	Export destination
Thailand	TMT	Pick-up truck (Hilux VIGO)	August 2004	280,000 units (including 140,000 units for export)	Europe, Asia, Oceania, The Middle East
		Sport utility vehicle	2005		
Indonesia	TMMIN	Minivan	September 2004	80,000 units (including 10,000 units for export)	Asia, the Middle East

Source: Toyota promotional material.

Notes: Worldwide IMV production, including in countries other than the above four, is expected to exceed 500,000 units in 2006. TMT: Toyota Motor Thailand Co., Ltd. TMMIN: PT Toyota Motor Manufacturing Indonesia.

certain models, those bound for the regional market in particular, will rise on a regional rather than national basis.

Localization of production and design is an important characteristic of Honda's general strategy and the company promotes the concept of producing locally for local consumers. Along with Toyota, who launched the Soluna in 1997, and Mitsubishi (Dynamic Family Wagon/Freeca), Honda has developed an 'Asian Car' for regional consumption. The City was launched in Thailand in 1996 and was well received by the market due to its price, which was generally 20 per cent less than the Civic. By 2003, the City was exported intra-regionally (Malaysia, Philippines, Indonesia, Taiwan) and to other areas (Middle East). Honda designed the City to be built with a high local content rate (65 per cent plus) and to reflect local conditions; Honda removed the heating system for example. Honda notes that localization of this nature is a valid strategy to reduce component costs and dependence on Japan. The City is also built in China (since 2003) where the local content rate was reported to have reached 80 per cent.

The City is designated to be superseded by the Fit which is already exported to Japan. Localization rates for this model were higher than for the City but no percentage was offered. It was also suggested that national local content is becoming less of an issue than the regional local content rate. Honda's strategy in ASEAN would allow it to raise (regional) local content rates close to 100 per cent in the medium term.

Thailand as a hub

The final trend considered is that of the emergence of Thailand as a regional automotive hub. Space restricts a more comprehensive comparison between the Thai experience and the policies employed by Malaysia but it is important to note that the Thai policy of liberalization and of not pursuing a national car project appears to be hugely successful. All manufacturers have focused investment on developing or expanding operations in Thailand. As noted above, Toyota chose Thailand to host the IMV project, Toyota Motor Thailand's (TMT) Gateway plant is now regarded as Toyota's main passenger car production plant in Southeast Asia and production capacity currently runs to 300,000 units in Thailand, more than in any other East Asian country including China. Thailand is also the first ASEAN country to produce a model completely relocated from Japan, in this case the Hilux. The increasing focus on Thailand as a regional hub and the commencement of the IMV project are largely premised on the implementation of AFTA. Although Toyota is focusing on Thailand in terms of production, it is important to recall that the Thai market is approximately a quarter the size of that observed in China.

Thailand has been the main beneficiary of Toyota's restructuring in Southeast Asia but this has been subject to some negotiation. For instance, Toyota delayed its decision to relocate Hilux production from Japan, the foundation of the IMV project, until Thailand made key (favourable) decisions on tax (the Hilux was to be taxed at a higher 4×4 rate rather than the preferential one-ton pick-up rate) and dismissed the likelihood of an investigation into allegations of transfer pricing by Japanese MNCs. Additionally, Toyota was able to secure certain incentives from the Thai Board of Investment reducing costs by 30 per cent. A number of new investments and further investments (or changes in ownership structures) in existing operations were reported by Toyota. As noted above, Thailand was chosen as the base for Toyota's first overseas R&D centre to be based outside of North America and Europe. The initial investment for this project was announced in 2003 as 2.7 billion Thai baht. Further developments in Thailand include the introduction of new shifts at both Toyota factories to ramp up IMV production and an increase in the number of dealerships from 240 to 310.

Mitsubishi's East Asian strategy (excluding Japan) is based on production in Thailand and China. Operations in ASEAN are being consolidated around Thailand as that region's main production centre and to facilitate this process Mitsubishi reported plans to increase production capacity in Thailand from 126,000 units to 180,000 units by 2005. A stronger focus on Thai operations inevitably suggests the possibility of disinvestment elsewhere in the region and beyond. Symbolic of this greater emphasis on Thailand, the local subsidiary, MMC Sittipol, was renamed Mitsubishi Motors (Thailand) Company Ltd in late 2003; a desire for brand consistency, as Mitsubishi utilizes Thai operations for additional exports, was identified as a further rationale for the name change.

However, when comparing the Southeast Asian and Chinese markets it was emphasized by interviewees that although SEA markets were growing quantitatively (Thai demand alone expected to reach one million units by 2006) and qualitatively (from pick-up trucks to passenger cars and MPVs), China was already a much larger market and growth there would far outstrip even the most optimistic projections for Southeast Asia. It was also suggested that production would be consolidated in China, although the data available at the time of writing and presented here suggests otherwise.

The stated twin-track approach of consolidating production in Thailand and China is further reflected in Mitsubishi's sales strategy for Thailand, which is consistent with the general strategy of bringing new products to market. Mitsubishi Thailand referred to its intention to initiate production and marketing of the Grandis (Space Wagon) in 2004, the first overseas production of the model, and the SUV/sedan crossover Outlander in 2003. Mitsubishi pointed to the introduction of these two models as evidence for a shift in focus away from the one-ton pick-up truck and towards what Mitsubishi hopes will emerge as a new, discerning customer base. Quantitatively, Mitsubishi is aiming to recover sales in Thailand to 40,000 units in fiscal year 2004/5, representing a 10 per cent market share, and to increase exports to 87,000 CBUs and 21,000 CKD kits.

In line with its general strategy of global expansion, Honda has announced or undertaken a number of investments in the region in recent years. These investments represent perhaps the most significant programme of expansion by any automaker in the region and reflect Honda's bullish stance on ASEAN's present importance and future potential. Between 2000 and 2004, Honda announced investments in all four main auto producing ASEAN states, in Vietnam and elsewhere in the region (China). The ASEAN investments are very much premised on regional trade liberalization under AICO and AFTA.

Significant investment in Thailand boosted capacity there from 55,000 units in 2002 to 120,000 in 2004. Although Honda, along with most other producers, had retained excess capacity in the immediate wake of the crisis, market recovery and increasing export sales suggest that this is no longer the case, even with this expansion. Honda's plant in Thailand is one of its biggest and is increasingly geared to export production. A US$169 million investment for the production of a further model on the compact platform for export to Europe was announced in 2004. This investment reflects the underlying strategy of locating 'world car' production for export in Thailand. Additional investments (317 million baht) have recently been made in human resource development (training) and R&D.

Summary and conclusions

This chapter has investigated the extent to which the changing political economy in East Asia has impacted on corporate strategy in the automotive sector. A secondary aim has been to test the validity of the approach adopted in this thesis: locating firm-level analysis in a political economy context. Within East Asia it is clear that Thailand is playing an increasingly central role in the regional strategies of all manufacturers, though for different reasons. Toyota has expanded capacity in Thailand to a point where it is the firm's third largest production centre after Japan and the United States. Mitsubishi has also elected to develop Thailand seemingly at the expense of other ASEAN countries. Honda, on the other hand, is pursuing a regional (ASEAN) strategy to make full use of the AFTA. As such, Honda has been investing considerably in increasing capacity albeit at a relatively small scale. The Asian financial crisis, while having an immediate and negative impact on regional sales, has in fact provided both automakers and host governments with an opportunity to restructure and rationalize. The removal of local content requirements and the accelerated implementation of AFTA have been welcomed by Japanese firms and, although yesterday's dream of the development of indigenous automakers has largely passed (Malaysia excepted), the region is well placed to grow in an increasingly competitive global environment. The emergence of ASEAN as a homogenous market under AFTA has further encouraged firms to reorganize their operations for the medium and long term.

The transformation of the region's political economy has, therefore, been shown to impact on corporate strategy in a number of ways. This conclusion appears to go beyond a straightforward assessment of locational advantages and suggests that it is the regional rather than the national unit of analysis that guides corporate strategy in the automotive sector. The development of regional headquarters and Asian cars, for instance, reflect much more of a regional perspective than a narrowly defined national strategy, although national product preferences persist. As the region develops and income levels rise even these disparities may recede. Therefore, as a methodological consideration, adopting a regional approach to corporate strategy simply reflects the regional orientation of automakers. This complex interaction between regionalization (regional economic integration) and regionalism (regional political integration), between state and non-state actors, and the asymmetries involved describes an increasingly complicated international (regional) division of labour. Accordingly, the Global Production Network (GPN) (Henderson *et al.* 2002; Coe *et al.* 2004) literature and its concern with economic and social dimensions of globalization and global production presents an attractive conceptual framework with which to analyse corporate strategy and international production in the era of bilateral and regional FTAs and suggests an intriguing research agenda.

This chapter has promoted a twin-track approach to the issue of Japanese FDI in East Asia that defines a clear role for the construction of a detailed context (the regional political economy) within which firm-level analysis can proceed. The central rationale for this has been a desire to gain a richer understanding and better grasp of the contemporary reality than that afforded by traditional approaches. Moreover, it has been suggested that the radical transformation of the region's political economy in the post-crisis era *necessitates* such a revised approach. The detailed analysis of the transformation provided in the first section and the subsequent analysis of firm-level data allows the reader to gain a clearer understanding of issues that are central to the decisions taken by firms to invest, produce and trade in the region. This is not to negate, for example, Dunning's Eclectic Paradigm.[5] Indeed, these approaches will continue to generate targeted and empirically sound data to aid our understanding of international production and corporate strategy. But in an increasingly interconnected business environment where strategies fall on a continuum between the global and the regional, failure to recognize the importance of the wider context may compromise any findings.

Notes

1 East Asia refers to the following countries: Brunei Darussalam, Cambodia, China, Democratic People's Republic of Korea (DPRK), Hong Kong (SAR), Indonesia, Japan, Laos, Malaysia, Myanmar, the Philippines, Republic of Korea (ROK), Singapore, Taiwan, Thailand and Vietnam.
2 The Singapore issues relate to investment, competition, government procurement and trade facilitation.
3 Cambodia, Laos, Myanmar and Vietnam.
4 Referring to Honda's strategy since the 1990s of organizing global production within six regions and the desire to locate production close to customers.
5 The Eclectic Paradigm provides a theoretical framework for the analysis of international production by MNCs. In short, the paradigm suggests that international expansion by MNCs may be understood with reference to some combination of ownership, location and internalization factors. See, in particular, Dunning (1988) for a fuller explanation.

References

ASEAN Secretariat (1999) *Joint Statement on East Asia Cooperation*, 28 November. Online. Available at: www.aseansec.org/5301.htm (accessed 24 April 2003).

ASEAN (2004) *ASEAN Statistical Yearbook*. Online. Available at: www.aseansec.org/macroeconomic/yearbook.htm (accessed 20 October 2004).

AutoAsia (2002) *AutoAsia Yearbook,* Singapore: AutoAsia.

Bernard, M. and Ravenhill, J. (1995) 'Beyond Product Cycles and Flying Geese: Regionalization, Hierarchy, and the Industrialization of East Asia', *World Politics,* 47: 171–209.

Bilaterals.org (2007) *Overview of Bilateral Free Trade and Investment Agreements*. Online. Available at: www.bilaterals.org/IMG/pdf/Overview.pdf (accessed 11 March 2007).

Charoenporn, P. (2001) *Automotive Part Procurement System in Thailand: A Comparison of American and Japanese Companies, Bangkok*: Faculty of Economics, Thammasat University.

Coe, N., Hess, M., Yeung, H., Dicken, P. and Henderson, J. (2004) 'Globalizing Regional Development: A Global Production Networks Perspective', *Transactions of the Institute of British Geographers*, 29(4): 468–484.

Dent, C. (2003) 'Networking the Region? The Emergence and Impact of Asia-Pacific Bilateral Free Trade Agreements', *The Pacific Review,* 16(1): 1–28.

Dunning, J.H. (1988) *Explaining International Production*, London: Unwin Hyman.

Freeman, N. and Bartels, F. (2004) *The Future of Foreign Investment in Southeast Asia,* London: Routledge.

Furman, J., and Stiglitz, J. (1998) *Economic Crises: Evidence and Insights from East Asia*. Online. Available at: rrwww.brookings.orgresrmacroeconomics/bpea/1.htm (accessed 2 November 2004).

Gamble, A. and Payne, A. (1996) *Regionalism and World Order,* Basingstoke: Macmillan.

Hatch, W. and Yamamura, K. (1996) *Asia in Japan's Embrace*, Cambridge: Cambridge University Press.

Henderson, J., Dicken, P., Hess, M., Coe, N. and Yeung, H. (2002) 'Global Production Networks and the Analysis of Economic Development', *Review of International Political Economy,* 9(3): 436–464.

Honda (2003) Annual Report, Honda Motor Co., Ltd.

Hook, G.D., Gilson, J., Hughes, C. and Dobson, H. (2001) *Japan's International Relations: Politics, Economics and Security*, London: Routledge.

International Monetary Fund (2004) *Direction of Trade Statistics.* Online. Available at www.imf.org/external/ns/cs.aspx?id=76 (accessed 15 January 2005).

Ito, T. and Krueger, A.O. (2000) *The Role of Foreign Direct Investment in East Asian Economic Development,* Chicago: The University of Chicago Press.

Jomo, K. (2003) Reforming East Asia for Sustainable Development, *Asian Business & Management,* 2(1): 7–38.

Krugman, P. (1999) *The Return of Depression Economics,* New York: Norton.

Noble, G. and Ravenhill, J. (eds) (2000) *The Asian Financial Crisis and the Architecture of Global Finance,* Cambridge: Cambridge University Press.

Pempel, T.J. (1999) *The Politics of the Asian Economic Crisis,* New York: Cornell University Press.

Petri, P. (1993) 'The East Asian Trading Bloc: An Analytical History', in J. Frankel and Miles Kahler (eds) *Regionalism and Rivalry: Japan and the United States in Pacific Asia,* Chicago: University of Chicago Press.

Robison, R., Beeson, M., Jayasuriya, K. and Kim, Hyuk-Rae (1999) *Politics and Markets in the Wake of the Asian Crisis,* London: Routledge.

Scally, A. and Wickramanayake, J. (2004) 'An Examination of the Impact of AFTA on Southeast Asian Foreign Direct Investment', in F. Bartles and N. Freeman (eds) *The Future of Foreign Investment in Southeast Asia,* London: Routledge.

Strange, S. (1993) 'Big Business and the State', in L. Eden and E. Potter (eds) *Multinationals in the Global Political Economy,* Palgrave Macmillan: Basingstoke.

Terada, T. (2004) 'Thorny Progress in the Institutionalization of ASEAN+3: Deficient China–Japan Leadership and the ASEAN Divide for Regional Governance'. Paper presented at *Creating an East Asian Community: Prospects and Challenges for Fresh Regional Cooperation* Conference at National University of Singapore, 8–10 January 2004.

Toyota (2003) *Annual Report,* Toyota Motor Corporation.

Urata, S. (2003*)* 'Regionalisation in East Asia and Japan's FTA Strategy'. Paper presented at PECC Trade Forum, Phuket, Thailand, 25 May 2003.

Weiss, J. and Shanwen, G. (2003) *People's Republic of China's Export Threat to ASEAN: Competition in the US and Japanese Markets,* ADB Institute Discussion Paper No. 2. Online. Available at: www.adbi.org/files/2003.01.02.dp002.prcthreat.competition.pdf (accessed 17 May 2004).

World Trade Organization (2004) *World Trade Report,* Geneva: WTO.

World Trade Organization (2007) *Regional Trade Agreements: Facts and Figure.* Online. Available at: www.wto.org/english/tratop_e/region_e/summary_e.xls (accessed 10 March 2007).

Wu, F., Poa Tiong Siaw, Yeo Han Sia and Puah, Kok Keong (2002) 'Foreign Direct Investments to China and Southeast Asia: Has ASEAN Been Losing Out?', *Economic Survey of Singapore* (Third Quarter): 96–115.

7 The future of monetary regionalism in Asia

A joint currency or limited cooperation?

Heribert Dieter

Introduction

At the beginning of the twenty-first century, the international financial architecture is characterized by continuing change. Perhaps the most profound difference compared with the preceding decade is that dollar hegemony can no longer be taken for granted. The successful introduction of the euro resulted in increasing competition for the dollar, and consequently the world is currently moving to a bipolar monetary arrangement (Bergsten 2005: 4). These changes are a challenge for East Asian and Southeast Asian countries. First, they demonstrate that monetary regionalism and the creation of a single currency is possible in practice, not just in theory. Second, Asia's traditional reliance on the dollar – as an external anchor for exchange rates, a reserve currency as well as the main invoicing currency – has to be evaluated from a new perspective. Is it sensible to tie one's currency to the dollar? Is the accumulation of dollar reserves a wise strategy? In addition, is it useful to continue emphasizing the ties to the dollar when the United States is confronted with an unsustainable balance of payments, the result of which will probably be a severe reduction of imports within the coming decade?

As pointed out in this volume, regional cooperation and integration has several dimensions. In recent years, monetary and financial regionalism has received substantial attention in East Asia. The reasons for the emphasis on this element of economic integration of a region are obvious: After decades of trade-driven rapid growth, the entire region experienced a traumatic shock when the Asian financial crisis hit in 1997. This event continues to be the most important factor for the advancement of regionalism in East Asia. The experience of being both put-up and let-down by Western countries – at least that is the perception of many observers in the region – drives the desire to develop regional safety nets as well as greater independence from Western financial markets in particular.

So what are the characteristics of monetary and financial cooperation in a region? Attention is focused on four goals:

- the facilitation of trade in goods and services by providing stable monetary conditions;
- the development of efficient, well-functioning financial markets;

- the prevention of financial crises;
- and finally the regional management of credit and currency crises.

Although these four goals are primarily economic, there is nevertheless much to be said against purely economic evaluations of monetary regionalism.[1] The process is essentially driven by political motives, and one-dimensional economic evaluations – for instance debating whether Asia satisfies the criteria to be an optimum currency area – do not fully grasp the contexts in which it evolves. As in Europe, a combination of political and economic motives can be observed in Asia. Monetary integration always had and still has a strong political connotation – both in Asia and in Europe. However, the key point driving the search for monetary regionalism is the perception of shared interests by policy makers.

Until today, steps toward monetary integration in Asia have been somewhat limited in scope. After the experience of the Asian crisis, governments have pursued a two-track strategy. The first and most obvious is the build-up of enormous currency reserves. Armed with staggering levels of cash, countries have significantly strengthened their first lines of defence. The second development has been a novel concerted effort to strengthen monetary cooperation in the region. There is the so-called Chiang Mai process, established in 2000 and aiming at creating a regional liquidity reserve. Although this appears to be useful – and mirrors a similar proposal by Giscard d'Estaing and Helmut Schmidt in the late 1970s – the goals of this process remain largely undefined. Is it aiming at providing liquidity in the event of an unexpected credit crunch, i.e. the simultaneous retreat of the majority of international lenders? Or is the stabilization of exchange rates the goal? The latter remains the more ambitious project and this chapter will need to explore which preconditions will have to be satisfied for the process to be a success. Again, political issues are at least as important as economic considerations, and leadership issues have to be resolved *before* further substantial steps can be taken.

However, even in the absence of a consensus on the further evolution of economic integration in general and monetary regionalism in particular, a surprising number of activities have emerged in the region in recent years. Similar to the cooperation of central bankers under the gold standard, which flourished despite reoccurring political tensions, today central bankers in Asia do work together. Again, there was very little, if any, cooperation of that kind prior to the Asian crisis. If central bankers exchanged views, it was in multilateral organizations, such as the Bank for International Settlements (BIS), not in regional ones. The shift to regional dialogue on monetary affairs – resulting in some rather concrete steps – can be observed at four levels:

- the networking of currency swaps under the Chiang Mai agreement;
- the monitoring of short-term capital flows and other surveillance measures;
- initiatives to strengthen the regional bond markets;
- cooperation on exchange rates.

This chapter will evaluate the debate on monetary regionalism as well as analyse the progress made to date. Of course, the discussion by now is so comprehensive that a selection has to be made with regard to the issues addressed. In the next section, emphasis will be on the rationale for monetary and financial cooperation. Why do Asian policy makers consider enhanced cooperation? What are the potential benefits? In addition, the sequencing of integration processes will be discussed. There is considerable debate on the merits of a swift shift to monetary stability. The following section will analyse the Chiang Mai process, one of the more tangible results of Asian monetary cooperation today. Subsequently, monitoring and surveillance as well as the evolution of regional bond markets will be discussed. The continuing rise of China leads to the question whether – given the unresolved leadership issue between China and Japan – we could one day see the emergence of a Greater Chinese Currency Union, comprising China, Hong Kong, Taiwan and perhaps Singapore.

The rationale for monetary regionalism and sequencing

There is virtual unanimity amongst academic and political observers that the Asian crisis of 1997 is the single most influential reason for pursuing more intensified monetary and financial cooperation in Asia.[2] As countries in Southeast and East Asia were receiving identical treatment by international financial markets – regardless of their individual merits or problems – this experience has laid the foundation for intensive monetary and financial cooperation.

Nevertheless, the Asian crisis alone would not have generated sufficient momentum for the current drive towards monetary regionalism. The frustration of Asian policy makers with the slow reform of the international financial architecture is probably equally important (Wang 2004: 940). It is becoming increasingly obvious that Asian elites resent the dominance of Washington in regional and global affairs. Eisuke Sakakibara, an important Japanese government official and former Deputy Finance Minister, sees a parallel between the decline of Britain after 1918 and America's decline today. Whereas the First World War symbolized the end of the British Empire, today's so-called War on Terror indicates the end of Pax Americana. The watershed was the Asian crisis, a position that Sakakibara spells out clearly:

> After the Asian crisis of 1997–98, Asian countries strongly perceived the vulnerability of their region, which does not have any viable regional cooperative scheme. They recognised that there is no global lender of last resort, that international organisations like the IMF and the World Bank were not of much use in preventing or addressing the crisis, and that the United States did not infuse much in the way of resources into Asian countries when the crisis broke.
>
> (Sakakibara 2003: 232f)

Therefore, the Asian crisis was not simply an unexpected and badly managed financial affair. Rather, it fundamentally altered the relationship between Asia and the USA. Governments and elites were reminded that America had a domestic agenda to deal with, and the interests of the American financial sector prevailed over the interests of America's allies in Asia.

However, there is more to monetary regionalism than resentment about past developments. Open capital markets, i.e. the absence of capital controls, have resulted in the need to improve governance structures, either on a national, regional or global level. The lack of effective global governance, including the development of a lender of last resort and the regulation of capital flows, will not disappear quickly. In fact, the main institution dealing with financial affairs, the International Monetary Fund, in 2007 is probably less relevant than at any previous point of its history.[3] National regulation can no longer provide sufficient regulation, but the region – from a theoretical perspective – is much more apt in providing these structures (Sakakibara 2003: 234). Although regional financial governance could be inferior to global financial governance, provided by the IMF in particular, this is not inherently the case. The superiority or inferiority of regional approaches depend on how the instruments of cooperation and the institutions created are structured in practice (de Brouwer 2002: 19). Considering the experience of the last decade, there is little evidence for the assumption that regions are less prepared for financial governance than the IMF.

Eric Giradin stresses the potentially positive contribution of monetary regionalism, when considered as public good:

> The gains from regional financial cooperation essentially stem from reducing regional systemic risk. Regional financial stability has the nature of a public good, in that no country would have an incentive to work toward it if others do not do it, while all benefit from it. Disruptions caused by financial crises, at a regional level, are a major incentive for cooperation. The public good nature of regional financial coordination is due to the fact that financial instability is a potential public bad that spreads across countries.
>
> (Giradin 2004: 334)

When analysing the rationale for monetary regionalism the issue of sequencing has to enjoy a prominent position. The conventional sequence for regional economic integration starts with trade, to be followed by monetary integration at a much later stage. This is the path Europe successfully took, but today the reverse strategy might be sensible. Since barriers to trade are much lower than they used to be in the 1960s and 1970s, the benefits from regional free trade are more limited. Furthermore, financial instability can cause severe damage to economies, and this potentially is an incentive for a different sequencing: finance first, followed by integration of markets for goods and services at a later stage (Dieter 2000; Shin and Wang 2002; Pomfret 2005).

So what would the advantages of monetary integration ahead of trade integration be? Shin and Wang suggest that a monetary union may speed-up intra-regional trade without requiring a free trade agreement or other measures (Shin and Wang 2002: 11). Reducing the costs of hedging against currency volatility – zero in a monetary union but high in the event of substantial exchange rate movements – is an advantage that can be quantified for individual companies as well as for countries. The cost of insuring against volatility can reach 5 per cent of the value of an export item, which is substantial by any standard.

An empirical study by Andrew Rose supports the expectation that a common currency has a dramatic positive effect on bilateral trade. Rose analysed bilateral trade over a 20-year time period in 186 countries. The results are surprisingly positive: other things being equal, a common currency more than triples bilateral trade. However, the samples that support his argument are somewhat atypical: they involved a very small economy that formed a currency union with a much larger neighbour, and that choice of sample distorts the findings (Pomfret 2005: 117). There is, however, no need to argue about the details of the quantitative results. The main finding is that monetary instability in space, i.e. a monetary union or a single currency between countries, is facilitating trade.

However, the lack of connection between trade and monetary integration in the literature makes this endeavour complicated. There are very distinct theoretical approaches. In trade the basic concepts go back to Jacob Viner's seminal book on customs unions, whilst the theory of monetary integration was first developed by Robert Mundell in the early 1960s (see Viner 1950; Mundell 1961). Nevertheless, this artificial separation does not seem sensible: trade flows are influenced by the prevailing monetary conditions, and capital flows are, to a degree, a function of trade.

A sequencing pattern that differed from the traditional trade-based model of integration has been suggested (Dieter 2000). Rather than starting with a free-trade area, followed by a customs union, a common market, an economic and monetary union and finally a political union, I have proposed starting with the pooling of foreign reserves, followed by the creation of a regional exchange rate regime, an economic and monetary union and a political union. Instead of postponing the benefits of monetary integration, this four-stage approach would begin with a monetary policy measure. A formal trade agreement would not be necessary in that scheme, although a differentiation has to be made: regional trade would be facilitated, but there would not be formal agreements, which would have severe negative side-effects, in particular in the case of bilateral preferential agreements.[4]

Yunjong Wang has suggested that regional monetary cooperation does not have to evolve into a regime that could be characterized as deep integration. The three pillars Wang identified – liquidity assistance, monitoring and surveillance and exchange rate stabilization – might not be fully implemented in a region. Some type of shallow financial cooperation, e.g. the pooling of foreign reserves without any exchange rate coordination, might be the maximum level of cooperation that a given group of countries is willing to engage in (Wang 2004: 940). Needless to say that such an approach to monetary regionalism is a low-risk and low-profit strategy: not much sovereignty is lost, not much is gained.

Table 7.1 Progress on the Chiang Mai Initiative (as of 31 August 2004)

Bilateral swap arrangement	Currencies	Conclusion dates	Amount (in US$ billion)
Japan–Korea	US$/Won	4 July 2001	7.0[a]
Japan–Thailand	US$/Baht	30 July 2001	3.0
Japan–Philippines	US$/Peso	27 August 2001	3.0
Japan–Malaysia	US$/Ringgit	5 October 2001	3.5[a]
China–Thailand	US$/Baht	6 December 2001	2.0
Japan–China	Yen/Rmb	28 March 2002	3.0 equivalent
China–Korea	Won/Rmb	24 June 2002	2.0 equivalent
Korea–Thailand	US$/Baht	25 June 2002	1.0
Korea–Malaysia	US$/Ringgit	26 July 2002	1.0
Korea–Philippines	US$/Peso	9 August 2002	1.0
China–Malaysia	US$/Ringgit	9 October 2002	2.0
Japan–Indonesia	US$/Rupiah	17 February 2003	3.0
China–Philippines	Rmb/Peso	29 August 2003	1.0
Japan–Singapore	US$/S$	10 November 2003	1.0
China–Indonesia	US$/Rupiah	30 December 2003	1.0
			Total 34.5

Source: Park and Wang 2005: 95.

Note:
a Amounts include credits agreed under the New Miyazawa initiative.

The Chiang Mai Initiative and the pooling of reserves

As already mentioned, during the Asian crisis the Japanese proposal for an Asian Monetary Fund was confronted with opposition by the United States and the IMF, as well as China, and was not implemented. Only two years after that experience, the leaders of ASEAN responded and invited China, Japan and South Korea to join in efforts to deepen economic and monetary cooperation. The ASEAN+3 Summit in November 1999 released a joint statement that covered a wide range of potential areas for cooperation (Wang 2004: 941). The first major result was presented by the ASEAN+3 finance ministers less than one year later.

In May 2000, the ASEAN swap agreement of August 1977 was reconsidered and strengthened. It was widened to cover all ASEAN members and the amount available was raised from $200 million to $1 billion in May 2001. The second development, also under the umbrella of the Chiang Mai Initiative (CMI), was the development of a full series of bilateral swap and repurchase agreements between the ASEAN+3 countries (Table 7.1). Countries can now swap their local currency for major international currencies for up to six months and for up to twice their committed amount (Pomfret 2005: 114).

The Chiang Mai Initiative was started as a very cautious endeavour. The amounts agreed on are modest compared to the enormous national reserves that central banks in Asia have accumulated.[5] Furthermore, the decision to limit the amounts available under the swap at the discretion of the two countries involved to 10 per cent of the total and to require IMF consent for the remaining 90 per cent has been surprising observers (e.g. Dieter 2001). The explanation for this decision has to be found not in economic rationality, but in diplomatic considerations. The ASEAN+3 countries had no desire to give the US government and the IMF an opportunity for renewed criticism. Functionally, the need for IMF consent does not make sense. It is not plausible to expect the IMF to be any faster or generous with the Chiang Mai funds than with its own loans. Thus, taking the experience of 1997 into account, there is much to be said for the exclusion of the IMF. Therefore, the requirement of the IMF could have been considered as a temporary measure (from the beginning), primarily for diplomatic reasons.

However, the CMI has additional shortcomings. Despite the fact that the CMI has now been operational for seven years, the project remains vague and ambiguous. It does not yet have an operational structure, in particular a monitoring and surveillance mechanism. But more important is that it is still unclear what its ultimate purpose is (Wang 2004: 948). Is the CMI the nucleus of an emerging process of monetary regionalism in Asia? Alternatively, is the goal much more limited, i.e. do the participating countries envisage a joint liquidity program?

Yet there has been some progress in recent years. During the annual meeting of the Asian Development Bank (ADB) in May 2005, the finance ministers decided to transform the bilateral swap arrangements to a multilateral fund. In the event of a crisis, individual decision processes to activate bilateral swaps were replaced by joint decisions patterns (*E&Z*, 46: 227). This is a significant step forward and adds a new spirit of community to the process. In addition, the part of the entire fund that does not require IMF consent was doubled to 20 per cent of the total amount. In 2006 the region's finance ministers decided to double the size of the Chiang Mai fund to $71.5 billion (*New Straits Times*, May 26 2006).

However, the sums that are available under the CMI continue to be small compared to the combined national reserves of Asian countries, which in 2006 exceeded $2,500 billion. Rajan and Siregar have emphasized that the pooling of reserves – accompanied by the reduction of national reserves – would result in a substantial reduction of fiscal costs (Rajan and Siregar 2004: 320). They have suggested a three-tier system of liquidity provision in the event of a financial crisis: First, the country will draw on its own national reserves, which can be used quickly and without consideration of conditionality. The second tier would be the regional liquidity arrangement, which would be subdivided into the country's resources placed with the pool and the other members' reserves. The third tier would be conventional IMF lending (Rajan and Siregar 2004: 320f).[6]

Today, many countries in Asia apparently have not fully embraced the concept of monetary regionalism, despite showing a keen interest in exploring its possibilities. If the countries participating in the CMI were to decide to go ahead and deepen integration, then the CMI could serve as a starting point and could be expanded into a regional liquidity pool, perhaps the first step of monetary regionalism (see Dieter 2000; Dieter/Higgott 2003).

Monitoring and surveillance

The rationale for regional surveillance – as opposed to national or global approaches – is not only based on the desire to integrate further, but also on the assumption that there is a risk of contagion. If there is a risk that a financial crisis in neighbouring countries will probably spread beyond the borders without the fundamentals providing an explanation, then regional surveillance makes sense. The Asian crisis was a powerful catalyst for increasing the understanding for the need of regional monitoring:

> The spread of a financial crisis to many countries can be due to externalities such as the transmission of domestic shocks to foreign countries through trade and financial flows; exposure to common shocks, such as a common external lender withdrawing liquidity, or informational imperfections on regional and international markets (pure contagion).
>
> (Giradin 2004: 345)

Monitoring and surveillance is part of the regional policy dialogue, without which policy formation in a region cannot function properly. Whilst it is true that regional surveillance is no substitute for efficient national banking supervision, the exchange of information nevertheless is essential for the development of regional responses to challenges that affect a number of countries.

It was nowhere more obvious than in Asia. Prior to the crisis of 1997, there was very little – if any – dialogue between finance ministers, central bankers and regulators. Paul Blustein has provided anecdotal evidence that shows the level of cooperation in the middle of the crisis. On 17 October 1997 Lee Kyung Shik, governor of the Korean central bank, was playing golf with his Taiwanese counterpart, Hsu Yuan Dong. Both central bankers kept talking to each other during the game, which was frequently interrupted by incoming phone calls for Hsu. On that very day Taiwan devalued its currency, and the fact that this issue was not debated between the two central bankers sheds a light on the lack of trust that prevailed in regional economic cooperation (Blustein 2002: 123).

There is an emerging consensus in Asia that an independent monitoring and surveillance process is an important element of any deepening of monetary and financial cooperation in the region (Wang 2004: 944). A distinction has to be made: there can be monitoring with agreed sanctions or there can be monitoring without any ex-ante agreed rules. In Asia the former type is difficult to implement in the short term. In Europe, by contrast, there is a well-developed set of institutions for supranational governance. The European Commission, the European Parliament, the European Court of Justice and not to forget the European Central Bank provide the institutional environment for governance above the level of the nation state. Although the European institutions are in continuing competition with the nation states, they nevertheless guarantee that the supranational perspective is not overlooked in any decision. There is no equivalent in Asia, and the lack of powerful supranational institutions has negative consequences for surveillance.

Monitoring and surveillance is of great importance in Asia because financial markets are not yet as developed as they ought to be for successful monetary integration. After the crisis of 1997, Eichengreen and Bayoumi pointed out that underdeveloped financial markets are major obstacles for the further integration of the region:

> The strongest argument against even a limited sacrifice of monetary autonomy is that domestic financial systems are less well developed than in Western Europe. The legacy of financial repression and capital controls continues to limit financial depth ... Currency pegs, whether unilateral or collective, are risky where governments are required to intervene in support of their banking systems.
>
> (Eichengreen and Bayoumi 1999: 364)

This assessment is less convincing in 2007 than it was immediately after the Asian crisis. There has been considerable effort to make national financial markets – and for the time being the regulation of these markets is a matter of national policy – more efficient. Nevertheless, the regional monitoring and surveillance processes that have emerged since the Asian crisis are useful stepping stones for monetary integration because they may create the functional basis for further integration.

Surveillance, however, should not be overestimated. Some institutions, e.g. the IMF, have expressed the expectation that surveillance can be a powerful tool in the prevention of future financial crises. At closer inspection, it cannot. In financial history, there are few examples of successful crisis prevention by efficient surveillance (Dieter 2005: 396). To take two prominent examples: there was no lack of data both during the Asian boom prior to 1997 or in the dotcom bubble before 2000. There simply is no formula that either does not predict too many crises or does not miss the main ones. To the present day, there is no forecasting model that could have predicted the Asian crisis (Frenkel and Menkhoff 2000: 29).

Initiatives for the deepening of regional bond markets

Before the Asian crisis many companies from the region borrowed funds from Western financial institutions, usually denominated in foreign currency. The absence of developed Asian bond markets left enterprises in Asia with little choice. Since 1997 the concept of an Asian bond market to keep the region's savings in Asia and to enable financing without currency risk has enjoyed renewed attention (Tourk 2004: 859). Financial systems that rely entirely on bank financing or foreign financial markets unduly concentrate risk (Stevens 2004: 68).

The development of regional bond markets has important advantages. Highly developed bond markets contribute to the deepening of regional financial markets, which gives borrowers more choice, and simultaneously stabilizes the markets. Rather than having to borrow in London or New York, being able to use the region's savings without either facing exchange rate risk or having to hedge against that risk would represent a major improvement of the region's financial architecture. It should be remembered that the combination of declining exchange rates and the unwillingness of international lenders to roll-over existing debt were the two most important factors in the financial meltdown of 1997.

The initiatives to create regional bond markets as well as strengthen national markets have taken various forms: The Asian Bond Market Initiative (ABMI), proposed by the Japanese Ministry of Finance in 2002, the Asian Bond Fund (ABF) and the initiatives of the Executives' Meeting of East Asia and Pacific Central Banks (EMEAP), which will be discussed in turn.

The ASEAN+3 finance ministers endorsed the creation of an Asian Bond Market Initiative (ABMI) in Manila in August 2003. The ABMI aims at the creation of a suitable environment for the emission of bonds in regional financial markets (Tourk 2004: 862). The ministers agreed not only on principles, but established six work- ing groups, including on standardized debt instruments, the creation of credit rating agencies and the setting-up of guarantee mechanisms (de Brouwer 2005: 7). For the development of improved bond markets, other problematic factors are weak finan- cial institutions and a lack of financial intermediaries such as insurance companies and pension funds, as well as the unwillingness of international ratings agencies to provide credit ratings for Asian companies, many of which are family-owned and unable to provide the data required for financial analysis by independent evaluators. Without an improvement of the conditions for bond emissions, companies in Asia will continue to be reluctant to use these instruments because unsecured corpora- tion bonds will simply be significantly more expensive than bank loans. The Asian Development Bank supports ABMI by issuing bonds denominated in Thai baht and Philippine pesos (*Financial Times* April 15, 2005: 9).

The Asian Bond Fund (ABF) was established in 2003. Nine Asian govern- ments agreed to contribute to this fund, which invests in Asian debt securities. Each country contributes 1 per cent of its foreign reserves to the fund. The par- ticipating countries are China, Japan, Hong Kong, Malaysia, Indonesia, the Philippines, Singapore, South Korea and Thailand (Tourk 2004: 865). Since foreign reserves are very high in the participating countries, the ABF will be a very liquid instrument attracting national and international investors. The ABF initiative underlines the willingness of Asian governments to promote actively the deepening of their financial markets. Rather than waiting for the private sec- tor alone to develop these structures, governments in the region seek to speed-up that process by creating the necessary market environment.

In contrast to the other projects, EMEAP is not a purely Asian venture. Membership is similar to the ABF, with the significant addition of Australia and New Zealand. There can be little doubt that these two economies have well- developed financial markets and that their central banks possess expertise which is very useful in the development of deeper financial markets. In fact, Bowman has argued that the Australian dollar today is as important in Asia as the yen, a development that could be observed after the Asian crisis (Bowman 2005: 84). In the post-crisis period, linkages between the Asian currencies and the Australian dollar have been significantly intensified. Whilst the yen was much more important for Asia prior to 1997, the Australian currency has caught up in all categories that were analysed by Bowman (2005: 96). The inclusion of Australia in the cooperation scheme of central bankers in the region is therefore not only justified by the expertise in financial markets the Australians possess, but also by the importance of the Australian dollar in the region.

Having been set up in 1991 at the behest of the Bank of Japan, EMEAP is one of the older dialogue institutions in the region (Castellano 2000: 1f.). During its first years of existence few concrete steps were taken, but since the turn of the century it has become an important – even if underrated – venue for central bank cooperation in the region. The importance of EMEAP has not escaped the attention of Washington, but the USA are excluded from this scheme today.

The first EMEAP Asian Bond Fund was launched in June 2003 with a capital of $1 billion, to be invested in a basket of *dollar denominated* bonds, which were issued by governments in all EMEAP countries except Japan, Australia and New Zealand, since these three had already well-developed bond markets. The fund was managed by the Bank of International Settlements (BIS) in Basle (Battellino 2004: 13; Tourk 2004: 860; de Brouwer 2005: 8).

The next phase is the Asian Bond Fund 2. This comprises a Pan-Asia Bond Index Fund (PAIF) and a Fund of Bond Funds (FoBF), which consists of investments in eight separate country sub-funds (Battellino 2004: 13). The implementation phase was announced on 12 May 2005. The PAIF is a single bond fund investing in sovereign and quasi-sovereign *local-currency denominated* bonds issued in the eight EMEAP markets, excluding again Australia, Japan and New Zealand. The single-market funds are also investing in local-currency denominated bonds. The EMEAP group has allocated $2 billion for the entire phase 2. The PAIF will be managed by State Street Global Advisors, domiciled in Singapore and initially listed in Hong Kong. The single-market funds will each be managed by a financial institution from the respective country and all nine funds will have the Hong Kong and Shanghai Banking Corporation as their master custodian (*EMEAP Press Statement*, 12 May 2005).

The importance of the EMEAP initiatives is significant. Central bankers from the larger economies of the region have taken active steps to broaden and deepen financial markets in the region. The aim of the initiatives is to reduce dependence on non-Asian financial markets and enable borrowing in domestic currency – both dimensions reducing the vulnerability of the region. If successful, in the long run these efforts will result in reduced risk and better management in Asian financial markets. At the same time, the willingness to exclude the American Federal Reserve underlines the willingness of central bankers to emancipate themselves from the mighty authority of the USA, and this dimension of the EMEAP process is as important as the bond market initiative itself.

However, despite the enthusiasm that has characterized the above-named processes, a note of caution is appropriate. Regional bond markets are not a substitute for the reform of national financial markets. Furthermore, even if the initiatives for the creation of regional bond markets are successful, the deepening of those will take time and further investment in the infrastructure of financial markets (Wang 2004: 947). Although the will to achieve can be observed today, there is no guarantee that this wave of enthusiasm will persist.

Exchange rate cooperation and an Asian currency

After the experience of 1997, when exchange rates of currencies from the region were under serious pressure, policy makers in Asia have been considering measures to stabilize exchange rates. Soon after the crisis, Barry Eichengreen and Tamin Bayoumi analysed the suitability of Asia for a currency area (Eichengreen and Bayoumi 1999).[7] They argue that Asia is as suitable for monetary union or a single currency as Europe:

> We find that the region satisfies the standard optimum currency area criteria for the adoption of a common monetary policy as well as Western Europe. Its small, open economies would benefit from the reduction in uncertainty that would result from the creation of a durable common peg. Intra-Asian trade and investment have reached relatively high levels. Adjustment to shocks is fast, and supply and demand disturbances are small and symmetric by European standards.
>
> (Eichengreen and Bayoumi 1999: 364)[8]

Although the political will for improved monetary arrangements in Asia can be identified, there is uncertainty about the potential shape of such a cooperation scheme. Furthermore, Barry Eichengreen has argued that Asia possesses none of the institutions that characterize integration in Europe. There is no administration implementing integration, no parliament and no regional court of justice. Consequently, Eichengreen takes a sceptical position with regard to the ability and plausibility of creating a monetary union in Asia (Eichengreen 2004a: 2). Whilst he certainly has a valid point, Eichengreen's assessment is both underestimating the (potentially) dynamic process of integration and is simplistic in the analysis of the paths available. As monetary regionalism is not a recipe cast in stone, it can be adopted to region-specific conditions. In Asia, it is true that there is limited willingness to initiate an integration process that imposes substantial limitations on national sovereignty. However, this does not imply that Asian governments are unable to agree on substantial monetary cooperation and a monetary union with fixed exchange rates. Consequently, Eichengreen's list of preconditions for monetary union in Asia is questionable. He states:

> The essence of monetary unification is therefore agreement to establish an international institution to which the participating national governments are prepared to delegate the relevant policy prerogatives.
>
> (Eichengreen 2004: 5)

Whilst the creation of a regional central bank is a precondition for the establishment of a common currency, it is not necessary for a monetary union. One can envisage an integration process that seeks to establish stable exchange rates as the final goal of the process, without aiming for a common currency. Of course, a monetary union, e.g. the establishment of a new (global reserve) currency, is a second-best solution in a number of areas but that second-best evaluation stems from economic, not political analysis. Asia, which includes a number of countries that were colonies of England, the Netherlands or Japan, might be better advised not to aim for goals that are too demanding. Recent European experience is underlining such caution. Whereas European policy elites have advocated further deepening and widening of integration, the negative referenda on the proposed European constitution in France and the Netherlands have shown that it is risky to assume everlasting support for a noble purpose.

It is, however, also true that fixing exchange rates without a common institution requires additional harmonization of economic and fiscal policy. In the Werner Plan of 1970, exchange rates were to remain stable, but economic and fiscal policy would be guided by a regional body. Rather than fixing certain targets for fiscal policy, the Werner Plan envisaged supranational control of national finance ministers. Furthermore, markets for capital and labour were to be integrated quickly (Eichengreen 2000: 204). The plan eventually implemented set a different emphasis: the treaty of Maastricht required the participating economies to observe set targets for fiscal policy.

The role of China in regional monetary cooperation

Apart from the development of region-wide cooperation in monetary and financial affairs, more limited schemes can also be considered. In particular, the continuing rise of China brings to mind the possibility of an integration scheme led by China. In recent years China's successful diplomacy has made such a development more plausible (see Thomas Moore's contribution on China in this volume).

At the beginning of the 1990s China's position in Asia was much worse than today. At that time, it did not enjoy full diplomatic relations with Indonesia, South Korea and even Singapore, whilst the relations with Russia, India and Vietnam were hostile (Shambaugh 2004: 66). In the first decade of the twenty-first century, this has changed dramatically. David Shambaugh has emphasized that China is the fundamental cause of change in Asia, altering the traditional underpinnings of international relations in the region. In contrast to the past, China is seen today as an opportunity and no longer predominantly as a threat:

> Most nations in the region now see China as a good neighbour, a constructive partner, a careful listener, and a nonthreatening regional power. This regional perspective is striking, given that just a few years ago, many of China's neighbours voiced growing concerns about the possibility of China becoming a domineering regional hegemon and powerful regional threat.

> (Shambaugh 2004: 64)

In the last two decades, China has become an economic hub in Asia. Both in trade and production, the countries in the region and elsewhere are increasingly benefiting from intense links with China. Today, nearly 50 per cent of China's trade is intra-regional, and there is no large trade surplus or deficit with any country in the region (Shambaugh 2004: 83). By opening itself to foreign investment and trade, China has not only become an indispensable trading partner, but also of strategic interest to many foreign companies (Zakaria 2005).

Chinese diplomacy has escorted this company-level development by portraying the country as the benign emerging giant in East Asia. Today, as David Shambaugh has put it, China is an exporter of goodwill and consumer durables instead of revolution and weapons (Shambaugh 2004: 65). China is investing in soft power: The efforts to popularize Chinese culture in the region and the attempts to lure future elites into Chinese universities are just two examples of that process. The rise of China's influence has been most significant where America's influence simultaneously declined – in South Korea and in Southeast Asia (Shambaugh 2004: 90). However, there is one area where China has not yet attempted to advance its position in the region and that is finance and monetary cooperation.

This, of course, is no coincidence. The financial sector in China requires comprehensive reform. The presence of capital controls enables the Chinese authorities to postpone reform because Chinese savers cannot export their savings, i.e. capital stays in China. However, if the Chinese government were to successfully reform the financial sector, there would also be room for a greater role for China in financial affairs. Considering the large foreign reserves of Beijing, which can partly be used for consolidating the state-owned banks, China could attempt to establish itself as the monetary and financial heart of the region within a decade.

In 2005 there has been a somewhat unexpected development in the Chinese financial sector. Foreign investors have started to make major investments in Chinese banks. The two largest ones, the Bank of China and the Industrial & Commercial Bank of China, have secured foreign investment of about €5,000 million in August 2005. The Industrial & Commercial Bank has sold a 10 per cent stake to a consortium of Goldman Sachs, American Express and Allianz, whilst the Bank of China has received a similar investment from Singapore's state-owned investment company, Temasek (*The Wall Street Journal*, 31 August 2005, pp. 1 and 8). Together with these two latest deals, foreign banks and other financial intermediaries have already invested around €12,000 million in the Chinese financial sector. The other foreign investors are equally well known: the Bank of America, the Royal Bank of Scotland and Merrill Lynch, as well as HSBC (*The Wall Street Journal*, 31 August 2005, p. 1). These are fundamental changes. Foreign banks are betting that the profit potential in China outweighs the legacy of bad loans and a state-controlled financial sector. By making substantial investments in China, foreign investors can be expected to intervene in the management of these banks – at least over time. With foreign capital and foreign management skills, the Chinese financial sector might be commercially run and be competitive much faster than many observers are expecting today. If this were to happen – and there cannot be any doubt that the risks for this process are formidable – the prospect of China becoming the financial hub in Asia suddenly looks much less futuristic and becomes far more plausible.

With hindsight, the Asian crisis has been a good opportunity for China, and it has exploited it. The decision not to devalue its currency in 1998 was wise and probably stopped the further spread of panic (Dieter and Higgott 1998). China offered aid packages to several Southeast Asian states, whilst the USA initially refused to participate in the bail-out of Thailand. The Chinese approach was appreciated in the region, and it stood in stark contrast to the authoritarian way the IMF and other international creditors imposed their programs (Shambaugh 2004: 68).

Cheung and Yuen have analysed the potential for a Greater Chinese Currency Union, comprising China, Hong Kong and Taiwan. They argue that these three economies have considerable complementary assets. China has low-cost resources and developed production facilities, Taiwan has advanced technological know-how and capital, and Hong Kong offers sophisticated financial services, modern management skills and a well-developed legal system (Cheung and Yuen 2004: 1). The two authors argue that Greater China is suitable for a currency union – from an *economic* point of view. The three economies already have extensive trade and investment linkages. Furthermore, business cycles are relatively synchronized, which would greatly reduce the negative impact of a common monetary policy (Cheung and Yuen 2004: 27).

Of course, suggesting a Chinese push for a prominent role in financial affairs is a highly speculative endeavour and can attract criticism for being unrealistic both with regard to economic *and* political conditions. Nevertheless, excluding such a possibility appears to be premature for a number of reasons. Greater China has all the features necessary: Hong Kong (and possibly Singapore) has the expertise in financial markets, Taiwan has the investment links to mainland China, and China proper has the political will to establish the country as the main regional power. An additional factor to be considered when evaluating the prospects of a Greater Chinese monetary union is that overseas Chinese represent the majority of dynamic entrepreneurs in Southeast Asia (Tourk 2004: 856).

As political friction continues to dominate the relationship between China and Taiwan, for the time being there is only a limited likelihood that such a project would be started in the near future. Nevertheless, in the recent past a softening of policies towards mainland China could be observed in parts of the Taiwanese political elites and, if such rapprochement continues, the likelihood of a Greater China Currency Union would increase rapidly. If that were to happen, it would represent a worst-case scenario for Japan, because Asia's largest economy would become dispensable for monetary integration in Asia – a worrying prospect.

Conclusions

The discussion on monetary and financial integration in Asia has shown a number of merits as well as the substantial technical problems that would have to be overcome. However, the most problematic obstacles continue to exist at the political level. As discussed in the preceding section, China's policies are one dimension to be considered. The other is doubtlessly the Japanese approach to regionalism.

Observers from the region continue to express doubts with regard to the motives of the Japanese government. Very serious are the suspicions raised in the region concerning the motives of Japan, as Wang has expressed them:

> There is also the suspicion that Japan is not interested in free trade and financial arrangements per se in East Asia for purely economic reasons. Instead, Japan is engaged in the discussion of those regional arrangements with other East Asian countries to maintain its leadership role as the region's largest economy by checking and balancing China's expansion. On top of this suspicion, Japan is perceived to be a country insensitive to and unwilling to resolve wartime legacies and disputes on historical and territorial claims. ... These developments combined with its lack of a strategy for East Asian development seem to undermine Japan's ability to pull East Asian countries together for regional cooperation and integration.
>
> (Wang 2004: 951f)

Wang raises a number of serious points. However, there are other issues to be considered. As much as Japan has failed to present a convincing strategy for the economic integration of the region, other players, namely China, have also not permitted such a development. The Chinese opposition to the Japanese proposal of a regional fund in 1997 provides an example. Furthermore, using anti-Japanese sentiment within some Asian countries is distracting attention away from their own atrocities, as well as providing legitimacy to existing regimes.

If Japan is serious about its regional policies, it has to top-up its offers. There is a risk that Japan is drifting towards some kind of isolation. While closely allied with the United States, it does not consider itself as an integral part of its own region, and tries to participate in regional processes without making serious, substantial commitments. Although this picture is a gross oversimplification of the Japanese position, what matters is that the regional policies of Japan might be perceived that way. In some ways the position of Japan is similar to that of the United Kingdom in Europe. There is a strong tendency – in England in particular – to have a very critical perception of European integration.[9]

Beyond that, there are some institutional questions to solve which might appear to be of secondary importance. However, the European experience has demonstrated that this is not the case. Institutions matter in any regional integration process. Without them it can be difficult to sustain the necessary momentum. In the absence of powerful institutions that can provide dynamic inputs into an integration process, these processes are solely dependent on the leadership provided by individual member countries.

In Asia, one issue that has to be solved in that context is the location of an ASEAN+3 secretariat. This is an issue of national pride as much as a functional issue. An ASEAN+3 secretariat will have a prominent function in the integration process and consequently there is considerable rivalry over this issue. De Brouwer has made some insightful proposals in this context (de Brouwer 2005: 20).

Another issue, which has to be addressed, is the name of the endeavour. ASEAN+3 is a temporary name, which does not properly reflect the regional dimension, i.e. there is too much emphasis on Southeast Asia. Considering that the region accomplished the first East Asia Summit in 2005, it seemed appropriate to change the name of the group to the East Asian Community. Again, one might argue that this is a minor issue. Drawing lessons from the European experience, it is clearly not irrelevant. The European Economic Community first dropped the 'Economic' and then changed to 'Union', and both changes symbolized a new phase in integration.

In this chapter, the options for monetary regionalism have been analysed and, where appropriate, the European model considered. Studying the European experience might not be useful when looking at the details. Nevertheless, there is one important lesson: technical details are far less important than political will to jump the hurdles that inevitably emerge in any integration process. Furthermore, the broad political will cannot be tied to precisely planned schedules. Too much rigidity of schedules and plans can backfire and harm the integration process.

The evaluation of monetary integration has to be based on the analysis of the positive and negative consequences of integration. There is no win-win model in monetary integration. Inevitably, countries that participate in monetary integration will lose some options when pursuing others. Creating a single currency causes – as some countries in Europe are currently experiencing – substantial cost. The analysis has to consider carefully the gains and losses of such a process.

The financial crises of the 1990s may have been a sufficiently traumatic learning experience – especially for some of the policy-making elites in weaker states – for the need to shed a little sovereignty to be recognized, in order to preserve wider state building capacity and regional stability. Vulnerability to financial market volatility is now the major challenge to policy autonomy. It may be this sense of vulnerability that is the key to the further development of regional collective action in the monetary sphere.

In conclusion, this analysis confirms the assumption that monetary regionalism in Asia will both be a complex endeavour and will – if at all – only be achieved in the long run. From today's point of view, it appears to be unlikely that Asian governments are willing to give up sovereignty over macroeconomic affairs, let alone push for the creation of an Asian supranational fiscal and monetary authority. At the same time, expecting Asian countries to bet solely on their own, national capabilities and the international financial institutions to support them in the event of crises is most probably a delusion. Asian countries will strengthen their ties, the main question being which shape that cooperation will take.

Notes

1 Monetary regionalism aims to contribute to the stability of currencies and financial markets in a region without the need for formalizing trade links. The terms regional financial cooperation and monetary regionalism can virtually be used synonymously – although

there is a difference: monetary regionalism is a broader approach with a more ambitious agenda.

2   See for example Dieter 2000; de Brouwer 2002; Milner 2003; Ryou and Wang 2003; Kohsaka 2004; Stevenson 2004; Wang 2004.

3   For a discussion of the IMF's future see Dieter 2006a.

4   The negative effects of bilateral trade agreements are now well documented. See, for example, Dieter 2006b.

5   It should be noted that accumulating high reserves has the drawback of high fiscal costs because the country effectively swaps high-yielding domestic assets for lower yielding foreign ones (Rajan and Siregar 2004: 293).

6   Jean Tirole has expressed doubts whether the concepts on which the regional liquidity pool is based make sense. The implicit assumption is that there are phases of illiquidity which can be distinguished from insolvency, the latter category not being a temporary shortage of liquidity, but a permanent one. Tirole argues that there is never illiquidity without the suspicion that insolvency may follow (Tirole 2002: 111). Although this is true, Tirole ignores the possibility that herd-behaviour and the procyclical tendencies of financial markets may turn illiquidity into insolvency without serious fundamental economic problems.

7   For a discussion on optimum currency areas, see Mundell 1961; Kenen 2002c; Ryou and Wang 2003; Pomfret 2005.

8   Ryou and Wang, as well as Ing, have supported the assessment that East Asia is not inferior to Europe in satisfying OCA conditions (Ing 2003: 399; Ryou and Wang 2003: 22).

9   For instance, there is no other EU country in which the main opposition party has suggested leaving the EU and joining NAFTA, as the Tories have in the United Kingdom. Britain has declined to participate in two major integration steps, the Schengen agreement and the Eurozone.

References

Battellino, R. (2004): 'Recent Developments in Asian Bond Markets'. Address to the 17th Australasian Banking and Finance Conference, Sydney, 15 December 2004.

Bergsten, C. Fred (2005): 'The Euro and the World Economy'. Paper presented at the conference *The Eurosystem, the Union and Beyond*, European Central Bank, 27 April 2005.

Blustein, Paul (2003): *The Chastening. Inside the Crisis that Rocked the Global Financial System and Humbled the IMF*. Oxford: Public Affairs.

Bowman, Chakriya (2005): 'Yen Bloc or Koala Bloc? Currency Relationships after the East Asian crisis', *Japan and the World Economy*, (17): 83–96.

Castellano, Marc (2000): 'East Asian Monetary Union: More Than Just Talk?', *Japan Economic Institute Report*, No. 12A (March).

Cheung, Yin-Wong and Yuen, Jude (2004): The Suitability of a Greater China Currency Union, CESIFO working paper No 1192, May 2004. Online Available at:www.cesifo-group.de/pls/guestci/download/CESifo%20Working%20Papers%202004/CESifo%20Working%20Papers%20May%202004/cesifo1_wp1192.pdf.

De Brouwer, Gordon (2002): 'The IMF and East Asia: A Changing Regional Financial Architecture', *Pacific Economic Papers*, No. 324.

De Brouwer, Gordon (2005): Monetary and Financial Integration in Asia: Empirical Evidence and Issues, Mimeo, March.

Dieter, Heribert (2000): 'Monetary Regionalism: Regional Integration without Financial Crises', Warwick: University of Warwick, Centre for the Study of Globalisation and Regionalisation (CSGR), Working Paper 52/00.

Dieter, Heribert (2001): 'East Asia's Puzzling Regionalism', *Far Eastern Economic Review*, 12 July 2001, p. 29.

Dieter, Heribert (2005): *Die Zukunft der Globalisierung. Zwischen Krise und Neugestaltung.* Baden-Baden: Nomos-Verlagsgesellschaft.

Dieter, Heribert (2006a): 'The Decline of the IMF', *Global Governance*, 12 (4): 343–349.

Dieter, Heribert (2006b): 'The Limited Utility of Bilateral Free Trade Agreements', *Journal of Australian Political Economy*, (58): 94–113.

Dieter, Heribert and Higgott, Richard (1998): 'Verlierer Japan, Gewinner China? Außenpolitische Konsequenzen der Asienkrise', *Internationale Politik*, 53 (10): 45–52.

Dieter, Heribert and Higgott, Richard (2003): 'Exploring Alternative Theories of Economic Regionalism: From Trade to Finance in Asian Co-operation?', *Review of International Political Economy*, 10(3): 430–455.

Eichengreen, Barry (2000): 'Vom Goldstandard zum Euro. Die Geschichte des internationalen Währungssystems', Berlin: Wagenbach.

Eichengreen, Barry (2004): 'Real and Pseudo Preconditions for an Asian Monetary Union'. Paper presented at the Asian Development Bank Conference on Asia's Economic Integration, Manila, 1–2 July 2004.

Eichengreen, Barry and Bayoumi, Tamin (1999): Is Asia an Optimum Currency Area? Can It Become One? Regional, Global and Historical Perspectives on Asian Monetary Relations', in: Stefan Collignon, Jean Pisani-Ferry, and Yung Chul Park (eds): *Exchange Rate Policies in Emerging Asian Countries.* London: Routledge, pp. 347–366.

Frenkel, Michael and Menkhoff, Lukas (2000): *Stabile Weltfinanzen? Die Debatte um eine neue internationale Finanzarchitektur.* Berlin: Springer Verlag.

Giradin, Eric (2004): 'Methods of Information Exchange and Surveillance for Regional Financial Co-operation', in: Asian Development Bank (ed.): *Monetary and Financial Integration in East Asia* (Vol. 2). Basingstoke: Palgrave MacMillan, pp. 331–363.

Ing, Joanne Tan Nuo (2003): 'The Possibility of an Asian Monetary Union Drawing from the EMU Experience', *Asia Europe Journal*, 1(1): 381–401.

Kenen, Peter B. (2002): 'What We Can Learn from the Theory of Optimum Currency Areas', in: HM Treasury, Submissions on EMU from leading academics, December, www.princeton.edu/~pbkenen/03UKTreasuryEMU.pdf.

Kohsaka, Akira (2004): 'A Fundamental Scope for Regional Financial Cooperation in East Asia', *Journal of Asian Economics*, (15): 911–937.

Milner, Anthony (2003): 'Asia-Pacific Perceptions of the Financial Crisis: Lessons and Affirmations', *Contemporary Southeast Asia*, 25(2): 284–305.

Mundell, Robert A. (1961): 'A Theory of Optimum Currency Areas', *American Economic Review*, 51 (1961): 657–665.

Park, Yung Chul and Wang, Yungjong (2005): 'The China Mai Initiative and Beyond', *The World Economy*, 28(1): 91–101.

Pomfret, Richard (2005): 'Sequencing Trade and Monetary Integration: Issues and Application to Asia', *Journal of Asian Economics*, (16): 105–124.

Rajan, Ramkishen and Siregar, Reza (2004): 'Centralized reserve pooling for the ASEAN+3 countries', in: Asian Development Bank (ed.): *Monetary and Financial Integration in East Asia* (Vol. 2). Basingstoke: Palgrave MacMillan, pp. 285–329.

Ryou, Jai-Won and Wang, Yunjong (2003): 'Monetary Cooperation in Asia: Major Issues and Future Prospects'. Paper presented at the bi-monthly workshop organized by the Study Forum on Monetary Cooperation in East Asia, 13 June 2003. Online Available at: www.cgu.edu/include/SPE_Ryou2004.pdf.

Sakakibara, Eisuke (2003): 'Asian Cooperation and the End of Pax Americana', in: Jan Jost Teunissen and Mark Teunissen (eds): *Financial Stability and Growth in Emerging Eocnomies. The Role of the Financial Sector.* The Hague: Fondad, pp. 227–244.

Shambaugh, David (2004): 'China Engages Asia', *International Security*, 29(3): 64–99.

Shin, Kwanho and Wang, Yunjong (2002): 'Monetary Integration Ahead of Trade Integration in East Asia?'. Paper presented at the conference *Linkages in East Asia: Implications for Currency Regimes and Policy Dialogue*, 23–24 September 2002, Seoul. Online. Available at: http://econ.korea.ac.kr/prof/shin/siles/sequemce.pdf.

Stevens, G.R. (2004): 'Regional Financial Arrangements: Recent Developments', *Reserve Bank of Australia Bulletin*, (May): 68–70.

Stevenson, Adlai E. (2004): 'Regional Financial Cooperation in Asia', *Journal of Asian Economics*, (15): 837–841.

Tirole, Jean (2002): *Financial Crises, Liquidity and the International Monetary System*, Princeton NJ: Princeton University Press.

Tourk, Khairy (2004): 'The Political Economy of East Asian Economic Integration', *Journal of Asian Economics*, (15): 843–888.

Viner, Jakob (1950): *The Customs Union Issue*. London: Stevens & Sons.

Wang, Yunjong (2004): 'Financial Cooperation and Integration in East Asia', *Journal of Asian Economics*, (15): 939–955.

Zakaria, Feareed (2005): 'Does the Future Belong to China?', Newsweek, 9 May 2005. Online. Available at: www.msnbc.msn.com/id/7693580/site/newsweek.

Part III
Regionalism and security

8 Trade and security in East Asia

Political (non-?) integration in an insecure region

Douglas Webber

Introduction

In January 2005, China overtook the United States to become Japan's biggest trading partner. In April 2005, with the evident connivance of the government (in a country where free political expression is tightly circumscribed), thousands of Chinese citizens took to the streets in some of the country's biggest cities to oppose Japan's claim to become a permanent member of the UN Security Council and to protest against the way in which Japan's Pacific War record was portrayed in a newly approved school history textbook. The confluence of these two events inspired this chapter.[1] Their occurrence, so close to each other, illustrates a striking trait of contemporary East Asia: while the countries in East Asia are rapidly becoming more and more economically interdependent, international politics in the region are volatile. Judgements as to exactly how volatile they are vary and there are in any case wide variations in the degree of their volatility within the region. But most observers of the region's politics would likely agree that, overall, political relations between East Asian states have not improved commensurately with the intensification of their economic ties and a significant number would not regard wars in East Asia as inconceivable.

For analysts of regional integration, the co-existence of a process of growing economic interdependence and continuing regional political volatility or instability raises two interesting puzzles, the one more theoretical, the other more empirical. The first, one of the issues that is at the heart of the disputes between international relations 'liberals' and 'realists', concerns the nature of the relationship between international economic and international political relations. The second is to what extent continuing political frictions and conflicts in the region, regardless of growing economic interdependence, may prevent closer regional political integration or even undermine that (modest) level of integration that has already been achieved, notably within the ASEAN+3 (APT) process.

While a voluminous literature is available on the regional integration of broadly economic (in particular trade and monetary) policies – in East Asia as well as elsewhere – and articles and books on security issues in East Asia abound, regional integration scholars in political science have not devoted a lot of attention to analysing the relationship between political integration and security. This is surprising, at least if one can safely make the assumption that, other things being equal, a country is less likely to be willing to link its fate inextricably with another, the more it fears that (with or without such integration) the other country threatens its own security. This chapter represents a preliminary attempt to explore this hitherto relatively uncharted terrain in the analysis of regional integration politics. The following section provides an overview of the current state of regional political integration in East Asia and the scholarly debate over its prospective future. The third section examines the relationship between political integration and security in post-Second World War Western Europe, as the world's hitherto politically most highly integrated region, to assess in particular whether political integration preceded or succeeded the resolution of politico-security conflicts among the states involved in the integration process. Two subsequent sections sketch the relationship between regional cooperation/integration and security in East Asia during and after the Cold War. In the conclusion, I return to the issue of whether, in the absence of 'improved' politico-security relations in East Asia, there is likely to be much progress towards closer political integration in the region.

Political integration in East Asia: The current situation and future prognoses

One could long have said of modern East Asia what Bismarck once said disparagingly of Europe, namely that it is no more than a 'geographical' concept. In general, political cooperation, let alone integration, between the states within the region was extremely limited.[2] The Cold War created similar divisions in East Asia as it did in Europe, although as the Sino-Soviet conflict developed, the Communist 'bloc' in East Asia itself split increasingly between allies of China and the Soviet Union respectively. Among the non-Communist states, political cooperation was confined to Southeast Asia, where ASEAN was founded in 1967, but with member states whose governments were extremely jealous of their policy-making prerogatives and certainly did not want to create a strong regional organization. In Northeast Asia, relations between the non-Communist states Japan and South Korea remained particularly 'under-institutionalized'. The construction of East Asia as a *political* region is a process that has really gathered momentum during the last decade, specifically since the 1997–98 Asian financial crisis, which played a catalytic role in convincing governments in South- and Northeast Asia of the extent of their countries' economic interdependence. Although tangible evidence of political integration is still limited, comprising in particular the Chiang Mai currency swap initiative, there has certainly been a significant increase in the level or volume of multilateral exchange or talks between East Asian governments and numerous ambitious collective projects have been adopted and are being negotiated, some relating to ASEAN alone, others to ASEAN's relations with Northeast Asia, most notably a free trade area linking ASEAN and China. In December 2005, Malaysia hosted an inaugural East Asia Summit, in which not only the APT states, but also the Indian, Australian and New Zealand heads of government participated. A second summit took place in the Philippines in January 2007. However, both meetings were very short and, apart from an agreement to commission a feasibility study on an East Asian free trade zone, produced no significant decisions.

Among scholars, opinions as to the likely future evolution of East Asian integration diverge considerably. Stubbs (2002), Cai (2003), Dieter and Higgott (2003), Terada (2003), Hamilton Hart (2005) and Pempel (2005) are all basically optimistic that the APT process will flourish and political integration will gather momentum. Stubbs, for example, identifies several variables, including 'common recent historical experiences and cultural traits', 'similar distinctive economic institutions and approaches to economic development', growing intra-regional trade and a growing sense of 'common purpose and identity' fostered by regular meetings of political leaders and government officials, that favour closer integration. Cai foresees an 'institutionalized East Asia' eventually becoming a 'third unified pole in the global economy' (2003: 401). Dieter and Higgott observe the growth especially of 'monetary regionalism' in East Asia following the 1997–98 financial crisis. Pempel (2005: 2–3) observes that East Asia has in recent years become 'considerably more interdependent, connected and cohesive' and that the region is 'ripe for cooperation' rather than rivalry, as in Friedberg's influential judgement (1993/94).

Most 'optimistic' analyses of East Asian integration emphasize growing economic interdependence and heightened, crisis-induced perceptions of common vulnerability and economic interest, both factors favourable to formation of a collective regional identity, as driving forces of this process. East Asian integration 'sceptics' typically acknowledge that economic forces are conducive to closer regional cooperation, but see countervailing obstacles in the form of competition for regional leadership between Japan and China, high levels of political, economic and/or cultural heterogeneity among East Asian countries, actual or purported American opposition to such cooperation, and fundamental strategic divergences. The present author (Webber 2001) was rather pessimistic in his first assessment of the prospective future of East Asian integration, while Ravenhill (2002) and Hund (2003) are much more unequivocally sceptical as to East Asia's integration potential. Webber concluded that 'overall ... the odds are against APT developing into a strong regional organization' (2001: 366). While not contesting that the APT 'dynamic' has had an impact on the political and economic landscape of East Asia, Hund (2003: 411) argues that the 'evolution of an exclusive East Asian identity seems to be a long way off'. For his part, Ravenhill (2002: 190) judges that to expect the formation of an East Asian 'bloc' comparable to the EU and NAFTA would be 'to confuse hyperbole with reality, a proliferation of meetings with institutionalization, and proposals with binding policy frameworks'.

Trade and security in regional political integration: Theories and (West) European practice

It would be an exaggeration to say that there is no common ground at all between these two 'camps' of East Asian integration scholarship. Both would agree that regional cooperation in East Asia is accelerating primarily in the domains of trade and financial crisis management policy and that progress in other domains, notably security or defence, is much less visible. Adherents of both camps would likely subscribe to Lipson's game-theoretic explanation of the greater scarcity of security compared with trade or economic cooperation, that security cooperation is rarer and weaker because on security issues the potential costs to a country that attempts to cooperate without reciprocation and the potential risks of inadequate monitoring of other countries' decisions and actions are higher (Lipson 1993: 72–73). East Asian integration 'optimists' and 'sceptics' also concur to a very large extent in terms of the variables that they identify as being conducive or hostile to closer integration in the region. They diverge, however, on the relative weight that they assign to these variables in determining the future path of international relations in the region. Basically, for the 'optimists', economics trumps politics, while for the 'sceptics', it is the other way round – politics trumps economics. Whereas for the 'optimists' growing economic interdependence gives East Asian states an ever greater reciprocal interest in stable and peaceful intraregional relations, making dangerous conflicts between them ever more unlikely, the 'sceptics' are much more guarded. They are not so gloomy as to suggest that major military conflicts are probable in East Asia, but they imply that contradictory trends of ever closer economic interdependence and growing political antagonisms can co-exist for indeterminate periods of time in intra-regional relations and that the fabric of regional cooperation and integration that has developed in recent times is reversible.

These opposed prognoses as to the likely evolution of East Asian integration of course reflect different theoretical stances. In terms of international relations theory, the 'optimists' are for the most part either 'commercial' or 'economic' liberals, for whom growing volumes of cross-border economic exchange grind down pre-existing interstate tensions and rivalries and produce increasingly common interests in the maintenance of international commerce and peace, or constructivists, for whom the burgeoning process of integration is the contingent outcome of a critical historical event or 'juncture', which has transformed collective identities and perceptions of interests in the region. The 'sceptics', for their part, are more akin to international relations realists, in as far as they attribute a critical role to (actual or perceived) distributions of power and fundamental security interests, perceptions of which are taken to be relatively stable and resistant to changing patterns of cross-border exchange. Or they may alternatively or also be at least implicit constructivists, who, however, attribute a more critical role in the formation of identities within the region to divisive historical legacies (above all the Japanese conquest and occupation of China from 1931/37 to 1945) than to 'uniting' recent ones, such as the Asian financial crisis.

The analysis of the historical experience of post-Second World War Western Europe, as the region which in the last half-century has developed the highest levels of political integration, may shed some light on the reciprocal relationship of intra-regional trade and security. To which of the two 'camps' on the future of East Asian integration does the Western European 'case' give greater credence? One reading of the history of European integration may be that, through a process of integration of trade and later of other aspects of especially economic policy, states that felt extremely insecure vis-à-vis each other gradually became economically so interdependent and developed relations of such mutual trust that they could no longer rationally fight or indeed wanted to fight each other. Extrapolated and applied to East Asia, this logic would lead one to predict that political integration would advance smoothly in step with growing economic interdependence, starting in the trade/monetary sphere and gradually extending into other policy areas. With a time lag, what happened in Western Europe after the Second World War would replicate itself in East Asia.

Such a reading of the history of European integration would, however, be erroneous. It is correct, of course, that the states that launched the integration process looked back on a long history of antagonistic relations, culminating in the two world wars that originated in conflicts between Germany and its neighbours. But several traits of international relations in Europe in the 1950s distinguished this period from earlier ones and created conditions in which the states involved in the integration process no longer viewed each other as fundamental mutual security threats. The reasons for this transformation of mutual security perceptions among the EU's founding states were threefold. First, with the extension of the Communist bloc into the heart of Europe after the Second World War and the outbreak of the Cold War from 1948 onwards, these states saw the principal threat to their security as no longer coming from each other (for the others, from Germany) but rather from the Soviet Union. Second, the country which had posed the most acute threat to security in Western Europe in the recent past, namely Germany, was divided and West Germany was occupied by the Western allied powers, without either a fully sovereign government or an army. And third, the security of the other member states – not only vis-à-vis the Soviet Union, but also against Germany – was guaranteed by the creation of the North Atlantic Treaty Organization (NATO) in 1949 and the American military presence in Western Europe for which the NATO provided. It is notable in this regard that the Western Europeans themselves, led by Britain and France, wanted the United States to guarantee their security through a formal military alliance and military presence in Western Europe (Herbst 1989: 52–57; Loth 1990: 68; Knipping 2004: 55).

It is doubtful whether, in the absence of the above conditions, the states that launched the integration process would have felt sufficiently secure vis-à-vis Germany to seriously envisage pooling sovereignty with it in a common regional organization. This supposition is supported by the fact that the project to create a European Defence Community in the early 1950s was defeated by a majority of French MPs, especially Gaullists and Communists, who feared that Germany would come to dominate a future common European army (Dedman 1996: 74–82). In fact, the road to the Treaty of Rome in 1957 was cleared only after Germany was incorporated into NATO through the Paris treaties and the other principal security-related issue dividing France and Germany, the status of the Saarland, was resolved in bilateral negotiations in 1955 (Spaak 1969: 283–285; Küsters 1982: 45–48, 91–95, 324–325; Herbst 1989: 179–180). Thus, European integration did not resolve the fundamental security-related issues that separated

Germany from its West European neighbours, above all France, but rather it was the resolution of these issues by other means that made closer political integration possible. The North Atlantio Treaty Organization, American military engagement in Western Europe, the division of Germany and the prior resolution of outstanding security conflicts with France were probably necessary, though not sufficient, conditions of European integration. Significantly, when German reunification became an issue in 1989–90, other EU members insisted very strongly then too that the newly united Germany remain a NATO member.

Security and political integration in Cold War East Asia

Non-Communist East Asia experienced little of the multilateral security cooperation and political integration that developed in Western Europe during the Cold War, albeit both regions were in the front-line of the confrontation between the two blocs. The only regional organization that emerged among the non-Communist states was the ASEAN (Association of Southeast Asian Nations), whose membership was limited, of course, to Southeast Asia. Although security issues – namely conflict-prevention within their own ranks – were uppermost in the minds of the political leaders who launched ASEAN, they consciously avoided granting it any conventional security (i.e. military) functions or for that matter any other powers that would have circumscribed the freedom of action of member governments.[3] Tentative steps towards the integration of trade policy among the ASEAN states had to await the end of the Cold War, as the organization searched for a new raison d'être, the GATT Uruguay Round was in difficulties, other regions, such as Europe and North America, were starting to integrate more closely, and Southeast Asia was confronted with the challenge of a rising China. The Southeast Asian Treaty Organization (SEATO) was founded as a non-Communist military alliance in 1954, but it contained only two 'core' regional states, namely Thailand and the Philippines, alongside the United States, the UK, Australia and New Zealand, never aspired towards the same degree of coordination of defence policy as NATO and was practically moribund well before it was formally wound up in 1977 (Duffield 2001: 73–74; Hemmer and Katzenstein 2002: 578). For multilateral security cooperation and political integration, non-Communist *North*east Asia (Japan, South Korea, Taiwan) was an even more barren terrain, in which no multilateral organization of any kind saw the light of day. Instead, security cooperation in non-Communist East Asia was organized bilaterally between the United States and various of its regional allies, first and foremost Japan. The only strictly multilateral military alliance linking non-Communist states in the Asia-Pacific (as opposed to East Asia) was the ANZUS, comprising Australia and New Zealand as well as the United States.

One explanation of the absence or relative weakness of multilateral security cooperation among non-Communist East Asian states attributes this phenomenon to a longstanding American preference for dealing bilaterally with its Asian allies. Much more powerful vis-à-vis its East Asian than its West European allies, the United States could therefore more easily achieve its goal of not creating any (multilateral) institutions that 'would have constrained independent decision-making in Washington' (Katzenstein 1996: 141–142). Hemmer and Katzenstein (2002: 575, 588ff.) also emphasize that, whereas US foreign policy makers saw their European allies as 'relatively equal members of a shared community', they viewed their Asian ones rather as part of an 'alien and, in important ways, inferior community'. Other analyses of the history of security and political cooperation in non-Communist East Asia do not agree that the United States was hostile per se to security multilateralism in East Asia and emphasize the role of other variables in explaining the absence of multilateral security cooperation. Pointing to the greater power disparities between non-Communist East Asian compared with West European states, they argue that the United States would like to have assembled the non-Communist East Asian states into multilateral organizations of economic and/or security cooperation, but that the smaller of these states resisted these endeavours because they feared falling – once again – under Japanese domination (Grieco 1998: 250–251; Duffield 2001: 78, 80–81). Another notes that, for different reasons, both Japan and Britain, still a colonial power in the region in the early Cold War period, also opposed a multilateral security organization such as the United States envisaged (Calder and Ye 2004: 206–207). Duffield (2001: 78–79) also highlights the significance of the comparative political geography of East Asia and Europe. First, Germany could more easily threaten the security of its non-Communist neighbours, with many of which it had common land borders, than could Japan that of other non-Communist East Asian states, which could expect the US Navy to protect them from possible Japanese aggression. Second, for similar, geographic reasons, (West) Germany, which bordered on the Soviet bloc, was much harder to defend against Communist attack than the island Japan so that its defence, as the industrial heartland of non-Communist Europe, required a more comprehensive, collective effort than did Japan's.

If there is much disagreement among scholars as to the *causes* of the relative absence or weakness of political and security cooperation in non-Communist East Asia during the Cold War, there is greater consensus over its *consequences.* Political relations between Japan and the other non-Communist Northeast Asian states, especially South Korea, and between these states, especially Japan, and the non-Communist Southeast Asian states continued to be distant and characterized by distrust and suspicion. Japanese foreign policy after the Second World War was low-key and 'reactive' (Calder 1988). Japan did not take the initiative in forging closer interstate cooperation until it joined forces with Australia to promote APEC (interestingly, a pan-Pacific rather than East Asian grouping of states) in the late 1980s. Attitudes of distrust and suspicion towards Japan in East Asia – shaped by Japanese aggression during the Pacific War and prior to that in Korea and China – were reinforced by the way in which Japanese political leaders dealt or did not deal with this legacy, a pattern of behaviour that may have its roots in the American occupation authorities' decision not to try Emperor Hirohito for war crimes after the war (Dower 1999; Bix 2000). Aided arguably by ASEAN, relations between the non-Communist states in *South*east Asia, by contrast, were characterized by growing mutual trust. An important contributory factor to this trend was the discreet leadership role played in the organization by the biggest Southeast Asian state, Indonesia (Anwar 2005). More importantly, however, the very foundation of ASEAN in the first place would not have been possible without the major change in mutual security perceptions among the non-Communist states that followed the regime change and foreign policy reorientation that occurred in Indonesia in 1965–66. As in Western Europe so too in Southeast Asia, regional integration or cooperation first became possible when the integrating or cooperating states no longer felt seriously threatened by each other but rather by a common other state or bloc.

Security and political integration in post-Cold War East Asia

The Cold War in East Asia did not end as abruptly or as completely as in Europe. The transition towards a market economy and integration into the global trading system had begun in China already in the late 1970s. The region still has several Communist one-party states, China included. But the ideological divisions that characterized the Cold War have faded enormously. In East Asia as well as in Europe, this process has facilitated growing economic and political exchange across the frontiers of the old Cold War blocs (thereby underlining the point that mutual security threat perceptions have an important impact on regional cooperation/integration) (cf. Mansfield and Milner 1999: 601). China in particular has been the engine of growing interstate cooperation in the region over the last decade, emerging from a position of relative diplomatic isolation to become a central player on the regional political stage and a key member of numerous (formal or informal) multilateral regional organizations (see especially Shambaugh 2004–05: 64–66). Alongside its participation in the Chiang Mai currency swap initiative, the prime example of China's support for closer regional cooperation is the ASEAN–China Free Trade Area project, initiated by China, accepted by the ASEAN member states, currently under negotiation, and intended to be implemented by 2010. But there is a significant list of other multi- or bilateral initiatives involving China, apart from its participation in the APT process, that testify to its promotion of closer regional cooperation: its accession to ASEAN's Treaty of Amity and Cooperation (TAC), committing it to the peaceful resolution of disputes within the region (2002), the negotiation by China and ASEAN of a 'code of conduct' relating to competing claims of sovereignty over the Spratly Islands (also 2002) and its negotiation of 'strategic partnerships' not only with ASEAN as such (2003), but also with the Philippines, Indonesia (and India, 2005). Given Sino-Japanese competition, China's efforts to promote closer cooperation with the ASEAN states have provoked Japan into offering the ASEAN states a 'Closer Economic Partnership', which is also currently being negotiated and should be implemented by 2012. ASEAN has also launched free trade area negotiations with India and Australia/New Zealand, leading to predictions that by 2020 there could be an Asia free trade zone comprising half of the world's population and stretching from 'Mumbai to Christchurch' (Australian Foreign Minister Alexander Downer, quoted in *Financial Times* 2005). Significantly, however, there has not yet been any agreement, as opposed to vague proposals, to create an East Asian Free Trade Area involving *both* Japan and China alongside the ASEAN states and South Korea.

To what extent these partly very ambitious trade liberalization projects will actually be implemented – which and how many sectors they will incorporate, how much flexibility there will be for the exemption of 'sensitive' products, to what extent non-tariff trade barriers will be dismantled, what procedures will be adopted to arbitrate disputes and enforce settlements – is uncertain. ASEAN's experience with its own trade liberalization project (AFTA–ASEAN Free Trade Area) in this regard is not entirely heartening (*The Economist* 2004; Severino 2006). Among the economically weaker ASEAN states, there are still significant fears that they will be negatively affected by the liberalization of their trade with China. Japan and South Korea are both highly protectionist on agricultural issues and therefore unlikely to agree to agricultural trade liberalization. Compliance with such trade liberalization agreements that are finally reached may be problematic, as there is little sign as yet at least that they will incorporate mechanisms that would effectively bind member states to implement their provisions, and the administrative capacity of some of the participating states to ensure implementation of the agreements 'on the ground' is limited.[4] It is questionable therefore whether these projects will lead to much political integration in East Asia. Forecasts that the inauguration of an East Asia Summit will launch a process that will culminate in the emergence of a 'European Union-style single market and community by 2020' (*Straits Times* 2004) are certainly extremely optimistic. Other things being equal, the expansion of the 'attendance list' of the inaugural summit from the original 13 APT states to encompass India, Australia and New Zealand makes closer political integration more unlikely by rendering the new grouping even more diverse – culturally, socio-economically and politically – than the pre-existing APT. The motives of the principal supporters of the East Asia Summit – Japan, Indonesia and Singapore – may have more to do with a common desire to dilute Chinese power in a larger, more inclusive grouping than with any goal of developing a strong and not just wide regional organization.

In the absence of a major crisis in the region, growing economic interdependence is likely to raise the pressure on governments to dismantle political barriers to intra-regional exchange. If the foregoing analysis is correct, however, how far governments accede to such pressures and bind themselves to pursue common regional policies will depend heavily on the extent to which they perceive their security as being threatened by neighbouring states. How has the decline of the Cold War in East Asia hitherto shaped their security perceptions? No major military conflict has occurred in East Asia since the end of the 1980s. Overall, mutual trust in interstate relations has almost certainly grown. This trend, however, has been neither unilinear nor uniform across the region. Thus, in the mid-1990s, the United States and North Korea came to the verge of military conflict over North Korea's nuclear weapon programme and tensions between China,

Taiwan and the United States escalated sharply over events or decisions that China perceived as being aimed at promoting Taiwan's formal political separation from China. Notwithstanding the agreement to freeze North Korean's nuclear weapons programme in exchange for international aid reached in the Six-Party Talks in 2007 and a recent de-escalation of tensions in the Taiwan Strait, neither the issue of North Korea's nuclear weapons ambitions nor that of the political status of Taiwan has meanwhile been durably resolved. Both arguably still contain the potential to fundamentally destabilize international relations in East Asia.

While, by and large, despite numerous divisive issues in various bilateral relationships, perceived politico-security threat levels in *South*east Asia may have *declined,* those in *North*east Asia have probably actually *risen.* For the fate of regional political integration, trends in interstate relations in Northeast Asia weigh more heavily than those in the southeast, as, without the participation of both regional 'heavyweights', Japan and China, political integration on a genuinely region-wide basis is inconceivable, as advocates of East Asian integration recognize. The issues dividing the two states include Japan's UN Security Council membership bid, Japanese history textbooks, prime ministerial visits to the Yasukuni war shrine in Tokyo and competing territorial claims regarding the Senkaku/Daiyoutai islands. Bilateral tensions over these issues reflect growing nationalism on both sides and have their roots not only in the Japanese conquest and occupation of China prior to1945, but also in the shifting balance of power between them, China's increasingly self-confident and ambitious regional diplomacy and rapid modernization of its armed forces, Japan's recent strengthening of its security ties with the United States and evidently increasing readiness to contemplate deploying military force abroad, and the growing competition between the two states for access to energy resources. In particular Japan's identification of China in a recent defence white paper as a potential threat to its security and suggestions that it may assist the United States in defending Taiwan if it should be attacked by China testify to the aggravation of bilateral politico-security relations. Both these steps, along with Japan's tightening military alliance with the United States, its increasingly close military ties with Australia, and its support for the inclusion of India, Australia and New Zealand in the East Asia Summit, point to Japan's concern to balance growing Chinese power in East Asia. Not just academic observers, but also practitioners such as the Chinese foreign vice-minister judge Sino-Japanese relations as having meanwhile reached their lowest point since the two states recognized each other diplomatically in the early 1970s (quoted in Roy 2005: 91). A reversal of this process of deteriorating bilateral relations presupposes a shift in the domestic balance of political power in Japan either from the conservative Liberal Democratic Party (LDP) to the opposition or within the LDP from more Sinophobic to more Sinophile currents and the renunciation by the Chinese Communist Party leadership of its exploitation of popular anti-Japanese sentiment in China as an alternative instrument of ideological integration to Communism – which seems unlikely in a period in which the party's authority is challenged by growing popular protests. Relations between Tokyo and Beijing seemed to warm a little when Junichiro Koizumi was succeeded as Japanese Prime Minister by Shinzo Abe in 2006 and the new Prime Minister made his first foreign trip to China and refrained initially at least from visiting the Yasukuni Shrine. However, Abe shares the same basic foreign policy orientation and stance towards China as Koizumi (Mallet 2007). In Sino-Japanese relations, an 'even more serious rift' may be as likely as a renewed rapprochement (Campbell 2005; see also Calder 2006).

The one security issue on which not only China and Japan, but also other states in or with interests in Northeast Asia, namely South Korea, Russia and the United States, have been able to cooperate is that of the North Korean nuclear weapons programme, which – for a variety of conflicting motives – all of these five states oppose. Their shared interest in disarming North Korea facilitated the staging of the 'Six-Party Talks' on this issue from 2003 onwards. These talks occasionally gave rise to speculation that they could lead to a longer-term institutionalization of security cooperation in Northeast Asia. Precisely the conflicting nature of the states' motives for wanting to curb North Korea's nuclear weapons aspirations made the broadening of cooperation on this one issue to durable cooperation on the whole range of security issues affecting Northeast Asia seem rather improbable.

As described above, China's relations with the Southeast Asian states have evolved very differently to Sino-Japanese relations since the early 1990s. Towards its other neighbours, barring Taiwan, and vis-à-vis Southeast Asia in particular, China has conducted a veritable 'charm offensive' (cf. Shambaugh 2005). Not least, given increasingly tense Sino-Japanese relations, Beijing's efforts to reassure the ASEAN states of the friendliness of its regional intentions may be motivated by a perception that in Southeast Asia it could counter what it sees as an American strategy of trying to 'contain' or 'encircle' China (Ott 2004). Convinced for their part that China's rise is 'inevitable', Southeast Asian states have decided that the best strategy for ASEAN is to engage China and 'entangle the dragon in as many ways as possible' (Shambaugh 2004/05: 76; also Acharya 2003/04: 152–153). Reciprocal strategies of engagement may be seen as providing conducive conditions for integration (at least between China and ASEAN), in the same way that such strategies facilitated integration between West Germany and its neighbours in Western Europe after the Second World War. However, engagement with China represents only one strand of the ASEAN states' foreign policy strategies. At the same time, despite the widespread unpopularity of the foreign policy of the Bush administration since 2001 in the region, several Southeast Asian governments – Singapore, Thailand and the Philippines – have intensified their security (and in some cases also trade) relations with the United States. Like Japan, several – Singapore and Indonesia in particular – also supported India's, Australia's and New Zealand's participation in the East Asia Summit, thus opposing China's preference for a more 'exclusive' grouping. Advocacy of an 'inclusive' concept of (East) Asian regionalism and the intensification of security links with the United States should not be taken as evidence that the ASEAN states are seeking together with the United States to 'contain' China. These strategies of 'hedging' against the possibility of China pursuing a more aggressive and unilateral foreign policy do indicate, however, that the Southeast Asian states continue to be uncertain about China's intentions and are not willing to link themselves inextricably to Beijing (IISS 2005). Aware that China, in the words of the former Singaporean leader Lee Kuan Yew (quoted in Thornhill and Tett 2001), is 'just too big' to be balanced even collectively by the ASEAN states, most of the latter have effectively converged on what the Singaporean foreign minister (Yeo 2005) has labelled a 'completely promiscuous' foreign policy strategy, aimed at maximizing their own freedom of action by maximizing the number of major powers engaged in the region and especially keeping the United States in the neighbourhood. By the same token, China's support for closer regional integration does not mean that Beijing has taken an irrevocable decision to pool its sovereignty with other states in the region, least of all on issues, such as the status of Taiwan, which it regards as relating to its 'core' national interests (Hughes 2005). With China and Japan at loggerheads and Japan aligning itself increasingly closely with the United States against China, with the ASEAN states hedging against a possibly hostile future China at the same time as engaging it and with China itself intent on keeping its hands free to deal as it wishes with Taiwan, the obstacles that will have to be overcome for a significantly more closely politically integrated East Asia to develop remain extremely formidable.

Conclusions

This chapter has not presented a comprehensive analysis of the forces working in favour of or against closer political integration in East Asia. The fate of this process will be shaped by the interaction of multiple international, regional and domestic-level variables that the chapter has not discussed. It has just one simple thesis: *states that view each other as security threats do not integrate.* This is a necessary condition of regional integration. As the absence of any strong cross-regional correlation between levels of intra-regional trade and political integration suggests, growing economic interdependence alone does not suffice to bring about corresponding political cooperation or integration. Certainly, Cold War-related, politico-security motives played a larger role than material–economic ones in the genesis of regional integration projects in non-Communist Europe and East Asia. Political integration in Western Europe became possible only when the non-Communist states perceived an acute threat to their security from the Soviet bloc and, following Germany's division and the creation of NATO, no longer felt threatened by a possible resurgent (West) Germany. In Southeast Asia, ASEAN's creation likewise became possible only when the non-Communist states in the region felt their security acutely threatened by Communist expansion and, following a regime change and foreign policy reorientation in Jakarta, the other states no longer viewed Indonesia as a threat to their security. Moderately strong regional organizations seem to develop only after formerly mutually antagonistic neighbouring states, for whatever reason (and especially because of a perceived powerful shared security threat), have reconciled themselves to co-existing peacefully alongside each other. Mainly because of the rise of China and the multilateral reorientation of its foreign policy, there have been profound changes in international relations in Asia during the last decade, most, but by no means all, of them conducive to regional stability and peace. Nonetheless, not only because China and Japan do not trust each other sufficiently and many other states in the region trust neither China nor Japan sufficiently, but also because, unlike in the case of the EU and ASEAN during the Cold War, there is no acute commonly perceived threat pushing states to cooperate more closely on a pan-regional basis, it is unlikely that East Asia will become a politically significantly more closely integrated region. Short of major convulsions, such as perhaps a war in the Taiwan Strait or on the Korean peninsula or a liberal-democratic revolution in China, international relations in the region are likely to continue to be characterized by an untidy mixture of rivalry and (ad hoc, limited and reversible) cooperation – but not political integration.

Notes

1 Much the same observation could be made about relations between China and Taiwan for most of the last decade or so.
2 I define the concept of 'regional political integration' as referring to the growing coordination of the policies of the governments of geographically proximate states. The coordination of trade policies to create a free trade area among such states is an example of *political* integration, as distinct from *economic* (i.e. market-based or -driven) integration. Regional *cooperation* refers to a less constraining pattern of relations, in which, contrary to what is involved in integration, the participating governments are not *bound* (by mutual agreement at least) to pursue the same or similar courses of action.
3 To this day, of course, ASEAN has renounced any ambitions to be or become a military alliance. An Indonesian initiative in 2003 to give the organization stronger military–security powers was largely blocked by other members (see Haacke 2005).
4 For an analysis of the inhibiting impact of weak state administrative capacities on regional integration in Asia, see Hamilton Hart 2003.

References

Acharya, Amitav (2003/04) 'Will Asia's Past Be Its Future?', *International Security*, 28(3): 149–164.

Anwar, Dewi Fortuna (2005) 'Leadership in the History of Southeast Asian Integration: The Role of Indonesia in ASEAN', in Bertrand Fort and Douglas Webber (eds), *Regional Integration in East Asia and Europe: Convergence or Divergence?*, London: Routledge.

Bix, Herbert P. (2000) *Hirohito and the Making of Modern Japan,* New York: HarperCollins.

Cai, Kevin G. (2003) 'The ASEAN–China Free Trade Agreement and East Asian Regional Grouping', *Contemporary Southeast Asia* 25(3): 387–404.

Calder, Kent (1988) 'Japanese Foreign Economic Policy Formation: Explaining the Reactive State', *World Politics*, 40(4): 517–541.

Calder, Kent (2006) 'China and Japan's Simmering Rivalry', *Foreign Affairs*, 85(2): 129–139.

Calder, Kent and Ye, Min (2004) 'Regionalism and Critical Junctures: Explaining the "Organization Gap" in Northeast Asia', *Journal of East Asian Studies*, 4: 191–226.

Campbell, Kurt (2005) 'Asia Needs a Trilateral Dialogue', *Financial Times*, 25 May.

Dedman, Martin J. (1996) *The Origins and Development of the European Union 1945–95: A History of European integration*, London: Routledge.

Dieter, Heribert and Higgott, Richard (2003) 'Exploring Alternative Theories of Economic Regionalism: From Trade to Finance in Asian Co-operation?', *Review of International Political Economy*, 10(3): 430–454.

Dower, John W. (1999) *Embracing Defeat: Japan in the Wake of World War II*, New York: W.W. Norton.

Duffield, John S. (2001) 'Why Is There No APTO? Why Is There No OSCAP?: Asia-Pacific Security Institutions in Comparative Perspective', *Contemporary Security Policy*, 22(2): 69–95.

The Economist (2004) 'Free Trade in Southeast Asia: More effort needed', 31 July: 25–26.

Financial Times (2005) 'New Asia Grouping Aims for Free Trade by 2020', 14 September.

Friedberg, Aaron L. (1993/94) 'Ripe for Rivalry: Prospects for Peace in a Multipolar Asia', *International Security*, 18(3): 5–33.

Grieco, Joseph (1998) 'Political-Military Dynamics and the Nesting of Regimes: An Analysis of APEC, the WTO, and Prospects for Cooperation in the Asia-Pacific', in Vinod K. Aggarwal and Charles E. Morrison (eds), *Asia-Pacific Crossroads: Regime Creation and the Future of APEC*, New York: St Martin's Press: 235–256.

Haacke, Jürgen (2005) 'The Development of ASEAN's Diplomatic and Security Culture: Not Beyond "Flexible Engagement"', in Bertrand Fort and Douglas Webber (eds), *Regional Integration in East Asia and Europe: Convergence or Divergence?*, London: Routledge.

Hamilton Hart, Natasha (2003) 'Asia's New Regionalism: Government Capacity and Cooperation in the Western Pacific', *Review of International Political Economy*, 10(2): 222–245.

Hamilton Hart, Natasha (2005) 'The Chiang Mai Initiative and the Prospects for Closer Monetary Integration in East Asia', in Bertrand Fort and Douglas Webber (eds), *Regional Integration in East Asia and Europe: Convergence or Divergence?*, London: Routledge.

Hemmer, Christopher and Katzenstein, Peter (2002) 'Why Is There No NATO in Asia? Collective Identity, Regionalism, and the Origins of Multilateralism', *International Organization*, 56(3): 575–607.

Herbst, Ludolf (1989) *Option für den Westen: Vom Marshallplan bis zum deutsch-französischen Vertrag*, Munich: Deutscher Taschenbuch Verlag.

Hughes, Christopher R. (2005) 'Nationalism and Multilateralism in Chinese Foreign Policy: Implications for Southeast Asia', *The Pacific Review*, 18(1): 119–135.

Hund, Markus (2003) 'ASEAN Plus Three: Towards a New Age of Pan-East Asian Regionalism? A Skeptic's Appraisal', *The Pacific Review*, 16(3): 383–417.

IISS (International Institute for Strategic Studies) (2005) 'China, America and Southeast Asia', *Strategic Comments*, 11(1) (February).

Katzenstein, Peter (1996) 'Regionalism in Comparative Perspective', *Cooperation and Conflict*, 31(2): 123–159.

Knipping, Franz (2004) *Rom, 25. März 1957: Die Einigung Europas*. Munich: Deutscher Taschenbuch Verlag.

Küsters, Hanns Jürgen (1982) *Die Gründung der Europäischen Wirtschaftsgemeinschaft*, Baden-Baden: Nomos Verlagsgesellschaft.

Lipson, Charles (1993) 'International Cooperation in Economic and Security Affairs', in David Baldwin (ed.), *Neorealism and Neoliberalism: The Contemporary Debate*, New York: Columbia University Press: 60–84.

Loth, Wilfried (1990) *Der Weg nach Europa: Geschichte der europäischen Integration*, Göttingen: Vandenhoeck & Ruprecht.

Mallet, Victor (2007) 'Japan Is Back – and Not Just as an Economy', *Financial Times*, 22 March.

Mansfield, Edward D. and Milner, Helen V. (1999) 'The New Wave of Regionalism', *International Organization*, 53(3): 589–627.

Ott, Marvin (2004) 'S-E Asia Must Wake up to the Rise of the Dragon', *Straits Times*, 8 September.

Pempel, T.J. (2005) 'Introduction: Emerging Webs of Regional Connectedness', in T.J. Pempel (ed.), *Remapping East Asia: The Construction of a Region*, Ithaca NY: Cornell University Press: 1–28.

Ravenhill, John (2002) 'A Three Bloc World? The New East Asian Regionalism', *International Relations of the Asia-Pacific*, 2: 167–195.

Roy, Denny (2005) 'The Sources and Limits of Sino-Japanese Tensions', *Survival*, 47(2): 191–214.

Severino, Rodolfo (2006) *Southeast Asia in Search of an ASEAN Community*. Singapore: Institute of Southeast Asian Studies.

Shambaugh, David (2004/05) 'China Engages Asia: Reshaping the Regional Order', *International Security*, 29(3): 64–99.

Shambaugh, David (2005) 'Rising Dragon, Flagging Eagle', *Straits Times*, 22 April.

Spaak, Paul-Henri (1969) *Combats Inachevés. De l'Indépendance à l'Alliance* (vol. 1), Paris: Fayard.

Straits Times (2004) 'Abdullah Sketches Vision for East Asia', 7 December.

Stubbs, Richard (2002) 'ASEAN Plus Three: Emerging East Asian Regionalism?', *Asian Survey*, 42(3): 440–455.

Terada, Takashi (2003) 'Constructing an "East Asian" Concept and Growing Regional Identity: From EAEC to ASEAN+3', *The Pacific Review*, 16(2): 251–277.

Thornhill, John and Tett, Gillian (2001) 'Asia's Colliding Interests', *Financial Times*, 27 April.

Webber, Douglas (2001) 'Two Funerals and a Wedding? The Ups and Downs of Regionalism in East Asia and Asia-Pacific after the Asian Crisis', *The Pacific Review*, 14(3): 339–372.

Yeo, George (2005) 'Making Things Crystal Clear', transcript of interview at a meeting of the Foreign Correspondents' Association, Singapore, *Straits Times*, 1 July.

9　The (in)effectiveness of security regionalism

Comparing ASEAN and the Pacific Islands Forum

Derek McDougall

This chapter poses the question of the effectiveness of security regionalism, with particular reference to Southeast Asia and the Pacific islands region. In recent decades regional organizations and groupings have emerged as an important element of international politics. Many of these organizations see themselves as contributing, either explicitly or implicitly, to the security of the regions within which they are located. There is a general issue as to whether this has in fact been the case. Assessing this issue involves a number of different dimensions. Given the broadening in the understanding of security, one needs to keep in mind the range of situations where regional organizations and groupings might be relevant. Then there is the question of how one judges effectiveness. Is it a matter of providing solutions to situations that arise? Or is it more to do with influencing norms so that situations do not arise (or are less likely to arise) in the first place? Taking into account both possibilities, one also needs to ask what factors lead to regional organizations or groupings being effective or not in dealing with security issues.

In this chapter these questions are addressed through a focus on two regional organizations in the Asia-Pacific context: the Association of Southeast Asian Nations (ASEAN) and the Pacific Islands Forum (PIF). ASEAN began in 1967 with five members (Indonesia, Malaysia, the Philippines, Thailand and Singapore). By 1999 it embraced all ten of the independent countries of Southeast Asia; currently the only independent country of Southeast Asia that is not a member is East Timor (under United Nations administration, 1999–2002, and independent since 2002). The Pacific Islands Forum dates from 1971 (known as the South Pacific Forum until 2000). The PIF covers all of the independent Pacific island countries (PICs), as well as a number of self-governing countries; Australia and New Zealand are also members. In 2007 the Forum membership was 16.[1] The contribution of each organization to regional security will be reviewed below.

As far as the general academic argument is concerned, ASEAN has received considerable attention. There is less analysis of the PIF's role, but some of the general arguments invoked in relation to ASEAN are also relevant to the PIF. Perhaps the two most significant writers on ASEAN's contribution to security regionalism are the late Michael Leifer and Amitav Acharya.[2] These writers are not necessarily diametrically opposed in their analyses but there is certainly a difference of emphasis. Leifer adopts a realist position, arguing that regional organizations (ASEAN and the ASEAN Regional Forum in particular) do not contribute significantly to regional security. The most that regional organizations can do is provide an 'adjunct' to ways of dealing with security issues that are grounded more in the 'realities of power'. This means focusing more on the involvement of the major powers, and the way in which the most significant regional powers relate to particular situations. Regional organizations might contribute to 'confidence building', but this is of marginal importance.

Acharya has a constructivist approach to these issues. Focusing on ASEAN, his argument is that the organization makes a contribution to regional security not necessarily in terms of resolving specific issues but in terms of contributing to norms that make it difficult for some types of conflicts to occur in the first place. Foremost among these conflicts would be issues that might lead to the use of armed force among ASEAN members. Acharya argues that ASEAN has become a security community, with the use of force among its members now precluded. This certainly means that regional security at one level is thereby enhanced.

While this issue has not been discussed in quite so explicit a way in relation to the Pacific Islands Forum, the arguments of Leifer and Acharya are also relevant in this context. Are security issues affecting the Pacific islands region dealt with primarily by the states exerting most power in the region (such as Australia), or does the PIF make a contribution comparable to that made by ASEAN in Southeast Asia?

Against this background this chapter argues that in the cases of ASEAN and the PIF, security regionalism does enhance regional security while not necessarily contributing significantly to the resolution of many of the more specific security issues that arise. In arguing thus, the perspective on security is that of comprehensive security, including human security (see Buzan *et al.* 1998). Traditional definitions of security focus on the protection of the state from external threats, using primarily politico-military means. Many of the situations in Southeast Asia and the Pacific islands region involve 'societal security', to use the term of Barry Buzan and his colleagues (Buzan *et al.* 1998: chapter 6). Security issues frequently arise within states and involve tensions between various social groups (often ethnic in some sense) and the state. Human security, focused on individuals, can be part of societal security in this sense, but also involves issues of human rights broadly defined. In assessing the effectiveness of ASEAN and the PIF as organizations contributing to regional security, much depends on the particular dimension of security. ASEAN contributes to norms inhibiting the use of armed force in dealing with conflicts among the ASEAN states. This issue (interstate conflicts where the use of armed force is a possibility) has not been particularly significant in the Pacific islands region. More recently the PIF has contributed to norms encouraging regional intervention as a means of upholding 'good governance', particularly where state failure or democracy might be an issue. ASEAN has been more circumspect on this matter, although not completely disengaged.

Where both ASEAN and the PIF have fallen down is in dealing with major conflicts affecting their regions. These conflicts have frequently led to the involvement of significant external powers and global organizations. The crisis in East Timor in 1999 is a good example in relation to ASEAN; at the level of human security the response to the tsunami of Boxing Day 2004 is also instructive. In the case of the PIF much attention has been given to the intervention in the Solomon Islands in 2003. Although less dramatic the situation in Fiji after both the attempted coup in May 2000 and the coup in December 2006, and concerns about Papua New Guinea as a failing state, also highlight the role of the PIF. In the case of ASEAN there are strong norms favouring a more traditional view of sovereignty; this is less the case in the PIF. In the ASEAN region the involvement of external powers relates to the lack of political will among member countries in dealing with the most serious crises; it is also a matter of lack of resources that can be readily deployed. The same situation would pertain in the PIF if membership were confined to PICs. However, the membership of Australia and New Zealand in the PIF has strengthened the organization's role in recent times. In the case of Southeast Asia, the United Nations has also had some involvement in dealing with crises, providing a vehicle for organizing and dispatching resources, while also embodying global norms relevant to the crises in question. The UN has been less involved in the Pacific islands in this respect, reflecting perhaps the limited significance of these issues on a world scale rather than the global norms not being relevant. With both ASEAN and the PIF, the two organizations have played some role in promoting regional responses to external powers. In the case of the PIF this is most obvious in relation to France from the 1970s to the mid-1990s. The PIF is also important as a context for interaction between the Pacific island countries and Australia and New Zealand. ASEAN has contributed significantly to ensuring that Southeast Asian issues receive attention in the broader Asia-Pacific and East Asian context, through Asia-Pacific Economic Cooperation (APEC), the ASEAN Regional Forum, ASEAN+3 and the emerging East Asia Summit.

In developing this argument I will focus first on ASEAN, providing an overview of the relevance of security regionalism in that context. Then I will undertake the same task in relation to the Pacific Islands Forum. Finally, I will use a comparative approach to highlight the factors that have made the two regional organizations either more or less effective in dealing with regional security issues. The point to emphasize is that while regional organizations have a significant impact on the development of relevant norms, the involvement of actors with the necessary political will and resources is required for specific crises to be dealt with effectively. Such actors are not necessarily based in the 'region' in question.

The experience of ASEAN

With both ASEAN and the PIF it is useful to put the experience of security regionalism in historical perspective. In both cases the chapter outlines the range of security issues to be found within the region in question, before proceeding to a discussion of the contribution made by ASEAN or the PIF.

Southeast Asia is a region where security often focuses on the domestic circumstances of the various states. Many groups challenge the legitimacy of particular states, or at least take issue with many fundamental policies. Some regionally based groups wish to secede and establish their own states, or at the very minimum have much more autonomy than they have had in the past (consider the situations of Aceh and West Papua in Indonesia, the Muslims in the southern Philippines, or the minority peoples in Burma). Authoritarian regimes of one kind or another have sometimes found themselves under challenge from pro-democracy movements, Burma being a notable example. Muslim groups vary in the way they relate to states; some groups have favoured change in an Islamist direction (such as PAS in Malaysia) while remaining in the state, and others have preferred separatism (southern Thailand, as well as the southern Philippines). The major Muslim groups within Indonesia (Muhammadiyah and Nahdatul Ulama (NU)) work within the framework of a secular state; in Malaysia UMNO supports preference for Malays and Islam, but within a pluralist context.

While state–society tensions constitute perhaps the most fundamental security challenge in many Southeast Asian states, there are also security issues of a more traditional kind in ASEAN. These focus on the relations among the Southeast Asian states, as well as the involvement of the major powers. There have been many tensions within Southeast Asia, involving both kinds of relationships. Sometimes these tensions have led to armed conflict. There was some low-level armed conflict during Indonesia's Confrontation (Konfrontasi) of Malaysia in the 1960s, and this has also been the case with the South China Sea issue. The various conflicts centred on Indochina involved significant use of armed force, beginning with the war between France and the Viet Minh from 1946 to 1954, continuing with US involvement in the 1960s and early 1970s, and culminating with the Cambodian conflict (Third Indochina War) beginning in 1978 and continuing through the 1980s. Indonesia's occupation of East Timor in 1975 also involved the use of armed force.

Given these various kinds of security issues, what contribution has ASEAN made to dealing with them since its formation in 1967? ASEAN has contributed significantly to reducing interstate tensions among its members. It has been less relevant to issues involving state-society tensions. It has played some role in conflicts directly involving the major powers in Southeast Asia but not necessarily in a decisive way. In some specific situations in Southeast Asia it has been necessary to call on external powers for assistance.

The political motivation for establishing ASEAN in 1967 was to develop a regional structure for including Indonesia as part of non-communist Southeast Asia. Indonesia's neighbours wanted to avoid another Confrontation. Of course, by 1967 Suharto's New Order was in place and the possibilities for establishing an organization such as ASEAN were more propitious. One measure of ASEAN's success as an organization with an implicit security role is that since 1967 Indonesia has not engaged in armed conflict with other ASEAN members.

In its early decades ASEAN's membership was restricted to the main non-communist countries in Southeast Asia; Brunei became a member in 1984. While a security community might have been developing within ASEAN itself, this did not extend to Southeast Asia as a whole. In fact, ASEAN saw itself as a vehicle for defending the interests of its members in relation to both security and other issues in Southeast Asia as well as in the wider world. When ASEAN emerged with an enhanced role after the Bali summit in February 1976, part of the motivation was the need to defend ASEAN members in a situation where the US role appeared less significant after the fall of Saigon in April 1975. ASEAN was soon called upon to honour that commitment when Vietnam intervened to depose the Khmer Rouge regime in Cambodia in late 1978. Among the ASEAN members it was Thailand that felt particularly threatened by this development. While ASEAN took a consistently anti-Vietnamese position throughout the Third Indochina War, countries such as Malaysia and Indonesia were more open to accommodation with Vietnam.

The possibilities for ASEAN becoming a security community encompassing the whole of Southeast Asia emerged in the aftermath of the Third Indochina War. With the settlement of that conflict, ASEAN's membership expanded to include Vietnam (1995), Burma and Laos (both in 1997), and then Cambodia (1999). Part of the rationale for the expansion of ASEAN was to provide a framework for peaceful conflict resolution that would include all of the Southeast Asian states. Given the conflicts that had centred on Indochina in previous decades, this was an ambitious objective. A decade on, however, this objective appears to have been realized.

The acceptance of Burma as a member suggested that ASEAN might be broadening the scope of the security issues with which it was prepared to deal. The continued suppression of the pro-democracy movement raised issues of human rights; these could also be seen as a matter of human security. ASEAN members believed that they would be better able to influence Burma to modify its policies by having the country join the organization. Given the lack of significant change in Burma, it is debatable as to whether the engagement strategy has worked. Nevertheless, this was the preferred ASEAN approach.

In the late 1990s the debate within ASEAN about 'flexible engagement' also raised issues relating to broader aspects of security. This approach, favoured mainly by Thailand and the Philippines, would have allowed some scope for ASEAN to become involved in 'domestic' issues where such issues had regional implications (Henderson 1999: 48–55). These issues could have included a number of matters encompassed by comprehensive security, such as human rights and environmental matters. However, most ASEAN members rejected this approach, preferring to adhere to a more traditional view of sovereignty; the new ASEAN members were particularly insistent on this point.

Despite the progress ASEAN had made in developing a security community among its own members, it proved incapable of dealing with some major crises. One of these was the East Timor crisis in 1999. Another was the Indian Ocean tsunami of Boxing Day 2004. Both these crises raised issues of human security, although the East Timor situation was also more clearly geopolitical in nature. In neither case was ASEAN very effective in its response.

In the case of East Timor, ASEAN lacked the political will to take action to deal with the crisis that ensued after the East Timorese voted overwhelmingly for independence on 31 August 1999 (see Dupont 2000). With Indonesian forces and their militia allies engaging in an orgy of destruction, many people were killed or forced to flee into the hills. It would have been within the capacity of the ASEAN countries to undertake humanitarian intervention in East Timor, but they were restrained by a concern not to offend Indonesia. While clearly there were differences within Indonesia over East Timor policy, the dominant view was that Indonesia should handle the situation on its own. The violence orchestrated by the TNI in East Timor was seen as a means of influencing international opinion, with Indonesia perceived as the only player legitimized to restore order. Given Indonesian attitudes on this issue it was very difficult for any ASEAN member to suggest that the organization should take the lead in dealing with the crisis. It was thus left to external powers to assume leadership on this issue. Despite past close relations with Indonesia, Australia became active in supporting and organizing intervention. This was due partly to strong public pressure in Australia on this issue, but also to the moral perceptions of the government. The crucial political pressure, however, came from the United States. Australia on its own could not persuade Indonesia to consent to intervention. The United States had the necessary political and economic 'muscle'. An Asia-Pacific consensus in favour of intervention was forged at the APEC summit meeting that was held fortuitously in Auckland in mid-September 1999. This prepared the way for a UN Security Council resolution authorizing Australian-led intervention (INTERFET); this was subsequently superseded by a UN intervention through UNTAET. ASEAN members were involved in both INTERFET and UNTAET, with Thailand and the Philippines being most prominent. The deputy commander of INTERFET was a Thai, and the commanders of UNTAET were a Filipino and then two Thais. Malaysia and Singapore also contributed forces. ASEAN involvement was important in giving the interventions a Southeast Asian dimension and thus some legitimacy in relation to ASEAN. However, ASEAN itself played only a minor role in relation to the East Timor crisis. (ASEAN similarly failed to play a leading role with the collapse of order in East Timor in May 2006; Australia was the main source of assistance, with contributions also from Malaysia, New Zealand and Portugal, and a renewed UN role through the United Nations Integrated Mission in Timor-Leste (UNMIT) from August 2006.)

Another crisis, with very much a human security dimension, was the tsunami of Boxing Day 2004. The worst affected region was Aceh, with some 130,000 estimated dead and almost 40,000 missing; among the Southeast Asian countries, several thousand people also died in Thailand. ASEAN had some involvement with this issue but it was relatively minor overall. The main need was to have resources deployed immediately to deal with the situation and then to implement reconstruction over the longer term. ASEAN countries did not have the resources to deal with this issue, nor could they provide the political leadership. Resources mostly came from the wealthier Western countries. Political leadership initially focused on a 'core group', led by the United States and including also Japan, India, Australia, Canada and the Netherlands. Singapore subsequently took the lead in organizing a summit under ASEAN auspices in Jakarta on 6 January 2005. This enabled the United Nations to assume the main coordinating role and also provided opportunities for countries other than those in the 'core group' to become involved (Huxley 2005: 124–125). At the summit the most significant promises of aid came from (in order) Australia, Germany, Japan, the United States, the United Kingdom, Sweden, Spain, France, Canada, China and South Korea (Huxley 2005: 125).

While ASEAN has not been particularly effective in dealing with these recent crises, it has had some impact in locating Southeast Asian security concerns within a broader context. The security community model within Southeast Asia has been relatively successful, but ASEAN's contribution within the broader 'Asia-Pacific' and 'East Asia' context should also be acknowledged. ASEAN has played an important role within some broader groupings. None of these constitutes a security community, but each has an implicit or explicit security dimension. At the explicit level the formation of the ASEAN Regional Forum in 1994 was important in providing a forum for discussing security issues in the broader Asia-Pacific context (see Leifer 1996[3]). As the title suggests, ASEAN played a crucial role in establishing the forum, and has subsequently provided the organizational framework. The annual meetings are held in an ASEAN country and are chaired by that country's foreign minister. While it would be difficult to argue that the ASEAN Regional Forum had played a decisive role in resolving any security issue in the region, it has contributed to confidence-building.

APEC (Asia-Pacific Economic Cooperation) was formed in 1989, ostensibly to promote economic cooperation in the region and to allow for an Asia-Pacific voice on global economic issues. In practice it has developed an implicit security role, particularly since the establishment of annual summit meetings for heads of government in 1993. These summits allow Asia-Pacific leaders to focus on the range of security issues affecting the region. With strong representation from ASEAN countries, ASEAN is in some position to have an influence on broader Asia-Pacific developments. Similarly the emergence of ASEAN+3 after the 1997 Asian financial crisis (and the East Asia Summit from 2005) was strongly influenced by a desire within ASEAN to deal with a number of issues (including security issues) within a broader East Asian context. Many issues could not be usefully dealt with by focusing on Southeast Asia alone. By placing Southeast Asia in a broader context, there was a better likelihood that the Southeast Asian countries themselves would benefit. Again it is difficult to point to specific security issues being resolved within this context, but the framework for contributing in a broad sense is developing. Contexts such as APEC, ASEAN+3 and the East Asia Summit (and the ASEAN Regional Forum for that matter) are also helpful to the Southeast Asian countries in strengthening their collective position in relation to the major powers, particularly China, Japan and the United States.

The experience of the Pacific Islands Forum

The types of security issues to be found in the Pacific islands region[4] overlap with those in ASEAN, but there are also some differences in emphasis. Keeping in mind that this region has a much smaller population than does Southeast Asia (about 9 million compared to nearly 570 million), and covers a very small land area (mainland Papua New Guinea being the largest single land mass), there is most obviously an overlap in relation to state-society tensions. Interstate conflicts involving the use of armed force have been virtually non-existent. Major power involvement in the region has been a security concern for the Pacific island countries on occasion. Post-Cold War there has also been an increasing emphasis on 'new international agenda' issues, many of which have a security dimension.

States in the Pacific islands region are mostly the legacy of colonial rule. A Western type of system has been imposed on the various indigenous societies. In Melanesia these societies are often very fragmented. A good indication of this is the number of language groups to be found in some countries: Papua New Guinea has 820 for a population approaching 6 million, the Solomon Islands 70 for over 500,000, Vanuatu 109 for over 200,000.[5] Polynesian countries such as Tonga and Samoa tend to have more unified societies. Settler populations in island countries such as Fiji (the Indo-Fijians) and New Caledonia (the Caldoches, descended from earlier French settlers, as well as more recent French immigrants) have sometimes been in conflict with the indigenous people. Throughout the Pacific islands region people tend to give their loyalty to their clan or tribe as their primary social group. Movements for secession can arise, the most obvious example being Bougainville in Papua New Guinea. The state is often seen as a vehicle for distributing benefits to one's particular group. Resentments about the domination of a particular group can cause conflict. Perceived advances by Indo-Fijians led to the coups in Fiji in 1987 and the attempted coup in 2000. Tensions between Malaitans and people from Guadalcanal were a key factor in the attempted coup in the Solomon Islands in 2000. The main decolonization struggle has been in New Caledonia, particularly in the 1980s when there were some violent episodes; the Matignon accords in 1988 were a compromise setting out a path to greater autonomy and possibly independence in the long term. More recently the pro-independence movement has also won greater support in French Polynesia.

Unlike Southeast Asia, the Pacific islands region has not experienced armed conflict among the local states. There have been political differences from time to time with some states but not to the point where the use of armed force was an issue. In fact most Pacific island countries do not have military forces (the main exceptions are Papua New Guinea, Fiji and Tonga). Domestic security is generally a matter for police forces. There have been tensions from time to time along Papua New Guinea's land border with Indonesia, mainly relating to the West Papuan independence movement.

The involvement of major powers in the region has posed security concerns for Pacific island countries. French nuclear testing at Mururoa atoll in French

Polynesia was a major issue from the late 1960s to the mid-1990s. French treatment of the Kanaks in New Caledonia during the 1980s also provoked hostility in the region, as did French involvement in Vanuatu at the time of that country's independence in 1980–81. During the Cold War there was a desire to prevent the spread of superpower rivalry to the Pacific islands region. This sentiment was strongest in the South Pacific; in the central Pacific the United States had a considerable military presence (Hawaii, Micronesia, Guam). In the post-Cold War era various major powers have been involved in the region but the security dimension of their presence has been less obvious. This involvement can relate to issues such as development assistance, licences for tuna fishing, or the China–Taiwan conflict (diplomatic recognition in particular).

A number of 'new international agenda' issues have been important in the Pacific islands region in the post-Cold War period, and some of these have a security dimension (see Firth 2003). Perhaps the most significant issue concerns state failure. While there have been no states that have definitively failed in this region, some states have been described as failing. The most notable example in this respect is the Solomon Islands where, both before and after the 2000 coup, many aspects of government failed to function and there was widespread corruption. In Papua New Guinea there have similarly been problems with corruption and a breakdown in 'law and order', particularly in the towns and in areas such as the Southern Highlands. In Nauru, once financially secure on the basis of phosphate earnings, there has been a financial collapse. Nuku'alofa in normally peaceful Tonga erupted in rioting in November 2006, with the situation fuelled by resentment at the failure of the monarchy to allow much progress towards a democratic constitution. In December 2006 the military deposed the elected government in Fiji. Weak states, even if they are not failing or failed, can have security consequences. Apart from 'law and order' problems, with clear implications for human security, weak states allow greater opportunities for criminal groups to operate. These might be involved in activities such as drug trafficking, money laundering and people smuggling. Terrorist groups might be able to make use of this situation too, although in the Pacific islands the main issue has been criminal activities.

Issues concerning fisheries and the environment also have a security dimension for the Pacific island countries. Having large exclusive economic zones (EEZs), many of these countries derive financial benefits from the fishing licences they issue, particularly in relation to tuna. Any threat to this revenue would have a significant economic impact. Similarly, low-lying Pacific island countries have major concerns about global warming, with countries such as Tuvalu potentially disappearing altogether.

Given this range of security issues, what contribution has the Pacific Islands Forum made since its inception as the South Pacific Forum in 1971? Two major aspects might be discerned. The first focuses on Pacific island countries' relations with France, covering both nuclear and decolonization issues. The second and more recent aspect concerns Forum involvement in dealing with 'domestic' issues that might have broader regional implications. In both cases the Forum influence has been mainly in relation to the development of relevant norms. In terms of more specific action, Australia and New Zealand as the leading regional powers have usually taken the lead, with the Forum playing a supportive role.

France's role in the South Pacific was an important factor in the establishment and early development of the South Pacific Forum. France had been a leading member in the South Pacific Commission, set up by the colonial powers in the region in 1947. France barred any attempt by the independent Pacific island countries to use the Commission for dealing with political issues; the focus was on development cooperation. Hence the Forum saw itself as having a major role in developing a political voice for the island countries. The major issue that engaged the Forum over its first two decades was French nuclear testing in the South Pacific. Opposition to testing encouraged the development of nuclear-free norms in the region, culminating in the Treaty of Rarotonga in 1985. This treaty provided for the establishment of a South Pacific Nuclear Free Zone (SPNFZ). The consensus in the Forum was on opposition to nuclear testing and the stationing of nuclear weapons in the region. Under Australian influence, SPNFZ did not prohibit the existing nuclear powers from transiting the region with nuclear-armed vessels or aircraft; this was most relevant to the United States. In terms of stronger steps against France on this issue, Australia and New Zealand mounted a case in the International Court of Justice in 1973–74 (on the Australian case, see Ryan 1980: 120–3; Parliament of the Commonwealth of Australia 1975). When France undertook a final series of nuclear tests in 1995–96, again it was Australia and New Zealand that were most active in campaigning, but with the Forum being strongly supportive (see Nossal and Vivian 1997; Thakur 1996).

Decolonization issues also caused tensions between France and the Forum, mainly in the 1980s. The Forum condemned the Santo rebellion in Vanuatu in 1980, involving some francophones who opposed independence under majority anglophone rule. France's position in relation to this rebellion was ambivalent to say the least. Papua New Guinea sent a small military force to assist Vanuatu in quelling this rebellion; Australia provided some logistical assistance. The Forum did not specifically approve the operation (see Gubb 1994; MacQueen 1988; Beasant 1984).

In relation to the New Caledonia issue the Forum's position during the 1980s was strongly against French policy. This largely involved condemnation of France in Forum resolutions, although the issue was also taken to the United Nations Decolonization Committee in late 1986 (Henningham 1992: 210). From the Forum's perspective the key issue was the right of the Kanak people to self-determination, an issue of human security and human rights.

From the late 1980s the Forum has gradually assumed a more significant role in relation to developments occurring within member countries, particularly if there is a perception that those developments have regional implications. At the same time, respect for the sovereignty of member states has meant that any involvement has been cautious. Specific action by the Forum as such has generally been minimal. Relevant situations have included Fiji, Papua New Guinea (Bougainville) and the Solomon Islands. In the 1987 Fiji coups there was some sympathy among the Pacific island countries within the Forum for the position of the indigenous Fijians; Australia and New Zealand were most adamant about upholding democratic norms. This was also the position at the time of the attempted coup in Fiji in 2000, as well as in the aftermath of the 2006 coup. The Forum sent an Eminent Persons' Group to Fiji in early 2007 to investigate the situation there, and to make recommendations about a return to democracy. In relation to the Bougainville secession issue the Forum did not even mention the matter in its annual communiqué until 1997, and then to note the progress being made (Firth 2003: 49). Upholding Papua New Guinea's territorial integrity appeared to be the main issue. In the case of the Solomon Islands the Forum did not become directly involved in dealing with the tensions between Malaitans and people from Guadalcanal ahead of the attempted coup in 2000. Similarly the Forum did not intervene in the situation in Tonga in late 2006.

The Forum's major contribution to dealing with these 'domestic' situations has been the development of norms. The Forum found itself compelled to take a stronger position on this matter after the attempted coups in 2000 in Fiji and the Solomon Islands. The most significant development was the adoption of the Biketawa Declaration at the Forum meeting in October 2000 in Kiribati. This declaration affirmed that the key to dealing with domestic security threats was 'good governance'. The PIF could assist through various diplomatic means extending to support for 'appropriate institutions or mechanisms' to achieve a solution (Biketawa Declaration 2000). The Nasonini Declaration on Regional Security (2002), adopted at the Forum meeting in Fiji in August 2002, gave particular attention to law enforcement cooperation, referring particularly to the need to tackle 'money laundering, drug trafficking, terrorism and terrorist financing, people smuggling, and people trafficking'. At the time of the Australian-led intervention in the Solomon Islands in 2003 it was support from the Forum that provided international legitimacy. In fact, PIF members, meeting on 30 June 2003, approved the operation before the Solomons parliament had given its consent (Fraenkel 2004: 165).[6]

When it comes to more specific actions dealing with these various security issues in the Pacific islands region, it has generally been Australia and New Zealand that have taken the lead. In the various Fiji situations this has mainly involved diplomatic pressure in various forms. In the case of Bougainville it was New Zealand that played the key role in concluding the Burnham accords in July 1997; Australia was too compromised by its support for Papua New Guinea to play the 'honest broker' role. The Burnham accords led to a ceasefire and the initiation of a peace process on Bougainville. A small peace monitoring force was composed mainly of Australians and New Zealanders, but there were also some Pacific island countries represented. In 2003 the decision to intervene in the Solomon Islands was taken primarily by Australia. The Regional Assistance Mission Solomon Islands (RAMSI) involved 1,745 Australians out of a total force of 2,225, with 140 from New Zealand, and small military contributions from Papua New Guinea, Fiji and Tonga, and some police personnel from Samoa, Vanuatu, Cook Islands, Nauru, Tuvalu and Kiribati (see further, McDougall 2004: 218–19). Subsequently Australia has also been active in dealing with the failing state issues in Papua New Guinea. An 'Enhanced Cooperation Program' has involved assistance in financial administration and policing (although Australian police had to withdraw in 2005 following a constitutional challenge in Papua New Guinea, it was agreed in 2006 that a number of Australian officers would occupy senior police roles). A contingent of 150 Australian and New Zealand military and police personnel provided assistance in Tonga after the riots there in November 2006.

As well as the Forum's involvement in issues concerning France from the 1970s to the 1990s and the more recent responses to various 'domestic' developments, Forum countries have worked together in relation to both the fisheries and environmental issues. The main vehicle for the fisheries issue has been the Forum Fisheries Agency, where a coordinated approach has considerably strengthened the bargaining position of the member countries. On the global warming issue the most affected Pacific island countries have worked through the Alliance of Small Island States, an international coalition bringing small island states from various regions together to support stronger measures to combat global warming (see Shibuya 2003: 146–147). Here they have found themselves opposed by Australia, which has not signed the Kyoto Protocol. With concerns about the impact of the Kyoto approach on its own economy, Australia has generally preferred to deal with the global warming issue through a strategy emphasizing technological solutions rather than targets for reducing carbon emissions.

Moves towards an 'enhanced regionalism' are an important part of the current scene in the Pacific islands region. The norms evolving within the context of the Forum have provided the justification for strengthening regional responses to the various challenges in the Pacific islands region. Australia has been very active in attempting to strengthen regional cooperation. Together with New Zealand it has the resources that can contribute to dealing with many of the situations that arise. Particularly in the context of the Solomons intervention and increasing concerns about Papua New Guinea, the Coalition government in Australia has decided that a more proactive approach is necessary for dealing with the problems of the region. Through its Secretary-General, Greg Urwin (an Australian), the Forum has developed a Pacific Plan that will provide for greater coordination among member countries in relation to a range of governmental activities, many of which have a security dimension. The first phase of the Plan was approved at the Forum meeting in Papua New Guinea in October 2005; regional cooperation would be strengthened but there was no commitment on proposals for greater political 'integration' at this point. The resources for implementing the Pacific Plan will come predominantly from Australia and New Zealand, but the Forum will play a crucial role in developing the norms that make 'enhanced regionalism' possible.[7] At the same time it remains to be seen whether there is the political will in the Pacific island countries to proceed very far in the direction of greater integration.

Comparison and analysis

Given this discussion of the role played by ASEAN and the Pacific Islands Forum in relation to security issues in Southeast Asia and the Pacific islands region respectively, what might we conclude about how these organizations contribute to security? In both cases the major contribution of the regional organizations has been to the development of norms that enhance security. In ASEAN's case its major weakness has been its inability to contribute significantly in dealing with specific crises that have arisen. The PIF has been more effective in this respect but mainly because of the involvement of Australia and New Zealand. The actors that have responded most effectively to security crises in Southeast Asia have been the states with resources, but not necessarily regional states. This conclusion thus sees merit in both the constructivist and the realist approaches to this issue. Shared norms have been important in the development of a security community in Southeast Asia and in the promotion of 'enhanced regionalism' in the Pacific islands region. The involvement of external powers and the UN has been important in dealing with crises in Southeast Asia; likewise Australia and New Zealand have taken the lead with many specific issues in the Pacific islands region.

On the issue of norms, there are both similarities and differences between ASEAN and the PIF. Both ASEAN and the Forum have promoted the goal of peaceful conflict resolution, especially among their member countries. In this respect the 'ASEAN way' and the 'Pacific way' have much in common. However, interstate conflicts have been much more significant in the history of Southeast Asia than in the Pacific islands region. This means that ASEAN's contribution in reducing the likelihood of such conflict is more remarkable than in the case of the PIF where interstate conflict was never a major issue. While both ASEAN and the PIF can be described as security communities, this term carries more weight in a situation where interstate conflicts were a more prominent feature of international politics. Apart from encouraging peaceful conflict resolution, ASEAN's norms have promoted a policy of non-interference in the domestic affairs of member states. Even where domestic developments clearly have regional implications, ASEAN's approach has generally involved facilitating regional cooperation in such a way that the infringement of national sovereignty is minimized. This is essentially the outcome of the debate about 'flexible engagement' that occurred in ASEAN in the late 1990s.

In the case of the PIF the development of norms has been in the direction of 'enhanced regionalism'. While Pacific island countries at one level are protective about their sovereignty, at another level their fragility makes them more open to external involvement. The dependence of many Pacific island countries on foreign aid is a good measure of this situation, but it is also relevant when one considers the responses within the region to the various security challenges. The Pacific island countries have been open to regional solutions that give some prominence to the leading role of Australia and New Zealand.

When dealing with specific security crises, the experience of ASEAN and the PIF has varied. Actors with the requisite resources and political will have generally played the most significant role in both regions, whether or not they are members of the relevant regional organization. In elaborating on this point one needs to be aware of some of the salient features of international politics in the two regions. Among the various ASEAN members Indonesia is the most significant but it is by no means a hegemon; at times it seems like a helpless Gulliver. In general, Indonesia has not taken the lead in dealing with regional security issues, and has opposed ASEAN involvement in situations directly affecting its own position (see further, Smith 2000). Other ASEAN members have attempted to influence the organization's position on various issues, particularly where they see their own interests affected, but none has had a dominant role. Apart from the difficulty in developing a clear ASEAN position on major issues, which relates to the question of political will, the ASEAN countries have generally lacked sufficient resources to deal with major crises. Non-Southeast Asian states involved in this region have been more decisive in dealing with crises, as both the East Timor and tsunami examples showed. Among the major powers the role of the United States is of particular note, with Japan also contributing financially and in other ways. Australia, although a middle power, has also played a significant role in relation to these crises. China has been less involved, although this might change if there were a serious security issue affecting mainland Southeast Asia. The other actor of note in the Southeast Asian situation is the UN, mainly because of its coordinating role in the deployment of resources and as a legitimizing agent for intervention.[8] Global norms manifested through the UN, as well as the regional norms developed by ASEAN, have been relevant to the responses to security crises in Southeast Asia.

In the case of the Pacific islands region, the island countries are all small states; they live in the shadow of Australia and New Zealand. Island countries can certainly have some influence on the direction of regional policies, but this is small compared with the influence of Australia and New Zealand. France's influence relates mainly to New Caledonia and French Polynesia. The United States and the United Kingdom generally play a minor role in the region's affairs; the former is significant in the central Pacific and in relation to territories such as American Samoa; the latter has some influence in relation to former colonial territories such as Fiji and the Solomon Islands. Island countries are generally most concerned about situations in their immediate vicinity. In relation to broader regional issues island countries might affirm the importance of the 'Pacific way', but a strong position articulated either by individual states or collectively tends to be lacking. Apart from the matter of political will, the island countries clearly lack the resources that would enable them to contribute significantly to the resolution of regional security crises. Any contribution of forces by island countries, as in Bougainville and the Solomon Islands, tends to be a token one. Australia and New Zealand have been in a better position to develop political will in relation to the security crises in the region. Relatively speaking, the Pacific islands have been a higher priority for New Zealand than for Australia. New Zealand has focused more on Polynesia, and Australia on Melanesia (Papua New Guinea being a former Australian colonial territory), but both countries also take a regionwide approach. With the deteriorating situation in a number of Pacific island countries since 2000 in particular, the region has assumed a more prominent place in the Australian political agenda. Given the political will, both Australia and New Zealand have the resources that can have an impact, at least in the short term, in dealing with security crises in the Pacific islands region. The PIF can act as a vehicle for translating that political will into action. The fact that the UN has been less involved in dealing with security situations in the Pacific islands than in Southeast Asia reflects the comparative significance of the two regions in world politics. Global norms are certainly relevant to a number of the situations in the Pacific islands and the UN could play a coordinating role as it has done in relation to crises in Southeast Asia, but it is a matter of priorities. The Pacific islands region is just far less important in world terms.

Given this assessment of the effectiveness of security regionalism in relation to ASEAN and the Pacific Islands Forum, are there any general lessons from these situations that might be relevant to security regionalism more broadly? This analysis has shown the relevance of both constructivist and realist approaches in studying security regionalism. Constructivist approaches highlight the importance of norms; realist approaches show how power affects the way in which security issues are dealt with. In the development of norms affecting security, regional organizations can be important even though the member states might be weak. In terms of responding to specific security crises the importance of political will and resources has been a key factor. Primarily, it is the most significant states that are in a position to exercise this kind of power and thus influence the outcome of crises. In Southeast Asia the most significant states were not regional states; in the Pacific islands it was Australia and New Zealand rather than the Pacific island states that played the most significant role. Australia and New Zealand could be seen as part of the South Pacific, even though they are not Pacific island states. In examining other regions the analysis in this chapter would suggest that it is important to assess where power relating to the region in question is located; this could be both inside and outside the region, or one or the other. No general conclusion on this point can be derived from an analysis of ASEAN and the Pacific islands region. If the discussion in this chapter provides any guide then it is that security regionalism has an impact on norms, but is not necessarily sufficient in developing the political will and deploying the resources necessary to deal with specific crises. Normally actors with the will and resources need to be involved if such crises are to be handled effectively.

Notes

1 The members of the Pacific Island Forum are Australia, Cook Islands, Federated States of Micronesia, Fiji, Kiribati, Marshall Islands, Nauru, New Zealand, Niue, Palau, Papua New Guinea, Samoa, the Solomon Islands, Tonga, Tuvalu and Vanuatu.
2 Michael Leifer's writings on this topic include Leifer 1989, 1999 and 2000. For Amitav Acharya's perspective, see Acharya 2001, 2003, 2005.
3 More recent studies include Emmers 2003: 30–39 and chapter 5; Caballero-Anthony 2005: chapter 4.
4 A useful recent reference on security in the Pacific islands region is Shibuya and Rolfe 2003.
5 Figures are from *Ethnologue.com*, www.ethnologue.com (accessed 28 September 2005).
6 The official Forum position is set out in 'Outcome Statement,' Forum Foreign Affairs Ministers Meeting, 30 June 2003, Sydney. Available at www.dfat.gov.au/geo/spacific/regional_orgs/ffam_solomons_0306.html (accessed 8 November 2003).

7 The PIF Special Leaders' Retreat adopted the goal of a Pacific Plan in Auckland, 6 April 2004. See Auckland Declaration, www.dfat.gov.au/geo/spacific/regional_orgs/spf_leaders_declaration.html (accessed 29 September 2005). For the final draft of the Pacific Plan as prepared by the Forum Secretariat for presentation to the Forum meeting in Papua New Guinea in October 2005, see http://pacificplan.org/tiki-page.php?page Name=PPDraft#_ftn3 (accessed 29 September 2005).
8 On the UN's role in Asia-Pacific security, including Southeast Asia, see Foot (2003). See also 'UN Peace Operations and Asian Security' (2005).

References

Acharya, A. (2001) *Constructing a Security Community in Southeast Asia: ASEAN and the Problem of Regional Order,* London: Routledge.

Acharya, A. (2003) 'Regional Institutions and Asian Security Order: Norms, Power, and Prospects for Peaceful Change', in M. Alagappa (ed.), *Asian Security Order: Instrumental and Normative Features,* Stanford: Stanford University Press.

Acharya, A. (2005) 'Do Norms and Identity Matter? Community and Power in Southeast Asia's Regional Order', *Pacific Review,* 18: 95–118.

Beasant, J. (1984) *The Santo Rebellion: An Imperial Reckoning,* Honolulu: University of Hawaii Press; Richmond, Vic.: Heinemann.

Biketawa Declaration (2000). Online. Available at www.dfat.gov.au/geo/spacific/regional_orgs/pif31_communique.pdf (accessed 28 September 2005).

Buzan, B., Waever, O. and de Wilde, J. (1998) *Security: A New Framework for Analysis,* Boulder, CO: Lynne Rienner Publishers.

Caballero-Anthony, M. (2005) *Regional Security in Southeast Asia: Beyond the ASEAN Way,* Singapore: Institute of Southeast Asian Studies.

Dupont, A. (2000) 'ASEAN's Response to the East Timor Crisis', *Australian Journal of International Affairs,* 54: 163–70.

Emmers, R. (2003) *Cooperative Security and the Balance of Power in ASEAN and the ARF,* London: RoutledgeCurzon.

Firth, S. (2003) 'Conceptualizing Security in Oceania: New and Enduring Issues', in E. Shibuya and J. Rolfe (eds), *Security in Oceania in the 21st Century,* Honolulu: Asia-Pacific Center for Security Studies.

Foot, R. (2003) 'The UN System's Contribution to Asia-Pacific Security Architecture', *Pacific Review,* 16: 207–30.

Fraenkel, J. (2004) *The Manipulation of Custom: From Uprising to Intervention in the Solomon Islands,* Wellington: Victoria University Press.

Gubb, M. (1994) *Vanuatu's 1980 Santo Rebellion: International Responses to a Microstate Security Crisis,* Canberra Papers on Strategy and Defence 107, Canberra: Strategic and Defence Studies Centre, Research School of Pacific and Asian Studies, Australian National University.

Henderson, J. (1999) *Reassessing ASEAN,* Adelphi Paper 328, Oxford: International Institute for Strategic Studies/Oxford University Press.

Henningham, S. (1992) *France and the South Pacific: A Contemporary History,* North Sydney, NSW: Allen and Unwin.

Huxley, T. (2005) 'The Tsunami and Security: Asia's 9/11?', *Survival,* 47(1): 123–32.

Leifer, M. (1989) *ASEAN and the Security of South-East Asia,* London: Routledge.

Leifer, M. (1996) *The ASEAN Regional Forum,* Adelphi Paper 302, Oxford: International Institute for Strategic Studies/Oxford University Press.

Leifer, M. (1999) 'The ASEAN Peace Process: A Category Mistake', *Pacific Review,* 12: 25–38.

Leifer, M. (2000) 'Regional Solutions to Regional Problems', in G. Segal and D.S.G. Goodman (eds), *Towards Recovery in Pacific Asia,* London: Routledge.

McDougall, D. (2004) 'Intervention in Solomon Islands', *Round Table,* 93(374): 213–23.

MacQueen, N. (1988) 'Beyond *Tok Win*: The Papua New Guinea Intervention in Vanuatu, 1980', *Pacific Affairs,* 61: 235–52.

Nasonini Declaration on Regional Security (2002). Online. Available at www.dfat.gov. au/geo/spacific/regional_orgs/pif33_communique.pdf (accessed 28 September 2005).

Nossal, K.R. and Vivian, C. (1997) *A Brief Madness: Australia and the Resumption of French Nuclear Testing,* Canberra Papers on Strategy and Defence 121, Canberra: Defence and Strategic Studies Centre, Research School of Pacific and Asian Studies, Australian National University.

Parliament of the Commonwealth of Australia (1975) *International Court of Justice, Nuclear Test Case, Australia v. France: Memorial of the Government of Australia,* Canberra: Government Printer.

Ryan, K. (1980) 'International Law', in W.J. Hudson (ed.), *Australia in World Affairs 1971–75,* Sydney: George Allen and Unwin, for the Australian Institute of International Affairs.

Shibuya, E. (2003) 'Climate Change and Small Island States: Environmental Security as National Security', in E. Shibuya and J. Rolfe (eds), *Security in Oceania in the 21st Century*, Honolulu: Asia-Pacific Center for Security Studies.

Shibuya, E., and Rolfe, J. (eds) (2003) *Security in Oceania in the 21st Century,* Honolulu: Asia-Pacific Center for Security Studies.

Smith, A.L. (2000) *Strategic Centrality: Indonesia's Changing Role in ASEAN,* Pacific Strategic Paper 10, Singapore: Institute of Southeast Asian Studies.

Thakur, R. (1996) 'Last Bang Before a Total Ban: French Nuclear Testing in the Pacific', *International Journal,* 51: 466–86.

'UN Peace Operations and Asian Security' (2005) Special Issue, *International Peacekeeping,* 12(1).

10 Regional peace through economic integration

The applicability of the European model in South Asia

Golam Robbani

Introduction

Regional integration arrangements are being seen as a major trend with a new, genuinely worldwide economic and political phenomenon having a significant impact on various issue areas (Hettne 2005). Region formation around the globe has now become a fashion of the day. Almost all countries in the world are members of at least one regional bloc (a notable exception is Mongolia). Apparently the world is becoming a 'world of regions' – though not replacing the significance of nation-states. While the number of such organizations is amazingly high, success in attaining their stated objectives is disappointingly low. The European Union (EU), of course, is an obvious exception. Nevertheless, as well as economic benefits, new hopes are hovering around the effectiveness of regional organizations in maintaining regional peace and security.[1]

The EU started its journey in early 1950s with a long-term view to 'make another war impossible' among European states. After half a century, it has been clear that another war among the EU states is indeed unlikely. Recalling this extraordinary success in attaining regional peace through economic integration, the EU is proclaimed as the most successful integration arrangement in the world (see Söderbaum *et al.*, 2005). As a corollary, it is also contemplated whether the EU experience is replicable elsewhere–particularly in South Asia where the decades-long Indo-Pakistani conflict resembles the century-long Franco-German rivalry.

The objective of this chapter is to position regional economic integration in the existing trade-conflict discourse in order to assess the relationship between regional integration and regional peace and security, and to examine the usefulness of the EU experience for South Asia in ending India–Pakistan rivalry, which has virtually blocked the progress in the 'South Asian Association for Regional Cooperation' (SAARC).

In the next section, I briefly introudce the basic idea behind the trade-promotes-peace proposition, followed by a short literature review. In the third section, I underline some changes in the traditional veiw on trade and conflict due to globalization. In the following sections I discuss positioning regional integration in the trade-conflict discourse, some features of regional integration in South Asia, and also in Europe. I then highlight the lessons to be learnt and the way forward, and, finally, draw some conclusions.

Trade-promotes-peace proposition: A brief introduction

The main argument in favour of the trade-promotes-peace hypothesis is attached to the idea of free trade.[2] Liberals argue that free trade has at least two effects – efficiency and interdependence–which, according to them, lead to peace.

According to this view, if free trade is allowed between two or more states, the gains from trade will be greater than in autarky. This will allocate scarce resources more efficiently, and will encourage international division of labour. As a result, states will become specialized in products over which they enjoy competitive advantage. If such a relationship is maintained, economists confirm that countries will export what they specialize in, and import the products in which they are less efficient than their trading partners. Eventually, increased trade will create mutual interdependence, and make it costly for states to break the relationship. Therefore, it is argued, trading states are most likely to look for peaceful alternatives to mitigate their disputes, rather than initiating conflict in the first place. A typical liberal argument in favour of the trade-promotes-peace hypothesis can be expressed as in the Box 10.1.

Box 10.1   Liberal view over trade and conflict relationship

Free trade → international division of labour → better gains from trade → specialization → interdependence → higher opportunity cost of conflict → relatively peaceful world.

(Here '→' indicates 'leads to')

This opportunity-cost argument is based on two basic implicit assumptions: (a) trade is a positive-sum game, therefore disruption of trade creates opportunity cost; and (b) trade automatically creates interdependence because substitutes are either non-existent or too expensive.

The benefits of trade can be demonstrated by means of David Ricardo's theory of comparative advantage. Although gains can be asymmetrical between nations, there are reasons to believe that international trade is a positive-sum game. Benjamin Franklin declared long ago (in 1774) that 'no nation was ever ruined by trade' (cited in Irwin, 2002: 225). There may be gainers and losers within a society; nevertheless, 'whatever hurt is suffered by particular groups, trade leaves the nation as a whole better off' (Destler 2005: 311). For instance, a careful analysis estimates that Americans are a trillion dollars better off, every year, due to the gains from international trade (Bradford *et al.* 2005; cited in Destler, 2005: 311). Thus, the widely shared view is that trade is beneficial to all– although not always equally. Based on this analysis, it is argued that these gains from trade create an opportunity cost of conflict, and hence discourage leaders to take military action against trading partners. At the domestic level, trade increases the influence of those economic groups who benefit most from trade and who therefore have an incentive to pressure the government to maintain a peaceful environment for trade (Rogowski 1989; Solingen 1998; cited in Levy 2003: 128).

The second assumption of the liberal view is problematic. The notion that trade automatically creates interdependence is based on the belief that a substitute is difficult to find due to prohibitive cost of transportation, lack of adequate information (imagine no Internet!), limited number of suppliers, standardization, ideological split (e.g. the Cold War), and above all, government regulations – restrictive trade policies and/or discriminatory trade politics. Although these arguments had merits in the past, due mainly to economic globalization,[3] they are losing their grounds. After the literature review below, I will elaborate on how such conditions are getting weaker day by day.

A brief literature review

The idea that free trade may reduce conflict dates back to the seventeenth century. As early as 1623, the French monk Emeric Cruce argued that the answer to decreasing the likelihood of war lay in free trade.[4] Subsequent philosophers like Baron De Montesquieu (in 1748),[5] Immanuel Kant (1795), British Statesman Richard Cobden (in 1846), John Bright (in 1858), Sir Norman Angell (in 1913) and Jacob Viner (in 1937) espoused the same view (cited in Polachek 2001). Former US President Woodrow Wilson also believed that 'a world open for commerce would be a world at peace' (Destler 2005: 6) and Franklin D. Roosevelt's Secretary of State, Cordell Hull, became convinced that 'unhampered trade dove-tailed with peace; high tariffs, trade barriers, and unfair economic competition, with war' (quoted in Destler 2005: 15). There is also a long history of sceptics to the liberal view. For example, Hamilton (in 1791), List (in 1842) and Hirschman (in 1945) are among those who were sceptical about and critical of the liberal proposition (cited in Schneider *et al.* 2003: 3).[6]

Numerous empirical studies have found that economically important trade has statistically significant and substantial benefits for reducing interstate violence (Oneal and Russett 2003a, 2003b; Robst *et al.* 2006).[7] Bruce Russett (2003: 159), for example, makes the claim that the effect of trade in reducing conflict is a strong and robust generalization. Erik Gartzke (2005) has shown a strong positive relationship between economic freedom and peace.

Several empirical studies have found evidence contrary to the liberal claim. For instance, Katherine Barbieri (2005) has not only challenged the existing liberal view but also counterclaimed that trade promotes conflict. Marxian-based theories contend that colonialism and imperialism go hand in hand. According to these models, powerful states use force to expand trade, which instigate conflict. Pointing to the high correlation between military spending and engagement in conflict, another set of models (gains-from-trade models) argues that trade gains are asymmetrically distributed. Gains from trade are used to build military capability, which ultimately raises coercion. A third set of arguments is based on game theory. Claiming trade as a zero-sum game, such models argue that trade creates gains, which has inherent distributional problems that instigate conflict.

Polachek and Seiglie (2006) counter argue that none of the claims contradicts the liberal view. First, according to these authors, Marxian-based thesis is not valid because trade is voluntary; second, the high correlation between military expenditure and conflict does not prove that trade increases conflict because nations seldom fight with trading partners; and finally, they suggest that game-theory based analysis is irrelevant because of its positive-sum nature, and multi-party involvement in international trades.

Although 'overwhelming evidence indicates that trade reduces conflict regardless of the proxies used to capture the gains from trade and conflict' (Polachek and Seigle 2006: 62), interdependence based trade-conflict analysis is losing its ground due mainly to rapid globalization. For example, Martin *et al.* (2005) demonstrate that 'countries more open to global trade have higher probability of war because *multilateral trade openness decreases bilateral dependence to any given country*' (emphasis added). In fact, massive liberalization, widespread privatization, and unprecedented technological innovation have changed the global scene remarkably. Clearly the proliferation of regional integration has appeared as a new phenomenon in the field of international political economy.

Changes due to globalization

One of the main problems with the existing trade-conflict analysis comes from the massive change due to globalization that removes restrictions on trade– leaving less opportunity cost of conflict. In fact, in the days of extensive restrictions, trade liberalization was thought to be a promoter to peace through creating increasing interdependence among states. Paradoxically when liberalization has been widespread, the power of creating sufficient interdependence through further liberalization has waned. This has been manifested by some recent findings where trade 'interdependence appears to be insignificant' (Goldsmith 2006: 547).

Following the so-called 'Washington Consensus' (in short, a prescription for 'stabilization, privatization, and liberalization; see Rodrik 2006), most developing countries have implemented extensive liberalization and substantial privatization programmes since the 1990s. Communication and transportation technologies have advanced so far that the world is now being called a global village. The terminologies such as 'death of distance' (Cairncross 2001), 'end of the nation state' (Ohmae 1995), 'silent takeover' (Hertz 2001) and 'borderless world' (Ohmae 1999) etc., are not free from controversies. These terms, however, at the very least indicate that the world has changed a lot–particularly during the last half of the twentieth century.[8] There has been a remarkable change in attitudes and beliefs as well. For instance, military coercion was more acceptable in a nineteenth-century international system than it is in the current period (Nye 1971: 78). States, though still the most important actor, are no longer the sole agent of international decision-making; there are private enterprises, various social organizations and NGOs, to press for the voice of the people to be heard. 'The international policy-making stage is increasingly congested as private and public non-state actors jostle alongside national governments in setting and implementing the agenda of the new century' (Thakur 2002: 268).

According to Nye (2002a) 'the information revolution, technological change and globalization will not replace the nation-state but will continue to complicate the actors and issues in world politics'. Kupchan (2003) argues that the ongoing economic, political and social change will call into question whether the nation-state will remain the world's dominant political unit. Apparently, states have been severely constrained in capacity and policy autonomy (Evans 1997; Rodrik 1997). There has been a massive policy shift as well: inward-looking strategy has been replaced by export-led growth strategy, and the conquest of foreign markets is being considered superior to the conquest of foreign territories (see Rosecrance 1986).

As a result of these changes, throughout the centuries and particularly since the Second World War, economics has gained substantial strength in influencing world (political) affairs. Bayne and Woolcock (2003: 4) assert that economic diplomacy is gaining increasing importance because of rapid globalization, particularly after the Cold War. This is not to claim that economics has overpowered politics, but to note that in a relative sense economics has become more influential on world affairs than ever before. As Gowa (1994: 116) notes:

> The pre-1914 and post-1945 worlds differed markedly. In the earlier period, the use of trade to influence the play of great-power politics was almost nonexistent. In the other period, the superpowers waged the Cold War not only on political-military but also on economic battlefields.

In reality, there are cases where commercial interest shapes political relations. For instance we may recall the détente between the USA and the USSR during the 1960s, and President Clinton's policy towards China in the 1990s.[9] The recent opening up of Nathu La Pass between China and India is also being seen as a way forward to minimizing political conflict between the two countries through bilateral trade gains via the Pass (Mohanty 2006).[10] The recent US offer of trade deals to entice Iran (Cooper 2006) is another glaring example along these lines.[11] Although there is widespread controversy over its effectiveness, the frequent use of trade sanctions against a number of belligerent states indicates that 'trade matters'. Consistent pro-trade policies and politics for decades have made almost every nation outward-looking, and as a result has created some kind of interdependence on the global system.

Interdependence and opportunity cost of conflict

The economic opportunity-cost argument is contingent on the degree of (inter)dependence–the more a country is dependent, the more the opportunity cost of conflict. Conventionally, it is assumed that trade automatically creates interdependence, which is not necessarily true unless some conditions are fulfilled. As Gowa (1994: 118) argues:

> Large volumes of trade between or among prospective belligerents, however, are not necessarily a valid indicator of the trade-related opportunity costs of

war. Instead, what really matters is whether close substitutes exist for the export markets and imports that prewar trading partners supplied. If such substitutes exist, then the trade related opportunity costs of war will be low.

Similarly, Crescenzi (2005: 24) notes that 'high levels of economic activity may not signal interdependence if both parties are able to access new markets at home and abroad in the event of a disruption in trade'. If we consider the current speed of globalization, increased trade cannot be taken as a valid barometer of interdependence. The main point is whether close substitutes are available or not. In the following section I explore why such substitutes are more easily available now than ever before.

Availability of close substitutes

Given the changes due to globalization described earlier, there are several reasons to believe that substitutes are more easily available nowadays than at any time before. As the cost of transportation has, and is still being, decreased, it is now feasible for more sources to be supplied at competitive prices. Due to the unprecedented development of telecommunication technology along with the magic of the Internet facilities, information has virtually become limitless. Moreover, because of extensive privatization,[12] Adam Smith's 'invisible hand' is much more efficient now in allocating scarce resources and responding to incentives. A great number of suppliers are readily available on equitable and affordable terms and conditions. The more the number of trading partners, the less the dyadic (inter)dependence, and hence, 'trade flows alone may not be an optimal measure of interdependence' (Gartzke *et al.* 2001: 394). Gowa (1994: 118) argues that 'if trade is to act as a significant deterrent to war, the opportunity costs of disrupting prewar trading patterns must be high'. Hence gains from trade alone cannot offer the desired peace dividend because similar gains may be extracted by building trade relations with states other than those that are belligerent. It appears that the gain from trade is a necessary but not a sufficient condition for peace. In short, when the number of (potential) suppliers is large, substitutes are available, and switching costs are negligible or not prohibitive, then even a large volume of dyadic trade does not create as much interdependence as liberals claim, and therefore, cannot raise the economic opportunity cost high enough to deter interstate conflict.

So far, mainly through dyadic analysis, most scholars have come to a conclusion that trade creates interdependence among trading partners, raises the opportunity cost of conflict, and hence promotes peace. But now the entire equation is changing due to globalization. As a consequence of substantial trade liberalization, the opportunity-cost argument is losing ground. While the dyadic analysis is becoming problematic, interestingly regional integration is appearing as another ingredient in the trade-conflict discourse, one that opens trade for a certain group of countries but not for others.[13] A question that naturally arises is: do regional economic integrations have any pacifying effect, within the group, and with outsiders? Now we will introduce regional integration into the debate and see how it interacts with the existing liberal view.

Positioning regional integration in the trade-conflict discourse

Among the many remarkable changes that took place during the 1990s, the proliferation of regional integration has been seen as a huge phenomenon in the field of international political economy, and this is gaining increasing attention in managing regional as well as global governance.[14] Economic implications of this new development have been widely studied and fiercely debated, but analyses of its impact on political–military relations have been sparse (Mansfield and Pevehouse 2003: 248).

The initial focus of the debate was basically confined to Jacob Viner's (1950) trade-creation versus trade-diversion arguments. Subsequently, proponents point to the 'dynamic effects' and argue that regional integration is something more than trade (i.e. trade-plus). Limao (2002: 30) observes that 'trade is not the only and often not even the main motivation for preferential trade agreements. Thus far we have neglected to model these other motives and the effects of such agreements on the multilateral trading system' (see also Limao 2007). Surprisingly, despite this recognition:

> while the economic effects of establishing PTAs [preferential trading agreements] have been debated at great length, the political effects of doing so have received far shorter shrift. However, there is ample reason to expect that the growth of these arrangements will promote peace and cooperation among member states, an important political benefit that has not been fully appreciated in debates on the consequences of regionalism
> (Mansfield 2003: 232)

Specifically, Mansfield and Pevehouse (2003: 235) warn that analyses ignoring the effects of PTAs risk arriving at misleading conclusions about the relationship between commerce and conflict.

Peace dividend via regional integration

Regional integration has several explicit and some implicit benefits. Through specialization, regional integration offers more gains from trade, and therefore creates more opportunity cost of conflict. Numerous studies find that neighbouring countries are more conflict-prone.[15] As integration is usually formed among closest neighbours, and 'most of the world's disputes tend to take place between neighboring states' (Kupchan 2003: 71), the pacifying effect of regional integration should naturally be substantial.

Trade is the strongest means of cooperation but it is not the only factor of interdependence in regional integration arrangements. Regional integration is said to be trade-plus, where many treaties or understandings, often with separate institutions, bind member states in a system of collective governance. As a result, states become markedly interdependent without necessarily increasing the share of trade. For instance, many regional integration arrangements notified to the WTO have achieved little progress in an economic sense. Nevertheless, their political impact is discernable (e.g. in Africa). In this line of reasoning, Bearce (2003) maintains that even apparently ineffective and economically-focused regional organizations can have a significant impact on conflict (cited in Goldsmith 2004).

Frequent interactions through various avenues created by regional integration build confidence among member states, which ultimately increases mutual trust to share sensitive/strategic goods and information. Furthermore, with widening and deepening of such relationships, countries gradually become dependent on a group of countries around them, rather than on any particular one. Small states enjoy a special benefit through tagging themselves to a regional group – frequently consisting of many of their potential enemies (e.g. regional hegemonies).[16] Nye (1971: 12) rightly points out that the temptation to foreign intervention and conflict could be removed if small states were amalgamated into larger regional units. Apart from these formal avenues, *elite socialization* through frequent inter-actions develops feelings of collective identity among the leaders/bureaucrats taking part (Nye 1971: 69). Bearce and Omori (2005) find a substantively strong and statistically significant effect in reducing the outbreak of military conflict when commercial institutions have more organs to bring high-level state leaders together on a regular basis.

Formation of a regional group may change the behaviour of a state towards its neighbours, because the power equation becomes one-versus-the-group. Attacking an integrated state becomes extremely risky as well as costly for another state. It becomes risky in the sense that hostile attitudes against any member state may make some others equally belligerent. It becomes costly because hostile activity adversely affects the whole region – 'leaders of integrated states who threaten a neighbor encourage investors to flee' (Gartzke and Li 2003a: 563).

In the occurence of any disagreements between some members over an issue, other member states quickly become an active mediator – either to press for, or help achieve, peaceful settlement. They are in a better position to take immediate and necessary action because they are better informed about the core issue and its background. Regional groups thus become a 'safety valve' to prevent further escalation of conflict. In this way, 'preferential groupings minimize conflict by both holding out the promise of economic gains and providing institutional mechanisms to deal with the negative political-military internalities stemming from economic interaction' (Mansfield and Pevehouse 2003: 235).

Regional integration has some implicit benefits as well. Through widening and deepening the process of integration, a region increases the economies of scale and scope, which makes it an attractive home for foreign investment from other regions. This increased inter-regional economic engagement, mainly through private initia-tives, ultimately creates pressure on the respective governments to solve disputes, if any, through peaceful means. For instance, one major reason of President Clinton's de-linking human rights issues from the annual extension of 'most favoured nation' status to China was the fierce business campaign (Destler 2005: 213).

Regional organizations can be a balancing element to the unipolar world as well. Obsessed with bipolarity and its potential risks, in the late 1960s some people started to see regional integration in Europe as an important step towards restoring multipolarity and flexibility of the international system (Nye 1971:12). However, what we have observed since the 1990s is rather a unipolar world under US hegemony – though paradoxically, with numerous regional integration arrangements around the globe. Although no regional organization can be considered strong enough to be called a 'polar' in the strictest sense against the USA, it would be unfair if we ignored the importance of such organizations in global governance. At least in an economic sense, many regional groups are playing significant roles, though implicitly, in balancing the present unipolarity. For instance, Nye (2002b: 244) is of the opinion that 'Europe is already well placed to balance the United States on the economic and transnational chessboards'.

Most regional agreements contain a conditionality or commitment to the promotion of democracy, the maintenance of the rule of law, and respect for human rights and so on. Almost all such arrangements include a strong desire to solve their disputes peacefully. In a number of initiatives, regional security appears as a policy objective. Examples include: the ECSC, the EEC, ASEAN, and MERCOSUR (De Lombaerde 2005). Turkey's keen interest to enter the EU umbrella is apparently driven by security concerns rather than just for economic gains. Likewise, a well-functioning ASEAN+3 might play a significant role in achieving political stability in North Asia. The same is true with SAARC in South Asia.

In short, mutual economic interest, political commitment, frequent communication, etc., collectively create a 'Perceived Regional Implicit Security Enclave' (PRISE, for short).[17] This notion of a security enclave (e.g. PRISE) acts as a security magnet not only for a particular region but also for its closest neighbours and, plausibly also for outsiders. Experience from around the world shows that PRISE works better in integration with strong institutional settings and pragmatic leadership.

Regional integration and liberal argument

The alternative routes to liberal argument through regional economic integration are shown in Box 10.2 (compare with the simple diagram in Box 10.1).

Box 10.2   Modified liberal view over trade and conflict with regional integration

Regional free trade → regional division of labour → better gains from trade (due to higher complementarity compared to bilateral relationship) → specialization within the region →less dyadic but more systemic (i.e. regional) interdependence → higher opportunity cost of conflict (one versus the group) → more incentive to retain regional as well as global peace.

(Here '→' indicates 'leads to')

By liberalizing trade among regional partners (or being committed to doing so), states implicitly create a security enclave among themselves. By being a party to a larger group of neighbours, a state becomes heavily dependent – not on any particular country, but on the regional group. Deeper economic engagements and frequent interactions of political leaders create a sense of 'community' (at least in an economic sense) among the member states. The common economic interests and new interdependence make a regional war costly, and, as a result, leaders are motivated to seek peaceful options to settle their internal disputes.

As the Box10.2 shows, the inclusion of regional integration in the analysis may change the definition and/or interaction of interdependence, but it does not necessarily change the basic idea of the commercial peace hypothesis. It supports, rather than contradicts, the liberal view. Apart from the EU, there are some other emerging initiatives along this line. The ASEAN Regional Forum (ARF), African Union, MERCOSUR and ECOWAS[18] are some of the notable endeavours for peace through regional integration.

Regional integration in South Asia and its security dilemma

South Asia joined the race for region formation in 1985 by establishing SAARC – the 'South Asian Association for Regional Cooperation'. SAARC is a seven-nation[19] regional forum comprising Bangladesh, Bhutan, India, Maldives, Nepal, Pakistan and Sri Lanka. Occupying only 3 per cent of the world's land, the region is the home of one-fifth of the world's population. With 55 per cent of adult literacy, more than 40 per cent of the population lives below the poverty line. The region shares 0.8 per cent of global trade, and the intra-SAARC trade is only about 5.3 per cent.[20]

On the economic front, SAARC initiated the 'South Asian Preferential Trade Arrangement' (SAPTA) in 1993. More recently, the South Asian Free Trade Area (SAFTA) has been operational since 2006. However, any progress has frequently been caught up by political deadlock, often between India and Pakistan.[21] In any case, past experience shows that politics has always been the main obstacle to progress in economic cooperation among South Asian nations.

The security dilemma in South Asia

In South Asia, the India–Pakistan conflict has been going on for more than half a century. The two nations have fought on several occasions but reached no solution. Apparently they are trapped in a security dilemma: independent action taken by one state to build up its own strength and security makes the other more insecure. The arms race between India and Pakistan has ended up with nuclear capability on both the sides. As a matter of fact, the belief that one can make oneself secure by amassing superior arms has proved to be false.[22] The conflict between India and Pakistan has not only been a problem between the two but has also appeared as a big obstacle in the overall development of the region, and in particular, in the progress in SAARC, with which the livelihood of millions of the poor is directly linked.

States could cooperate to avoid this security dilemma; that is, they could agree that none should build up its defences and all would be better off (Nye 1993: 12). In reality, however, it is difficult to achieve. Many factors, such as mistrust and miscalculation, become a hindrance to such a mutual agreement. Nye (1993: 37) therefore argues that a better solution to avoid war is to pursue economic growth in an open trading system without military conquest. Japan has demonstrated that economic strength is no less powerful than military might (see Rosecrance 1986).

After two decades it has become clear that the progress in SAARC is far from satisfactory, if not disappointing.[23] A popular saying goes, 'SAARC will never get momentum until the problems between India and Pakistan are solved' (see Bhatta 2004; Naik 2004). A contrary view is that problems between India and Pakistan will never be solved until SAARC gains momentum (Dahal 2004). This is clearly a 'chicken and egg' problem. Hitherto, political attempts to resolve the Indo-Pakistani enmity over half a century have not been successful. The poorest of the poor people in the region cannot afford to allow politicians another half a century to solve the problem. Therefore, there is a pressing need to look for alternatives. As mentioned before, one such alternative is popularly known as the commercial peace hypothesis, i.e. the use of economic interdependence to minimize political rivalry. This is a soft and indirect way of tackling hardcore political problems. The unprecedented success of the EU in bringing political tensions down to zero among member states could be a good guide for other regions, and this is particularly true for South Asia. The following section will examine how the EU succeeded in the initial years of region formation and how economic, as well as political objectives, were achieved.

Regional integration in Europe

The destruction of two World Wars within a quarter of a century forced the Europeans to unite against the possibility of such a recurrence. As the founding fathers rightly envisaged that political integration at the first stage would be difficult to carry out, they decisively took an indirect (i.e. economic) route to the accomplishment of their goal. In the words of Baldwin and Wyplosz (2004: 26), 'While the goals were always political, the means were always economic'. The idea of a 'United States of Europe' came up in discussion several times in the aftermath of the First World War, but it did not gain enough momentum before hostilities began again in 1939. At the beginning, the idea of forming a federation or confederation among European States led the move. In reality, however, leaders experienced extreme difficulty in 'selling' their idea of forming such a 'federation' among warring nations. Consequently, a 'piecemeal' approach through functionalism tested the ground by establishing the European Coal and Steel Community (ECSC) in 1951 by virtue of the Schuman Plan and the public relations excellence of Jean Monnet. The ECSC offered the first gratifying taste of cooperation among European nations, the success of which encouraged the signing of the Treaty of Rome in 1957 to form the European Economic Community (EEC) – the precursor of today's EU. The first decade of the EEC was very successful with the Common Agricultural Policy (CAP) being adopted, and a common external tariff (e.g. customs union) established.

The progress, however, was not always as smooth as expected. It is widely believed that the 'empty chair' policy of France followed by the 'Luxemburg Compromise'[24] in the late 1960s, the breakdown of the Bretton Woods System,[25] and the oil shocks in the 1970s slowed down the progress of European integration. Nevertheless, through a series of bold measures such as the Single European Act in 1987, the Maastricht Treaty in 1992, introduction of the euro as a common currency in 1999, and, finally, the wide enlargement in 2004, the EU has achieved stability, peace and prosperity in Europe.

The pressure to accept the idea of a 'united Europe' came forth from many factors. First, the horrors of frequent war with huge human and economic losses compelled the Europeans to think of uniting against such events ever happening again. Indeed, the Second World War was the fourth time in 130 years that France and Germany had been at the core of horrifying wars. The Second World War claimed 8 million people in Western Europe. Eastern Europe lost 9 million, and the Soviet Union alone lost 20 million people (Baldwin and Wyplosz 2004: 3). The economic and humanitarian situation in Europe was equally dire in the years of 1945–47, especially in Germany. Much of Europe's infrastructure, industry and housing lay in ruins. Hunger was widespread. All this suffering was the prime motivation to accept any proposal to avoid such a situation. Therefore, when the French proposed the ECSC, the Germans accepted.

Second, the threat of the spread of communism was another issue that forced the Western Europeans to unite. The East–West divide in Europe due to the Cold War between the USSR and the USA was one of the main reasons behind European unity.[26]

Third, the conditions laid down in the Marshall Plan required European countries to act collectively in the deployment of the financial assistance provided under the plan. The financial support through the plan was extremely important to Europe in recovering from the wreckage of the war. However, in the aftermath of the Korean War in the early 1950s, it was clear that the support was not without cost. European leaders could recognize the value of the generous US support, but at the same time they took into account the potential political price subtly attached to it. This sense of US hegemony made the European leaders consider a supranational structure for the ECSC. Probably they rationally thought that it was better to accept European supranationality, rather than live under US hegemony. These factors made politicians more committed towards unity in order to regain the lost dignity of Europe.

Are there any such motivations for South Asia to be united?

Obviously, not all the motivating factors that drove the Europeans to be united are entirely present in South Asia. However, if we look closely, we may find similar, if not the same, pressures to be united regionally.

First, India and Pakistan have also fought at least three major wars since their independence in 1947. Although human loss was not comparable to that in Europe, given the nuclear capability now of both the sides, the potential human and economic loss is enormous. Needless to say, existing tension and uncertainty is no less detrimental to the economies in the region.

Second, globalization has forced all the South Asian countries to open up. The South Asian nations are competing against other Asian and non-Asian regional groups (e.g. African, Latin American) in the world market: a rising China, growing ASEAN, and developing ASEAN+3, plus a growing number of other regional groups in Africa and Latin America, are all potential threats to South Asian exports. The situation appears to be such that when other nations around the world are getting together to fight for the global market, it makes little sense to continue hostility against close neighbours. As former US President, Jimmy Carter (2002),[27] asserts, 'war may sometimes be a necessary evil. But no matter how necessary, it is always an evil, never a good'.

Third, at present, of course, there is no threat from communism; however, China silently 'taking over' the world market is no less threatening to poorer countries in the south than territorial occupation.[28] Nevertheless, if China eventually merges with ASEAN to make it 'plus three', there will be little option left for South Asia but to unite under a regional umbrella.

Finally, aggressive pushing of bilateralism by the USA, and promotional support for regionalism by the EU[29] has become obvious. Recent US policy of taking 'one-by-one' through bilateralism–undermining multilateral systems–should be a genuine concern to the leaders in South Asia. Being a superpower, bilateral economic/security support by the US is most likely to produce asymmetric results against developing countries. Regional integration could be an 'escape clause' for weaker countries from the bilateral trap. As Farrell (2005) observes, 'In absence of any direct challenge to hegemonic rule, inter-regional cooperation remains an indirect reaction to the pervasive influence and might of the world's super-power'.

Key success factors of the ECSC

Above, we have seen why the Europeans accepted supranationality and sacrificed sovereignty. Here, we will detail some of the success factors that contributed to the emergence of supranationality. The well-thought-out Schuman Plan, excellent 'selling' capability of Jean Monnet and the long-term vision, commitment, and courage of the then leaders in Europe made the plan readily acceptable. The French proposed the plan and the Germans accepted: when 'big brothers' (France and Germany) took a big credible step forward, the smaller countries followed. The Messina Conference asserted greater cooperation among the six members that gave birth to the EEC. All this happened because of the positive externalities demonstrated by the ECSC. Below, we will see some of the factors that made the Schuman Plan a success.

Important and strategic industry

Coal and steel were two of the most important and strategic sectors during the immediate post-war period. These two sectors were strategically essential for military purposes, and important for industrial development. In addition, they were the provider of substantial employment and business opportunities for European citizens. The ECSC, therefore, took charge of highly contentious, but equally beneficial, sectors for cooperation. Demonstration of benefits through cooperation in such an important, strategic and sensitive industry offered enough credibility to extend further cooperation in other areas.

Supranational structure

The most important factor in the success of the ECSC was probably the supranational power of the High Authority, through which Monnet separated the politics from economic decision-making. Appointed by common agreement by the then six governments, its nine members exercised their power directly over the coal and steel companies and European citizens. The High Authority, not the member states, had the final say on the functioning of the ECSC. This was very important in maintaining neutrality, enhancing credibility and gaining acceptability.

Checks and balances

Although the High Authority had 'super power' in theory, it was not imbalanced. The founding fathers had created several other institutions to balance the power of the High Authority. A Council of Ministers was created to coordinate between the coal and steel sectors and the other economic branches of member countries. A Common Assembly was also set up to follow democratic norms and, finally, a Court of Justice was established to ensure that the treaty was respected, and to resolve differences among the member countries and the High Authority. The well-thought-out and balanced structure offered enough avenues for unexpected bubbles to disappear.

Financial liberty

Another interesting fact about the ECSC was that it had financial liberty from the member states. The tax-collecting power gave the High Authority much more freedom of action. The Schuman–Monnet team must have had a hard time persuading the political leaders to agree. However, they finally succeeded in convincing them and this financial liberty provided the ECSC with true supranational power. The financial liberty allowed the High Authority to allocate funds to minimize adjustment costs and displacement effects due to the massive overhauling programme.

Political will, pragmatic leadership

In addition to a superb plan and the excellent public relations of Jean Monnet, political will and pragmatic leadership were very important factors behind the success of the ECSC. Particularly, the prompt acceptance of the then German Chancellor, Konrad Adenauer, offered sufficient credibility to the plan for it to be accepted by some smaller states. Above all, the European leaders could put their regional interest above national interests, and 'the European [integration] revolution left no victims, celebrated no conquests, and avoided the temptations of violence' (Schmitt 2005).

Supranationalism in the EU versus intergovernmentalism in the SAARC

There are several ways of integrating and/or managing integration of a region. Supranationalism and intergovernmentalism are two such competing propositions for managing regional integration arrangements. Functionalism with a supranational structure played an important role in the initial years of the EU formation. As mentioned earlier, the idea of uniting Europe started in line with intergovernmentalism. Eventually, however, the federalist idea prevailed, and the ECSC, a functional organization, was established with a powerful High Authority. The separation of politics from economic decision-making through the supranational structure of the High Authority is considered to be the most important reason for the success of the ECSC. As noted before, a slight derogation from this principle in the late 1960s through the 'Luxembourg compromise' slowed down the integration process and cost a 'lost decade'.

By contrast, since its inception SAARC has been following the intergovernmental method of governance. Needless to say, it has hardly achieved anything special to celebrate its twentieth anniversary. Mediocre achievements through SAPTA show that SAARC failed to achieve economic integration as expected, let alone political coherence. The unprecedented success of functionalism in the formation of the EU and the miserable performance of intergovernmentalism in SAARC are persuasive arguments that functionalism could be a better option, at least at the formation stages. This is particularly true for South Asia where mistrust is high, the effect of deeper economic integration is a grey area, and progress is frequently hindered by political deadlock.

Lessons to be learned

The first and the most important lesson to be learned from the EU experience is the necessity of separating politics from economic decision-making. The ECSC and, in that sense, the EU itself could not be so successful without a supranational authority. The setback due to the Luxemburg compromise proves this.

The inter governmental method of governance has severe limitations. In intergovernmentalism everything is seen through a 'political prism'. More often than not, it is dictated by the 'public choice theory'[30] where political elites are more concerned either with staying in power or with being re-elected in the next election, rather than with supporting policies for overall development or the common good. Therefore, the first and foremost task is to separate politics from economic decision-making. In reality, any move beyond an FTA would eventually need a supranational structure. For that reason, it would have been better if supranationality had been introduced from the beginning.

Another important lesson from the EU experience is that the supranational authority should not only be free from the political ambit but also have an independent source of income. Otherwise unstable flows of funds may interrupt the smooth functioning of the organization.

While sufficient power should be assigned to the supranational authority, it should not be an unbridled horse. The High Authority of the ECSC used to possess supreme power, but there were several other institutions in the system to maintain checks and to balance the power of the High Authority. Leaders in South Asia should keep this in mind.

The way forward

If someone asks whether the EU model is straightforwardly applicable in South Asia, then the plain answer is 'no', simply because the two regions are different in many respects. However, the experience of the EU, could of course, be a good guide to solving the political problems in South Asia and elsewhere. Before arguing further, I would like to restate a few things.

First, the EU could solve political problems through economic integration. By contrast, India and Pakistan have political problems over Kashmir but could not reach any solution for more than half a century. Second, separation of politics from economic decision-making (e.g. with a supranational structure, at least in the ECSC) worked well in case of the EU, but intergovernmentalism has grossly failed to do so in South Asia. Third, coal and steel industries were important in a strategic and economic sense in Europe in the 1950s. At that time, politics played a very important role in controlling economic affairs. Today, globalization is the most important vehicle for growth, and now economics plays a much more important role in controlling politics. Fourth, it was not easy to separate politics from economics in the 1950s. Now private enterprises, not governments, do business. Therefore, it should not be that difficult to separate the two. Fifth, we do not know yet the exact impact of the South Asian Free Trade Area (SAFTA) – its adjustment cost or displacement effect, particularly on the poor. If leaders cannot agree on specific sectoral cooperation, how can they agree on thousands of industries at a time? Hence, it is logical to adopt a step-by-step approach rather than doing it all at once. Finally, the opportunity cost of conflict is much higher now than ever before; therefore, it is logical to think of mitigating political conflict through peaceful (e.g. economic) means.

Conclusion

The economic world is taking a new shape through regional integration. New waves of globalization are putting enormous pressure on states to cooperate regionally. Regional organizations have been playing important roles in mitigating interstate conflict. Research on the commercial peace hypothesis has strongly demonstrated that interdependence reduces political conflict. Regional integration has strengthened these arguments.

While the EU has been successful in mitigating interstate conflict through deeper economic integration, on the contrary, based on the intergovernmental method, SAARC has grossly failed to do so. Due to huge size asymmetry in the region, the ultimate effect of SAFTA is hard to calculate beforehand.[31] Though desirable, the acceptance of free trade all at once may cause huge adjustment cost and displacement effect. Hence, it might be easier to absorb probable shocks gradually through a piecemeal approach – where successful integration of key sectors may eventually pave the way for wider and deeper integration.

Sectors in which member states have the most interest should be selected first to start cooperating within a limited supranational authority.[32] This 'pooling' (not necessarily sacrificing) of sovereignty will abolish unnecessary reservations on the issue and, most likely, will show the high opportunity cost of non-cooperation. There are reasons to believe that ability is not a problem in replicating the EU model in SAARC, but the willingness certainly is. What is desperately needed is the visionary mind of putting regional or collective interest above the national interest and a readiness to allow some kind of supranationality. If it becomes possible, then that must be a 'paradigm shift' in the right direction. Such a supranational organization for SAARC should contain stakeholders from governments, the business community and NGOs.

While the world is often amazed by the so-called 'grand successes' of summit meetings of SAARC, little is known about the functioning of its Secretariat. This indicates that the organization has been assigned few tasks and given insufficient power compared with the EU Commission. This is certainly at odds with the often-mentioned vision of establishing a South Asian Economic Community (SAEC). In this respect, although the EU model is not fully applicable to SAARC, its invaluable experience could certainly be a good guide for South Asia.

Despite all these arguments, if South Asian leaders do not see the potential of peace through economic integration, then they have failed to notice at least two points. First, they have overlooked the unprecedented opportunity through globalization in the twenty-first century. Second, they have disregarded the desires of millions of poor people who are eagerly waiting to move out of poverty – setting aside fruitless, egoistic political tensions in the region. Globalization has offered a 'golden duck' especially to the developing countries; but without a favourable environment she will never lay the desired egg. Without immediate and peaceful settlement of contentious issues, South Asia's road to further progress is certainly bumpy, if not blocked. We must not forget the teachings of Mahatma Gandhi: 'There is no way to peace. Peace is the way'.[33] It is to be seen whether the present leaders in South Asia show enough courage to recognize the past weaknesses and take corrective actions now for a brighter future for the people in the region.

Notes

1 The issue of global governance through regional organizations gains new impetus when the United Nations (UN) places special emphasis on regional organizations in managing regional conflict. See at www.un.org, news on the Sixth High-Level Meeting with Heads of Regional and Other Intergovernmental Organizations at New York on 25 July 2005.

2   For a comprehensive coverage of the recent debate, see Mansfield and Pollins (2003), and Schneider *et al.* (2003).
3   Economic globalization implies an international market of goods and factors of production, financial capital moving across national borders with relatively little friction, production networks spread over several states, and elaborate communication networks linking people around the globe (Gartzke and Li 2003b: 124).
4   Contrary to this, most early Christian theologians questioned the legitimacy of commerce. St Augustine went as far as saying that 'For they are active traders ... they attain not the grace of God' (quoted in Irwin 1996; cited in Schneider *et al.* 2003: 6).
5   'Commerce cures destructive prejudices ... the natural effect of commerce is to lead to peace' (Montesquieu 1989 [1748]), cited in Irwin 2002: 45–46).
6   Critics of free markets, such as V.I. Lenin (1970 [1916]) and Patrick Buchanan (1998), argue that globalization generates not amity, but added international antagonism (cited in Gartzke and Li 2003a: 562). Kenneth Waltz (1979) belongs to this group.
7   For a list of various studies related to trade and conflict, see Table 1.2 in Schneider *et al.* 2003: 17.
8   The world is changing at a speed never before experienced by the human race (Hiranuma 2000).
9   In his 27 January 2000 State of the Union Address, President Bill Clinton exhorted: 'Congress should support the agreement we negotiated to bring China into the WTO, by passing Permanent Normal Trade Relations with China as soon as possible.... [because] it will plainly advance the cause of peace in Asia' (www.gpo.gov/ congress/sou/sou00.html, accessed on 14 July 2006).
10 'But at the moment most agree that there are more immediate political benefits rather than economic.' BBC News: http://news.bbc.co.uk/2/hi/south_asia/5150682.stm (6 July 2006).
11 To ease the problems of the North Korean nuclear issue, Nye (2007) suggests 'offering gradual economic integration in return for a freeze in the production of fissile material'.
12 'Firms not states trade' (Krugman 1996; cited in Schneider *et al.* 2003: 4).
13 While Article 24 of GATT/WTO does not allow member states to raise trade barriers for outsiders, by removing trade barriers among themselves, in a relative sense, they give the appearance of erecting barriers to outsiders.
14 For example, the recent UN emphasis on the role of regional organizations in partnering to manage regional conflicts, the role of ECOWAS, the African Union, MERCO-SUR, SADC, etc.
15 Vasquez (1995: 280) finds that contiguity is the single largest factor promoting interactions and contiguous states are more likely to have serious disputes and war. Buzan *et al.* (1998: 11) note that 'Insecurity is often associated with proximity and most states fear their neighbors more than distant powers'. Nye (1971: 17) observes that 'Proximate states are the ones more likely to become involved in conflict and thus they have the greatest need for [such a] functional link'.
16 The position of Uruguay and Paraguay in the MERCOSUR was similar during the 1990s (see Schirm 2002 Chapter 4).
17 Nye (1971: 11) also argued that 'regional economic organizations may create islands of peace in the international system'.
18 ECOWAS : Economic Community of West African States.
19 The number becomes eight after Afghanistan joined SAARC in 2007.
20 See 'SAARC Postponement' (16–28 February 2005). *World Trade Review* (Editorial). Available at: www.worldtradereview.com/news.asp?pType=S&sID=13 &iID=101&i Type=A&lType=D
21 For example, the postponement because of New Delhi's 'grave concerns' of the 13th SAARC Summit (which was supposed to be held in Dhaka in early 2005) raised scepticism in neighbouring countries about the progress in economic cooperation through intergovernmental dialogue.

22 The balance-of-power theory could not prevent these two countries from fighting each other. The American President during the First World War, Woodrow Wilson, felt that the balance of power was an evil principle because it encouraged statesmen to treat nations like cheeses to be cut up for political convenience regardless of the concerns of their people. Wilson also disliked the balance-of-power because he believed it caused war (Nye 1993: 49). Nevertheless, the Cold War was conducted on the basis of balance- of-power principles – and the superpowers managed to avoid an outright confrontation as a result.

23 For a detailed discussion on the progress of SAARC, see Rodrigo (2004).

24 See www.ena.lu/mce.cfm

25 See www.econ.iastate.edu/classes/econ355/choi/bre.htm or http://canadianeconomy. gc.ca/english/economy/1944Bretton_woods.html (accessed on 22 September 2005).

26 See how the Cold War began at: http://history.acusd.edu/gen/20th/coldwar1.html (accessed on 22 October 2005).

27 Nobel Peace Prize Acceptance Speech at Oslo on December 10, 2002. Available at: http://nobelprize.org/peace/laureates/2002/carter-lecture.html (accessed on 22 October 2005).

28 For example, China already has captured a lion's share of the world textile and clothing market, raising serious concern in some of the least developed as well as developing countries in South Asia.

29 We can recall here the policies and agreements of the EU with various regional organizations in Africa.

30 For a short introduction see: www.econlib.org/library/Enc/PublicChoiceTheory.html

31 Unfortunately, there does not yet appear to be any considerable research on the impact of SAFTA.

32 A 'South Asian Economic Community' (SAEC) could be established with a view to separate economic matters from politics. While such a community is good in theory, in practice it is difficult to convince concerned stakeholders to agree to it. Therefore, at the beginning, a specific sector in which most member states have substantial interest could be selected. For some practical reasons, the writer proposes a 'South Asian Textiles and Apparel Community' (SATAC) for regional cooperation, which would have positive spillover effects on other areas of potential cooperation before the wide functioning of the aforementioned SAEC.

33 Cited in: www.dadalos.org/frieden_int/ (accessed on 1 October 2005).

References

Baldwin, Richard and Charles Wyplosz, 2004. *The Economics of European Integration*. London: McGraw-Hill.

Barbieri, Katherine, 2005. *The Liberal Illusion: Does Trade Promote Peace?*. Ann Arbor, MI: University of Michigan Press.

Bayne, Nicholas and Stephen Woolcock, 2003. *The New Economic Diplomacy*. Aldershot: Ashgate Publishing Ltd.

Bearce, David H., 2003. 'Grasping the Commercial Institutional Peace', *International Studies Quarterly* 47(3): 347–370.

Bearce, David H. and Sawa Omori, 2005. 'How Do Commercial Institutions Promote Peace?', *Journal of Peace Research* 42(6): 659–678.

Bhatta, C.D., 2004. 'Regional Integration and Peace in South Asia: Cooperation versus Conflicts', *Journal of Peace, Conflict and Development,* July.

Bradford, Scott C. Paul L.E. Grieco and Gary Clyde Hufbauer, 2005. 'The Payoff to America from Global Integration', in C. Fred Bergsten (ed.), The United States and the World Economy. Washington, DC: Institute for International Economics, Chapter 2.

Buchanan, Patrick J., 1998. *The Great Betrayal: How American Sovereignty and Social Justice are being Sacrificed to the Gods of the Global Economy.* Boston, MA: Little, Brown.

Buzan, Barry, Ole Waver and Jaap de Wilde, 1998. *Security: A New Framework of Analysis.* London: Lynne Rienner.

Cairncross, C. Frances, 2001. *The Death of Distance: How the Communications Revolution Is Changing Our Lives.* London: Texere.

Cooper, Helene, 2006. 'US. Is Offering Deals on Trade to Entice Iran', *New York Times,* 6 June.

Crescenzi, Mark J.C., 2005. *Economic Interdependence and Conflict in World Politics.* Oxford: Lexington Books.

Dahal, Navin, 2004. 'Indo-Pak Ties and SAARC', *Kathmandu Post,* 20 January.

De Lombaerde, Philippe, 2005. 'Regional Integration and Peace', *Peace and Conflict Monitor.* Costa Rica: University of Peace (www.monitor.upeace.org/innerpg.cfm?id_article=268).

Destler, I.M., 2005. *American Trade Politics* (4th edition). Washington, DC: Institute of International Economics.

Evans, Peter, 1997. 'The Eclipse of the State? Reflections on Stateness in an Era of Globalization', *World Politics* 50(1): 62–87.

Farrell, Mary 2005. 'The EU and Inter-regional Cooperation in Search of Global Presence', in Erik Jones and Amy Verdun (eds), *The Political Economy of European Integration Theory and Analysis.* London: Routledge, pp. 128–148.

Gartzke, Erik, 2005. 'Economic Freedom and Peace', in James D. Gwartney and Robert Lawson (with Erik Gartzke) *Economic Freedom of the World: 2005 Annual Report.* Canada: Fraser Institute.

Gartzke, Erik and Quan Li, 2003a. 'War, Peace, and the Invisible Hand: Positive Political Externalities of Economic Globalization', *International Studies Quarterly* 47: 561–586.

Gartzke, Erik and Quan Li, 2003b. 'How Globalization Can Reduce International Conflict', in Gerald Schneider, Katherine Barbieri and Nils Petter Gleditsch (eds), *Globalization and Arms Conflict,* Lanham, MD: Rowman and Littlefield, pp. 123–140.

Gartzke, Erik, Quan Li and Charles Boehmer, 2001. 'Investing in the Peace: Economic Interdependence and International Conflict', International Organization 55(2): 391–438.

Goldsmith, Benjamin E., 2004. 'Democracy, Interdependence, International Organizations and Asian Security', Asia Pacific School of Economics and Government Discussion Paper No. 04–08. Canberra: Australian National University.

Goldsmith, Benjamin E., 2006. 'A Universal Proposition? Region, Conflict, War and the Robustness of the Kantian Peace', *European Journal of International Relations* 12(4): 533–563.

Gowa, Joanne, 1994. *Allies, Adversaries, and International Trade.* Princeton, NJ: Princeton University Press.

Hertz, Noreena, 2001. *The Silent Takeover.* London: William Heinemann.

Hettne, Bjorn, 2005. 'Regionalism and World Order', in Mary Farrell, Bjorn Hettne and Luk Van Langenhove (eds), *Global Politics of Regionalism: Theory and Practice,* London: Pluto Press.

Hiranuma, Takeo, 2000. 'Challenge of the New Age and Japan-Singapore Free Trade Agreement', remark by the Minister, MITI, Japan (www.meti.go.jp/english/speeches/index.html).

Irwin, Douglas A., 1996. *Against the Tide: An Intellectual History of Free Trade.* Princeton, NJ: Princeton University Press.

Irwin, Douglas A., 2002. *Free Trade Under Fire*. Princeton, NJ: Princeton University Press.

Kant, Immanuel, 1927 [1795]. *Perpetual Peace: A Philosophical Sketch*. The Grotius Society Publications, no. 7, Helen O'Brien (trans.). London: Weet and Maxwell.

Krugman, Paul R., 1996. *Pop Internationalism*. Cambridge, MA: MIT.

Kupchan, Charles A., 2003. *The End of American Era: U.S. Foreign Policy and the Geopolitics of the Twenty-First Century*. New York: Vintage Books.

Lenin, V.I., 1970 [1916]. *Imperialism: The Highest Stage of Capitalism*. New York: International.

Levy, Jack S., 2003. 'Economic Interdependence, Opportunity Costs, and Peace', in Edward D. Mansfield and Brian M. Pollins, (eds), *Economic Interdependence and International Conflict: New perspectives on an Enduring Debate*. Ann Arbor, MI: University of Michigan Press, pp. 127–147.

Limao, Nuno, 2002. 'Are Preferential Trade Agreements with Non-trade Objectives a Stumbling Block for Multilateral Liberalization?' (www.wam.umd.edu/~limao/lspta_ciewp0202.pdf).

Limao, Nuno, 2007. 'Are Preferential Trade Agreements with Non-trade Objectives a Stumbling Block for Multilateral Liberalization?', *Review of Economic Studies* 74(3): 821–855.

Mansfield, Edward D., 2003. 'Preferential Peace: Why Preferential Trading Arrangements Inhibit Interstate Conflict', in Edward D. Mansfield, & Brian M. Pollins, (eds), *Economic Interdependence and International Conflict: New perspectives on an Enduring Debate*. Ann Arbor, MI: University of Michigan Press, pp. 222–236.

Mansfield, Edward D. and Pevehouse Jon. C., 2003. 'Institutions, Interdependence, and International Conflict', in Gerald Schneider, Katherine Barbieri and Nils Petter Gleditsch (eds), *Globalization and Arms Conflict*, Lanham, MD: Rowman and Littlefield, pp. 233–250.

Mansfield, Edward D. and Brian M. Pollins (eds), 2003. *Economic Interdependence and International Conflict: New Perspectives on an Enduring Debate*. Ann Arbor, MI: University of Michigan Press.

Martin, Philippe, Thierry Mayer and Mathias Thoenig, 2005. 'Make Trade not War?', CEPR Discussion Paper No. 5218.

Mohanty, Satyajit, 2006. 'Nathu La: The Road Ahead', Article No. 2054. India: Institute of Peace and Conflict.

Montesquieu, Baron De, 1989 [1748]. *The Spirit of the Laws*. Translated by A.M. Cohler, BC. Miller and H.S. Stone. New York: Cambridge University Press.

Naik, Niaz, A. 2004. 'A Security Organization for South Asia: Mechanism for Conflict Resolution in South Asia'. In Ramesh Thakur and Oddny Wiggen (eds), *South Asia in the World: Problem Solving Perspectives on Security, Sustainable Development and Good Governance*. Tokyo: United Nations University Press. pp. 269–278.

Nye, Joseph. S. 1971. *Peace in Parts: Integration and Conflict in Regional Organization*. Boston: Little Brown.

Nye, Joseph S. Jr, 1993. *Understanding International Conflict: An Introduction to Theory and History*. New York: HarperCollins College Publishers.

Nye, Joseph S. Jr, 2002a. 'The New Rome Meets the New Barbarians: How America Should Wield Its Power. *The Economist*, 23 March.

Nye, Joseph S. Jr, 2002b. 'The American National Interest and Global Public Goods', *International Affairs* 78(2): 233–244.

Nye, Joseph, 2007. 'Japan Faces Two Big Security Concerns', Op-ed. Cambridge, MA: JFK School of Government, Harvard University (www.ksg.harvard.edu/ksgnews/Features/opeds/012207_nye.html).

Ohmae, Kenichi, 1995. *The End of the Nation State: The Rise of Regional Economies.* New York: McKinsey & Company.

Ohmae, Kenichi, 1999. *The Borderless World.* New York: McKinsey & Company.

Oneal, John.R. and Bruce Russett, 2003a. 'Assessing the Liberal Peace with Alternative Specifications: Trade Still Reduces Conflict', in While the world is often amazed by the so-called 'grand successes' of summit meetings of SAARC, little is known about the functioning of its Secretariat. This indicates that the organization has been assigned few taskes and given insufficient power compared with the EU Commission. This is certainly at odds with the often-mentioned vision of establishing a South Asian Economic Community (SAEC). In this respect, although the EU model may not be fully applicable to SAARC, its invaluable experience could certainly be a good guide for South Asia. pp. 143–163.

Oneal, John R. and Bruce Russett, 2003b. 'Clear and Clean: The Fixed Effects of the Liberal Peace', *International Organization* 55(2): 469-485.

Polachek, Solomon W., 2001. 'Trade Based Interactions: An Interdisciplinary Perspective. Revised version of the Presidential Address delivered at the Annual Meeting of the Peace Science Society International, October 2000, New Haven, CT. (www.binghamton.edu/econ/wp02/WP0202.pdf).

Polachek, Solomon W. and Carlos Seiglie, 2006. 'Trade, Peace and Democracy: An Analysis of Dyadic Dispute', IZA Discussion Paper No. 2170. Bonn: The Institute for the Study of Labor.

Robst, John, Solomon Polachek and Yuan-Ching Chang, 2006. 'Geographic Proximity, Trade and International Conflict/Cooperation', IZA Discussion Paper No. 1988. Bonn: Institute for Study of Labor.

Rodrigo, Nihal, 2004. 'SAARC as an Institutional Framework for Cooperation in South Asia', in Ramesh Thakur and Oddny Wiggen (eds), *South Asia in the World: Problem Solving Perspectives on Security, Sustainable Development and Good Governance.* Tokyo: United Nations University Press, pp. 279–291.

Rodrik. Dani, 1997. *Has Globalization Gone Too Far?.* Washington DC: Institute for International Economics.

Rodrik, Dani, 2006. Goodbye Washington Consensus, Hello Washington Confusion? A Review of the World Bank's Growth in the 1990s: Learning from a Decade of Reform,' *Journal of Economic Literature* 44(4): 973–987.

Rogowski, Ronald, 1989. *Commerce and Coalitions: How Trade Affects Domestic Political Alignments.* Princeton, NJ: Princeton University Press.

Rosecrance, Richard, 1986. *The Rise of the Trading State: Commerce and Conquest in the Modern World.* New York: Basic Books.

Russett, Bruce, 2003. 'Violence and Desease: Trade as a Suppressor of Conflict when Suppressor Matter', in Edward D. Mansfield and Brian M. Pollins (eds), *Economic Interdependence and International Conflict: New Perspectives on an Enduring Debate* Ann Arbor, MI: University of Michigan Press.

Schirm, Stefan A., 2002. *Globalization and the New Regionalism.* Cambridge: Polity Press.

Schmitt, Hans A. 2005. Memories of A Tranquil Revolution. *The Virginia Quarterly Review.* www.vqronline.org/viewmedia.php/prmMID/8432 (accessed August 26, 2005)

Schneider, Gerald, Katherine Barbieri, and Nils Petter Gleditsch eds, 2003. *Globalization and Arms Conflict.* Lanham, MD: Rowman & Littlefield.

Soderbaum, Fredrik, Patrik Stalgren and Luk Van Langenhove, 2005. 'The EU as a Global Actor and the Dynamics of Interregionalism: a Comparative Analysis', *European Integration* 27(3): 365–380.

Solingen, Etel, 1998. *Regional Order at Century's Dawn: Global and Domestic Influences on Grand Strategy*. Princeton, NJ: Princeton University Press.

Thakur, Ramesh, 2002. 'Security in the New Millennium', in Andrew F. Cooper; John English and Ramesh Thakur, (eds), *Enhancing Global Governance: Towards a New Diplomacy*. New York: United Nations University Press pp. 268–286.

Vasquez, John, 1995. 'Why do Neighbors Fight? Proximity, Interaction, or Territoriality', *Journal of Peace Research* 32(3): 277–293.

Viner, Jacob, 1950. *The Customs Union Issue*. London: Stevens & Sons.

Waltz, Kenneth N., 1979. *Theory of International Politics*. New York: McGraw-Hill.

Index

For Product Safety Concerns and Information please contact our EU
representative GPSR@taylorandfrancis.com
Taylor & Francis Verlag GmbH, Kaufingerstraße 24, 80331 München, Germany

www.ingramcontent.com/pod-product-compliance
Lightning Source LLC
Chambersburg PA
CBHW050435280326
41932CB00013BA/2123

9 780415 664004